UNITED NATIONS CONFERENCE ON TRADE AND DEVELOPMENT
GENEVA

TRADE AND DEVELOPMENT REPORT, 2004

Report by the secretariat of the
United Nations Conference on Trade and Development

UNITED NATIONS
New York and Geneva, 2004

Note

PER
UNI
TD
T62

- Symbols of United Nations documents are composed of capital letters combined with figures. Mention of such a symbol indicates a reference to a United Nations document.

- The designations employed and the presentation of the material in this publication do not imply the expression of any opinion whatsoever on the part of the Secretariat of the United Nations concerning the legal status of any country, territory, city or area, or of its authorities, or concerning the delimitation of its frontiers or boundaries.

- Material in this publication may be freely quoted or reprinted, but acknowledgement is requested, together with a reference to the document number. A copy of the publication containing the quotation or reprint should be sent to the UNCTAD secretariat.

UNCTAD/TDR/2004

UNITED NATIONS PUBLICATION
Sales No. E.04.II.D.29
ISBN 92-1-112635-5 ISSN 0255-4607

FOREWORD

After years of slow growth, a global recovery that includes many developing countries now appears to be under way. If it is sustained and widened, the recovery could be a step forward on the way to meeting the Millennium Development Goals by the internationally agreed target year of 2015.

The current acceleration of growth in world output and trade reflects the recovery in the United States and faster growth in a number of developing countries in Asia, especially China and India. But many other countries have not enjoyed similar improvements. And far too many, especially in Africa, remain marginalized from the process of globalization, making it much more difficult to achieve the Millennium Development Goals.

These and other key issues were addressed at the eleventh session of the United Nations Conference on Trade and Development, which was held in São Paulo in June. The agreements reached there – the São Paulo Consensus, and the political declaration, the Spirit of São Paulo – emphasize the need for genuine progress in international trade negotiations and for much greater coherence, both in the international economic system and between international regulations and national development strategies.

This year's *Trade and Development Report* is intended as a contribution to the debate on policy coherence. It examines how international trading relations are affected by the international monetary and financial systems, and shows that monetary and financial instability can have a serious impact on the ability of developing countries to participate successfully in the international trading system and reap the benefits of globalization. The *Report* stresses the importance of building a truly multilateral monetary system, in which all countries, not just a few, have a voice in the decisions affecting their lives and prospects. By complementing the multilateral trading system, this would strengthen the impact of trade and capital flows on development. The *Report* also discusses exchange-rate management at the national and international levels, and shows how it can contribute significantly to job creation and poverty reduction.

Effective action in these areas would greatly enhance the prospects for achieving the Millennium Development Goals. Now that an economic recovery is on the horizon, we must move swiftly to pave the way for an extended phase of growth that generates gains in all countries and for all parts of society. In that spirit, I commend this *Report* to the widest possible global readership.

Kofi A. Annan
Secretary-General of the United Nations

Contents

Part One

GLOBAL TRENDS AND PROSPECTS

Chapter I

List of tables

List of figures

List of figures (concluded)

List of boxes

Explanatory notes

Classification by country or commodity group

The classification of countries in this *Report* has been adopted solely for the purposes of statistical or analytical convenience and does not necessarily imply any judgement concerning the stage of development of a particular country or area.

The major country groupings distinguished are:

» Developed or industrial(ized) countries: in general the countries members of OECD (other than the Czech Republic, Hungary, Mexico, Poland, the Republic of Korea, Slovakia and Turkey).

» Transition economies: the countries of Central and Eastern Europe, the Commonwealth of Independent States (CIS) and the Baltic States.

» Developing countries: all countries, territories or areas not specified above.

The term "country" refers, as appropriate, also to territories or areas.

References to "Latin America" in the text or tables include the Caribbean countries unless otherwise indicated.

Unless otherwise stated, the classification by commodity group used in this Report follows generally that employed in the UNCTAD *Handbook of Statistics 2003* (United Nations publication, sales no. E/F.03.II.D.33).

Other notes

References in the text to *TDR* are to the *Trade and Development Report* (of a particular year). For example, *TDR 2003* refers to *Trade and Development Report, 2003* (United Nations publication, sales no. E.03.II.D.7).

The term "dollar" ($) refers to United States dollars, unless otherwise stated.

The term "billion" signifies 1,000 million.

The term "tons" refers to metric tons.

Annual rates of growth and change refer to compound rates.

Exports are valued FOB and imports CIF, unless otherwise specified.

Use of a dash (–) between dates representing years, e.g. 1988–1990, signifies the full period involved, including the initial and final years.

An oblique stroke (/) between two years, e.g. 2000/01, signifies a fiscal or crop year.

A dot (.) indicates that the item is not applicable.

Two dots (..) indicate that the data are not available, or are not separately reported.

A dash (-) or a zero (0) indicates that the amount is nil or negligible.

A plus sign (+) before a figure indicates an increase; a minus sign (-) before a figure indicates a decrease.

Details and percentages do not necessarily add to totals because of rounding.

Abbreviations

AMECO	Annual Macro-economic Database of the European Commission
ASEAN	Association of South-East Asian Nations
CEEC	Central and Eastern European countries
CFA	Communauté financière africaine
CIS	Commonwealth of Independent States
CMEA	Council for Mutual Economic Assistance
CPI	consumer price index
ECE	Economic Commission for Europe
ECLA	Economic Commission for Latin America
ECLAC	Economic Commission for Latin America and the Caribbean (CEPAL in Spanish)
ECOSOC	Economic and Social Council (of the United Nations)
EIU	Economist Intelligence Unit
ESCAP	Economic and Social Commission for Asia and the Pacific
ESCWA	Economic and Social Commission for Western Asia
EMU	(European) Economic and Monetary Union
EU	European Union
FDI	foreign direct investment
GATT	General Agreement on Tariffs and Trade
GCC	Gulf Cooperation Council
GDP	gross domestic product
GNP	gross national product
GFCF	gross fixed capital formation
GLS	generalized least square
IBGE	Instituto Brasileiro de Geografía y Estatística
IBRD	International Bank for Reconstruction and Development
IDA	International Development Association
IEA	International Energy Agency
INDEC	Instituto Nacional de Estadística y Censos (Argentina)
ILO	International Labour Organization
IMF	International Monetary Fund

ISI	import substituting industrialization
ITO	International Trade Organization
LDC	least developed country
M&A	merger and acquisition
MDG	Millennium Development Goal
MERCOSUR	Southern Common Market
MFA	Multi-Fibre Arrangement
MFN	most favoured nation
NAFTA	North American Free Trade Agreement (or Area)
NEPAD	New Partnership for Africa's Development
NIE	newly industrializing economy
ODA	official development assistance
OECD	Organisation for Economic Co-operation and Development
OPEC	Organization of the Petroleum Exporting Countries
PPP	purchasing power parity
R&D	research and development
REER	real effective exchange rate
SDR	special drawing right
SSA	sub-Saharan Africa
TDR	Trade and Development Report
TNC	transnational corporation
UN	United Nations
UNCTAD	United Nations Conference on Trade and Development
UN/DESA	United Nations Department of Economic and Social Affairs
UNDP	United Nations Development Programme
UN-HABITAT	United Nations Human Settlements Programme
USITC	United States International Trade Commission
WPI	wholesale price index
WTO	World Trade Organization

OVERVIEW

Global trends and prospects

The situation of the global economy is brighter than it was a year ago. Since growth in world output and trade recovered in 2003, there is now widespread optimism that the acceleration of growth in 2004 could lead to a return of the performance experienced at the end of the last decade and that the world economy may enter an extended period of growth.

In reality, however, the outlook for a sustained recovery is more clouded and uncertain than at the beginning of the 1990s. Large disparities in the strength of domestic demand persist among the major industrial countries, and increasing trade imbalances between the major economic blocks could lead to new protectionist pressures and increase instability in currency and financial markets, with adverse implications for developing countries. The sharp increase in oil prices and uncertainty about their future development, as well as their possible impact on inflation and interest rates, are an additional reason for concern.

Moreover, income growth is unequally distributed both among developed countries, where the euro area continues to lag behind, and among developing countries, where fast and sustained growth continues to be concentrated in East and South Asia. At the same time, per capita income in most of sub-Saharan Africa is stagnating, and the basis for sustained growth in Latin America is still very fragile. Indeed, the improvement in the global economy has been the result of exceptionally good performance in a small number of countries, with great variations in the spillover effects on other economies.

The recovery of the world economy has been driven largely by the United States economy and continued fast expansion in East and South Asia. Through its increasing fiscal and trade deficits, the United States economy has provided a strong demand stimulus to the rest of the world. On the other hand, several developing economies in Asia, in particular China, have been able to increase not only their imports – with strong spillover effects in economies in the Asia and Pacific region – but also their exports at double-digit rates.

The dependence of the global economy on the performance of the United States economy is not a new phenomenon, but United States deficits are much larger today than they were in the late 1990s. This is a matter for concern, since the high budget deficit of the United States will require fiscal adjustments and the unusually expansionary monetary policy stance may also need to be revised in light of inflationary pressures stemming from a surge in import prices and in particular from oil prices.

Geopolitical tensions and speculative forces explain much of the sharp rise in oil prices, which during the first half of 2004 reached their highest level since the early 1990s, but the rise has also been driven by the global recovery and rapidly rising demand from China. Substantially higher oil prices carry the risk of compromising growth in oil-importing countries, especially those in the developing world that are facing serious balance-of-payments and external financing constraints while benefiting to a relatively small extent from potentially higher exports to oil-exporting countries. Moreover, as in past episodes of rapidly rising oil prices, the oil-exporting countries may not be able immediately to translate additional oil revenues into higher demand for goods produced in oil-importing countries. Although higher oil prices have not had an immediate impact on inflation in the industrialized countries, such an effect cannot be ruled out should prices remain at current levels in the medium term. This in turn might lead to increases in interest rates.

Greater financial and exchange-rate instability may also result from the fact that the United States is increasingly immersed in trade-financial dynamics with East Asia. Expansionary fiscal and monetary policies in the United States have been providing a significant boost to exports from East Asia, including Japan, and are contributing to the large current account surpluses in the region. On the other hand, the East Asian developing countries have been following a policy of keeping their exchange rates at a competitive level following the currency depreciations in the late 1990s. This has required heavy intervention in the foreign exchange market, leading to fast reserve accumulation. As a result, East Asia has been recycling its current-account surpluses directly to the United States, thereby financing a large part of the United States current-account and budget deficits through the investment of increasing foreign exchange reserves in United States Treasury securities. In 2003, East Asian developing countries, including China, bought more than $210 billion of foreign currency, compared to a United States budget deficit of $455 billion and a trade deficit of $490 billion. This pattern is unlikely to be sustainable in the long run, especially if pressure on the dollar to depreciate mounts as a result of further rising United States deficits, which, in turn, could induce Asian central banks to minimize risks by diversifying their foreign exchange holdings into assets denominated in other currencies, in particular the euro.

Because of the recycling of balance-of-payments surpluses of the East Asian and a number of other developing and transition economies through an unprecedented increase in reserve accumulation in 2003, there has been a continued net capital outflow, in the order of $230 billion, from developing and transition economies to the developed countries. This has occurred despite a substantial rise in the net inflow of private capital to the developing and transition economies, which has reached its highest level since 1997. On the other hand, although foreign direct investment (FDI) remains the most important type of private capital inflows to developing countries, it fell to its lowest level since 1996 as the wave of privatization, which had been a driving force behind FDI during the 1990s, levelled off. Conversely, credits and short-term capital flows rose considerably, but the bulk of these flows were directed to a small number of emerging-market economies, attracted by high interest rates or the expectation of currency appreciation. Indeed, a substantial proportion of private external financing did not flow to economies with external financing needs or low investment rates. Instead these flows were mainly directed to economies with often sizeable current account surpluses resulting from fast export expansion, adding to their foreign exchange reserves. This is another indication that capital markets cannot be counted on as a stable source of development finance. Moreover, the obvious fear of many developing countries with regard to floating their currencies in the presence of sharply fluctuating expectations on the international financial markets should give rise to increased efforts to strengthen the coherence between the international trading system, on the one hand, and the international monetary and financial system, on the other, an issue that is taken up below.

With East and South Asia forming a de facto dollar block, adjustments of global imbalances may require more pronounced exchange-rate changes in the rest of the world. In order to maintain the growth momentum in the world economy without constantly growing United States deficits and mounting pressure on the dollar, demand growth would need to be strengthened in the other major industrial countries. However, growth in most European economies continues to be itself dependent on exports. The euro area has benefited from the recent United States recovery, despite the appreciation of the euro vis-à-vis the dollar, confirming the competitiveness of its industries, but domestic demand remains sluggish, mainly due to the inability of economic policy to lift the income expectations of consumers in the three largest economies. Without a reorientation in the euro area away from fiscal and monetary orthodoxy, the rising imbalances in world trade will force further and even more dramatic changes in real exchange rates.

Regional trends and the new geography of trade

An exceptionally strong fiscal stimulus and a reduction of interest rates to their lowest level in 50 years have helped the United States economy overcome the phase of weakness that began in 2000. Rising government expenditure due mainly to a surge in defence spending, higher company profits that finally led to the long-awaited rise in business investment, and a recovery in household consumption all converged to produce a substantial rise in domestic demand. By contrast, despite the weakening of the dollar vis-à-vis the euro and the yen in 2003, external demand grew at a much slower rate than imports. The large and rising trade deficit thus remains a major concern, as it is likely to exert further downward pressure on the dollar.

Moreover, given the size of the United States budget deficit, fiscal policy will need to adopt a more restrictive stance, and a switch towards a more restrictive monetary policy would aggravate the high indebtedness of households, which could prove to be a major obstacle to sustained expansion. There are thus serious doubts that United States growth and its positive impact on the world economy will continue with the same strength as has been the case during 2003 and the first half of 2004.

In the euro area, domestic demand has remained flat. The European Central Bank was reluctant to follow a more aggressive expansionary policy. Despite slower growth, real short-term interest rates in Europe have been consistently higher than in the United States, while the space for expansionary fiscal policies is restricted by the Stability and Growth Pact. This is in contrast to the United Kingdom, where countercyclical fiscal policy in response to the global slowdown after 2000 contributed to considerably higher growth rates than those in continental Europe. The current attempt of many European companies to improve their international competitiveness by cutting wages will aggravate the weakness of domestic demand. Eventually, as the financial markets realize that the world economy is not receiving the stimulus needed to overcome the existing imbalances, the probability of a strong overvaluation of the European currency will rise significantly. In this case, the euro area and its major trading partners will run the risk of being trapped in a low-growth, high-unemployment scenario.

After a decade of stagnation, the Japanese economy finally achieved considerable recovery of output growth in 2003. Although there has been a rebound of corporate investment, the recovery was largely based on higher external demand. While exports to the United States fell in 2003, the export drive was mainly due to continued strong demand from China, suggesting a change in trade patterns within Asia and between Asia and the United States. However, given the strong reliance on foreign demand, the Japanese export-led recovery is vulnerable to changes in external conditions, particularly currency fluctuations.

GDP growth in the developing countries rose in 2003 and is likely to do so again in 2004. While growth has accelerated in a large number of developing countries, its level differs considerably across and within regions. Growth has been the strongest in East and South Asia, as a result of further expansion of domestic and external demand, and it is set to accelerate further in 2004. Economic policy in most countries of the region has maintained an expansionary stance through public investment in infrastructure development and the creation of favourable monetary conditions. The stability of exchange rates within the region, together with significant growth of investment and GDP, has favoured the trend towards specialization in the context of rapidly growing intraregional trade and investment.

China is playing a central role in this process. Indeed, in 2003 and the beginning of 2004, it was a major engine of growth for most countries in the region. A large proportion of its imports, which have been growing even faster than its exports, are coming from the rest of Asia. In 2004 rapid growth is likely to continue in East and South Asia, and particularly in the two largest economies, China and India. However, in China there is now overheating in certain sectors of the economy, and the policy stance is becoming more restrictive, with attendant effects on other countries in the region, including Japan.

Although exports to the United States continue to be an important component of total output growth in East and South Asia, this region has generated an intraregional pattern of demand and specialization that should allow it to maintain a relatively stable growth path independent of cyclical and structural problems in the rest of the world.

After two years of negative per capita growth, economic activity in Latin America began to improve in the second half of 2003. Several countries have regained international competitiveness and have increased their room for manoeuvre in macroeconomic management by shifting away from rigid exchange rate regimes and overvalued currencies. While improved trade balances in 2002 were largely the result of import compression, further improvement of trade performance in 2003 was mainly due to a rise in exports, stimulating economic recovery. Although for the region as a whole growth is expected to accelerate further in 2004, serious obstacles to a return to high and sustained growth rates in Latin America persist. Despite improved monetary conditions, in several countries fixed capital formation has fallen to its lowest level in decades. The new policy initiatives taken in some of the major economies in the region could lead to a more sustainable recovery if they succeed in stimulating domestic demand. In order to achieve a substantial recovery of both investment and private consumption, it will be necessary to ease the public debt burden, reform fiscal structures in some countries, and enhance the supply of domestic credit at lower interest rates than in the past, as well as achieving a more equitable distribution of income.

The African continent benefited from the recovery in the world economy less than other developing regions. The moderate rise in African growth was driven by higher prices of primary commodities. Growth in North Africa increased substantially as a result mainly of improved weather conditions, higher oil prices and a revival of tourism, whereas in sub-Saharan Africa, where poverty and social deprivation continue to take their greatest toll, real GDP growth remained sluggish, implying a further stagnation of per capita incomes. Given the severe financing constraints of most sub-Saharan economies, investment rates remain too low to achieve the required degree of diversification into higher value-added production and more dynamic products in international markets that would allow for faster integration into the world economy and a reduction of the persistent vulnerability of the region to external shocks. The required rise in the level of both public and private investment cannot be achieved by relying on domestic savings and private capital inflows. Debt relief and the additional provision of official development assistance in the form of grants are indispensable for alleviating poverty and improving social conditions in these countries. In light of the persisting weakness of per capita income growth, it now appears increasingly unlikely that sub-Saharan Africa can attain the Millennium Development Goals, in particular that of halving poverty by 2015. In most countries, growth would need to be doubled and sustained over a decade in order to meet those goals.

The transition economies of Central and Eastern Europe also registered higher growth rates in 2003, and their GDP should accelerate again in 2004, thanks to higher exports and strong domestic demand. In the countries members of the Commonwealth of Independent States, growth was strongly supported by considerably higher revenues from oil exports. European Union enlargement and the relocation of activities to the low-wage transition economies are facilitating their closer integration into a new division of labour on the continent.

The processes that have led to the recovery of the world economy and the regional growth patterns in the developing world confirm the importance of proactive fiscal and monetary policies. The economies that provided growth stimuli to the rest of the world were those where monetary and fiscal policy supported domestic demand growth. This is true for both developed and developing countries. Moreover, a competitive exchange rate can play a decisive role in forestalling external constraints and creating policy space for monetary easing.

The introduction of a large number of security-related measures since late 2001 is likely to have an adverse impact on the cost of trade and the movement of goods, in particular from developing countries. Nevertheless, world trade expanded significantly in 2003 and the first half of 2004, but unlike the second half of the 1990s, when rapid trade expansion was mainly the result of increasing export volumes, two thirds of trade growth in 2003 was on account of a surge in the dollar unit value of exports. Trade expansion was driven by the recovery in the United States and the phenomenon that has come to be called the "new geography of trade". Developing and transition countries have played a more important role in the expansion of world trade than ever before: in 2002 and 2003, they accounted for around three quarters of the increase in export volume and for 60 per cent of the increase in import volume. This reflects the increasing relocation of manufacturing production to some regions, especially East and South Asia and the transition economies of Central and Eastern Europe, as well as the international pattern of demand growth. Indeed, a number of developing countries, especially in East and South Asia, have become important markets for a wide range of manufactures and commodities, while expanding their own manufacturing industries at a very rapid pace. Consequently, their growth is more energy-intensive and requires more primary-commodity inputs, such as metals and agricultural raw materials, than growth based on an expansion of the services sector. Moreover, given the size of these countries in terms of population, the demand for food products has been expanding vigorously.

Commodity prices in current dollar terms rose for the second consecutive year in 2003 as a consequence of higher demand, particularly from the rapidly expanding Asian economies. However, as the dollar prices of manufactures exported by developed countries also rose, overall commodity terms of trade did not improve, and for some commodity groups they even worsened. Moreover, the development of commodity prices quoted in dollars has to be seen against the depreciation of the dollar against other major currencies. For many large consumers, the rise in dollar prices has been offset by these exchange-rate movements, and the export earnings of commodity producers whose currencies are pegged to the euro, in particular the African commodity producers in the CFA zone, have been negatively affected. Moreover, the situation in financial and currency markets has also increased speculative demand for commodities, and this may be reversed as the conditions in international financial markets change. In any case, in real terms non-oil commodity prices still remain at very low levels and considerably below their level of the early 1980s.

Policy coherence, development strategies and integration into the world economy

Since the mid-1980s, many developing countries have made close integration into the international trading system a pillar of their economic reform agenda. They have sought to achieve this not only through active participation in multilateral trade negotiations, but also through rapid unilateral trade liberalization. In many countries, this has been accompanied by an opening up of their financial sector and capital account. To date, this strategy – which may be called the "openness model" – has not enabled most developing countries, with some notable exceptions such as Chile, to establish the virtuous interaction between international finance, domestic capital formation and export growth that underpinned the catching-up process of Western Europe after the Second World War and of the East Asian newly industrializing economies (NIEs) as from the 1980s.

A feasible development agenda requires a more complex analytical and policy framework than that offered by the "openness model". A fundamental question is how to reinforce coherence between national development strategies and global processes and disciplines, as well as policy coherence among and within the various sectors of the global economy that impact on development prospects of developing countries. Of particular importance is the interface between the international trading system and the international monetary and financial system.

Openness, integration and national policy space

A coherent treatment of the interdependence between trade, macroeconomic and financial issues was an important element in the debate leading to the post-War international economic system. The set-up of the post-War international trade regime was predicated on the belief that, in conditions of strictly limited private international capital flows, an international monetary system with convertible currencies at fixed, but adjustable, exchange rates would provide a stable environment conducive to trade and investment. Under the aegis of the General Agreement on Tariffs and Trade (GATT), this regime considered tariffs as the only legitimate trade policy measure. The adopted exchange rate regime supported the GATT approach, as participants in international trade negotiations could predict the full extent to which the competitive position of domestic industries would be affected by tariff cuts without having to be unduly concerned about other exogenous factors.

The specific problems of developing countries participating in the post-War international trading system were largely absent from the mandates of the intergovernmental institutions created immediately after the Second World War. This was despite the fact that, with international private capital flows constrained and official development assistance still limited (and often tied), the role of international trade was attracting increasing attention as a dependable means of removing the resource constraints on economic growth in developing countries. Multilateral efforts at designing a trading system that would take account of the policy options of developing countries, for which slow growth and adverse terms-of-trade movements were distinctive features, culminated in the First United Nations Conference on Trade and Development in 1964. The Report to the Conference spelt out a strategy designed to help poorer countries develop outwardly through strong capital formation and continuing and accelerated expansion of exports – both traditional and non-traditional. Central to that agenda was the idea that developing countries can base economic development on their own efforts only if they have sufficient policy space to accelerate capital formation, diversify their economic structure and give development greater "social depth". This agenda also emphasized the interdependence between trade and finance, given that, particularly in the early stages of industrialization, imports would almost certainly grow faster than exports, and financing the gap would be key to accelerating growth.

The need for coherence between the international trading system and the international monetary and financial system has gained in importance with the abandoning of the system of fixed, but adjustable, exchange rates and the adoption of widespread floating, combined with a return of private international capital flows to levels similar to those that had caused much economic and social instability in the inter-war period. In particular, the liberalization of capital movements has, on balance, had little impact on levels of development finance, and the balance-of-payments constraint of developing countries has not been removed. Rather, there has been a de-linking of financial flows from international trade. This is most clearly the case with short-term flows, where over 80 per cent of transactions relate to round-trip operations, motivated by hedging, arbitrage and speculative considerations. Moreover, the increased level and volatility of short-term private international capital flows, associated with the often sharp swings in exchange rate expectations of international investors, have an adverse bearing on the principle of non-discrimination in trade and on developing-country trade performance.

Thus, an evaluation of the functioning of the international trading system should take account of the way in which its rules have been modified to deal not only with changes in international trading relationships, but also with international monetary and financial relationships that have an impact on trade.

Fostering coherence between the international trading, monetary and financial systems

An important lesson from the experiences of countries that combined successful integration into the world economy with sustained growth is the critical role of active and well sequenced policies to augment the stock of physical and human capital, enable the use of more efficient technologies, and shift resources away from traditional, low-productivity activities towards activities that offer a high potential for productivity growth. Under some circumstances, and particularly when a period of real currency appreciation has hampered export performance, real currency depreciations can improve international cost competitiveness and boost exports.

One condition for successful trade performance is that developing countries are able to manage their exchange rates in a way that allows them not only to sustain competitive rates over the longer term, but also to retain enough policy space to be able to make orderly adjustments when faced with exogenous shocks. The post-War institutional set-up had thought to achieve this through the creation of an international monetary system on an intergovernmental basis with convertible currencies at fixed, but adjustable, exchange rates and strict limitations on private international capital flows. However, partly due to the liberalization of capital flows in the last 30 years and to the sizeable increase in the scale and variety of cross-border financial transactions, whose direction can change rapidly in response to shifts in expectations of international portfolio investors, the currencies of financially open developing countries have been subject to strong volatility and gyrations. Such volatility has frequently contributed to problems in managing interest rates and exchange rates and to financial crises, including in countries with track records of macroeconomic discipline. These currency movements have often been characterized by prolonged periods of exchange rate appreciation followed by abrupt and sharp devaluations.

Given that real currency depreciations can generally be expected to improve a country's trade balance, it could be assumed that sharp depreciations of the real exchange rate will provide an even greater impetus to the international cost competitiveness of domestic exporters and a boost to a country's exports. However, effects that accompany large depreciations of the real exchange rate can, at least in the short term, seriously compromise the ability of domestic exporters to benefit from their increased international cost competitiveness stemming from the depreciation.

Such effects can occur at two levels. At the level of individual enterprises, nominal exchange rate changes can have a major impact on investment and international competitiveness, as they affect the instruments that firms can use to foster international cost competitiveness in a sustainable way. Firms may not be able to benefit from sharp real currency depreciations if the goods that they export have a high import content, so that the net effect on their international cost competitiveness is small. More importantly, recent experience shows that sharp real currency depreciations can compromise the ability of firms to expand production capacity or even maintain production at pre-depreciation levels. This is so because the easing of capital controls will have seriously compromised the availability of trade finance from international sources in the aftermath of sharp currency depreciations. Moreover, the tightening of domestic monetary conditions associated with the depreciation has often made it difficult for domestic lenders to maintain their provision of short-term credit.

With regard to effects at the macroeconomic level, discussions on the impact of exchange rate changes on trade flows have frequently emphasized the effect of exchange rate volatility on trade, or the contribution of currency depreciations to the removal of temporary imbalances in a country's current account. Typically, the focus has been on the impact of exchange rate changes that are relatively small, whereas since the early 1990s developing countries' real exchange rates have frequently undergone large gyrations, adding an additional dimension to the traditional debate for at least two reasons. First, sharp exchange rate changes in one economy can adversely affect the external trade position of other economies where the exchange rate remains relatively stable. For example, evidence from the Asian crisis points to competitive depreciations as an important form of contagion through trade linkages, as countries whose exporters compete directly with those in the crisis-affected country also face pressure to depreciate their currencies in order to avoid a loss in international competitiveness. This also means that exporters in the crisis-affected country do not experience the rise in demand for their products hoped for.

Second, the domestic impact of a sharp and abrupt exchange rate depreciation is more complex than the adjustments resulting from small exchange rate fluctuations, because sharp currency depreciations are typically associated with a drop in domestic economic activity and a need to cut imports of intermediate and capital goods. Combined with the sharp decline in the availability of trade finance, this is likely to hamper the domestic supply response. Thus, while the trade performance of developing countries generally improves after "normal" depreciations, major real currency depreciations do not generally result in proportionally larger improvements, as they tend to undermine the ability of exporters to take advantage of the rise in international cost competitiveness.

In effect, volatility in international financial markets and particularly in short-term private capital flows can reduce international competitiveness and the profit incentive for investors to undertake productivity-enhancing investment in developing countries. Hence, there is inconsistency in the policy advice that encourages developing countries to adopt rapid financial liberalization and yet to increasingly rely on productivity-enhancing investment to strengthen their competitiveness for improved trade performance.

Existing modalities in the multilateral trading system do not address the problems of trade performance that originate in the monetary and financial system. Moreover, there are no mechanisms under the existing system of global economic governance for dispute settlement or redress regarding these impulses. One possible solution could be a review of the balance-of-payments provisions of the GATT. Otherwise, developing countries that have liberalized their capital account at an early stage of their integration process may have to adopt measures to limit the impact of private capital flows on exchange rate movements that adversely affect their trade balance and the international competitiveness of their exporters.

The changes required in the international trading, monetary and financial systems to enable a more equitable distribution of the benefits from international trade and to maximize the developmental effects of globalization for developing countries call for an integrated treatment of trade problems and the increasingly interlinked issues of development and overall payments balances. Decisions on the international monetary and financial system should not be circumscribed by narrow monetary and financial considerations, but should take account of the fact that they have a strong and lasting impact on the real sectors in both developed and developing countries.

Measures at the national level cannot substitute for appropriate trading, monetary and financial arrangements. Nevertheless, avoiding currency overvaluation has become the chosen strategy of an increasing number of developing countries. East Asian countries pioneered this approach. They did not apply the "open capital market strategy" at an early stage of their catching-up process and tried to avoid dependence on foreign capital flows. This gave them the possibility of simultaneously managing the real exchange rate, a key determinant of exporters' international cost competitiveness, and the real interest rate, a key determinant of domestic investment.

Managed floating, however, faces an adding-up problem at the global level. Not all countries can simultaneously manage the movements of their exchange rate and achieve their targeted rates. The exchange rate is, by definition, a multilateral phenomenon, and attempts by many countries to keep their currencies at an undervalued rate may end up in a race to the bottom – or in competitive devaluations – that would be as disastrous for the world economy as the experience of the 1930s. Moreover, given the size and inherent volatility of international short-term capital flows, only those developing countries that are big and competitive enough to withstand strong and sustained attempts of the international financial markets to move the exchange rate in a certain direction will be able to manage the floating successfully. A small and open developing economy will hardly be able to continue fighting a strong tendency for its currency to appreciate over a longer period of time.

Since exchange rate policies have the same international dimension as trade policies, multilateral or global arrangements similar to those of the multilateral trading system would be the best solution to this problem. Indeed, the main idea behind the establishment of the IMF in the 1940s was to avoid competitive devaluations. In a well-designed global monetary system, the advantages of a currency devaluation in one country have to be balanced against the disadvantages for the others. As changes in the exchange rate that imply deviation from purchasing power parity affect international trade in a way comparable to tariffs and export duties, such changes should also be governed by multilateral regulations. Such a multilateral regime would, among other things, require countries to specify their reasons for real depreciations and the dimension of necessary changes. If such rules were strictly applied, substantial changes in the real exchange rate of individual countries could be avoided.

In a world without a multilateral solution to the currency problem, the only way out for high-inflation or high-growth countries that are not members of a regional monetary union is to resort to controls on short-term capital flows or to follow a strategy of undervaluation and unilateral fixing. If developing countries are able to prevent destabilizing inflows and outflows, either by taxing those flows or by limiting their impact through direct intervention in the market, the hardest choices and misallocations due to erratic exchange rate changes may be avoided; but resort to controls or permanent intervention should not replace the search for an appropriate exchange rate system at the regional and global levels.

Rubens Ricupero
Secretary-General of UNCTAD

GLOBAL TRENDS AND PROSPECTS

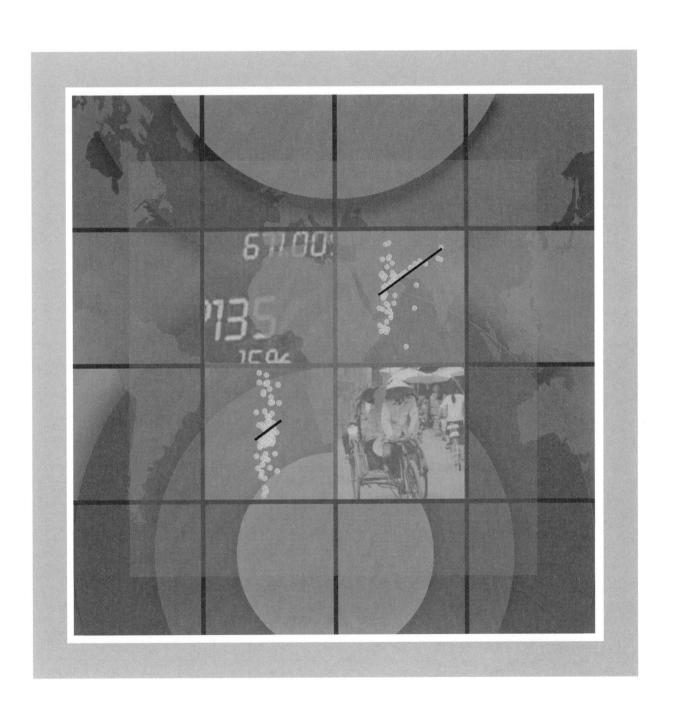

THE WORLD ECONOMY: PERFORMANCE AND PROSPECTS

A. Introduction

The world economy, after two years of slow growth and rising unemployment, is regaining momentum. Global GDP grew by 2.6 per cent in 2003, up from 1.7 per cent the year before. For 2004, a growth rate of nearly 4 per cent is forecast, similar to the pace experienced at the end of the 1990s (table 1.1). Rising domestic demand in large parts of the world should stimulate the economies of developing countries. In particular, the strong recovery of private investment spending in the United States, combined with increased consumer confidence, looks set to provide a large positive spillover effect on the rest of the world.

The second engine of growth is East and South Asia, where the Chinese economy is surging (at an estimated rate of 8.5 per cent in 2004), India is on a high and stable growth path (of about 7 per cent in 2003–2004) and most of the other emerging-market economies are following close behind (table 1.2). This region is not entirely dependent on the performance of the developed world; rather, it has generated a dynamic that would allow it to push ahead even while the rest of the world still struggles with cyclical and struc-

tural problems. In 2004, its average growth rate should approach 7 per cent, and the investment ratio, spurred by an unprecedented investment boom in China, could reach an all time high. In recent years, industrial production growth has been especially important in emerging-market economies in Asia and Europe as well as in Japan, but it has been weak in the euro area, the United States and Latin America (fig. 1.1).

Driven by the dynamism of East and South Asia, and recovery in the United States, global trade expanded significantly in 2003 and well into 2004. World exports of goods increased in volume by nearly 5 per cent in 2003, while prices in dollar terms, for commodities – with some notable exceptions – as well as manufactures, were on the rise. Beyond growth, the good trade performance of China, East Asia and the transition economies of Central and Eastern Europe reflects an ongoing process of relocation of production of manufactures. In some countries of Africa, South America and the Commonwealth of Independent States (CIS), investment in mining and hydrocarbons boosted exports. At the same time, currency

Table 1.1

WORLD OUTPUT GROWTH, 1990–2004[a]

(Percentage change over previous year)

	1990–2000[b]	1998	1999	2000	2001	2002	2003[c]	2004[d]
World	**2.3**	**2.2**	**3.0**	**4.0**	**1.4**	**1.7**	**2.6**	**3.8**
Developed countries/regions	**2.4**	**2.5**	**2.9**	**3.5**	**1.0**	**1.2**	**2.0**	**3.2**
of which:								
Japan	1.4	-1.1	0.1	2.8	0.4	-0.3	2.5	4.3
United States	3.5	4.2	4.4	3.7	0.5	2.2	3.1	4.0
European Union	2.1	2.9	2.9	3.6	1.7	1.0	0.7	2.0
of which:								
Euro area	1.9	2.9	2.8	3.5	1.6	0.9	0.4	1.8
France	1.8	3.5	3.3	4.0	2.2	1.2	0.2	2.3
Germany	1.6	2.0	2.0	2.9	0.8	0.2	-0.1	1.5
Italy	1.6	1.8	1.7	3.0	1.8	0.4	0.3	1.0
United Kingdom	2.7	3.1	2.8	3.8	2.1	1.6	2.2	3.1
Transition economies	**-2.5**	**-0.8**	**3.6**	**6.8**	**4.5**	**3.9**	**5.9**	**5.9**
Developing economies	**4.9**	**1.3**	**3.6**	**5.6**	**2.4**	**3.5**	**4.5**	**5.8**
Developing economies, excluding China	**4.1**	**0.3**	**3.0**	**5.1**	**1.5**	**2.6**	**3.6**	**5.2**

Source: UNCTAD secretariat calculations, based on World Bank, *World Development Indicators, 2004;* OECD, *Quarterly National Accounts,* June 2004; ECLAC, *Preliminary Overview of the Economies of Latin America and the Caribbean 2003;* ECE, *Economic Survey of Europe,* No. 1, 2004; ESCWA, *Survey of Economic and Social Developments in the ESCWA Region, 2004;* ESCAP, *Economic and Social Survey for Asia and the Pacific, 2004;* IMF, *World Economic Outlook,* April 2004; OECD, *Economic Outlook No. 75,* 2004; the Project LINK Meeting, April 2004; JP Morgan, *Global Data Watch,* June 2004; Economist Intelligence Unit (EIU), *Country Forecast,* June 2004; and national sources.

a   Calculations are based on GDP in constant 1995 dollars.
b   Average.
c   Preliminary.
d   Forecasts.

depreciations in several Latin American countries resulted in major improvements in competitiveness. Impressive export growth from developing countries was mainly related to favourable short-term factors. This could be sustained by the success of ongoing multilateral trade negotiations.

Developing and transition economies played a prominent role in the recovery of world trade in 2002 and 2003: they accounted for around three quarters of the increase in the volume of world merchandise exports. Moreover, some developing countries have become important markets for a wide range of manufactures and commodities. Among the most rapidly growing economies are large developing countries such as China and In-

dia. Unlike expansion in the developed regions where the services sector is of key importance, growth in Asian developing economies is generally concentrated in the industrial sector, which is relatively energy-intensive and requires more inputs of primary commodities, such as metals and agricultural raw materials. Moreover, given the size of these countries in terms of population, their level of development and the pace of growth of their real per capita income, some global patterns of consumption may change substantially. For instance, animal and plant sources of energy are being replaced by fossil fuels, especially oil, while higher demand for food and changes in its composition are causing exports of food products to pick up after having remained at low levels. Latin

American food producers have been among those who have benefited from this turnaround.

Based on strong recovery in the United States and Asia's outstanding performance, many observers expect an extended period of growth. But unlike the sustained expansion of the 1990s, when growth in the United States economy at the beginning of the upswing was accompanied by rather small current account deficits, the current global recovery is marked by huge external imbalances.

For its part, the United States economy is increasingly immersed in a trade-financial dynamic with Asia. Expansionary fiscal and monetary policies in the United States are helping to boost demand for Asian goods. Due to the aim of Asian countries to keep their real exchange rates at a competitive level, considerable revenues from trade with the United States have been directly recycled by central banks to the United States in the form of official purchases of United States Treasury bonds. As a consequence, developing countries reported an overall net outflow of capital of $200 billion. This was despite an increase in net private capital flows to developing countries to $83 billion in 2003, compared to the very low level of $13 billion in 2002. This increase was not driven by a recovery of FDI, which actually fell to its lowest level since 1996, but by a surge in "other private capital flows" including credit and short-term capital flows.

Private flows have targeted countries with high domestic interest rates, such as Brazil and Turkey, or those where a currency appreciation is expected, as China. A substantial share of private external financing went to economies that did not need external financing, since they had huge external surpluses in their current account balances and a high rate of domestic investment. In many developing countries, monetary authorities' attempts to avoid a real appreciation of their currencies – that would result in a loss of national competitiveness – can be interpreted as emulating the Asian policy strategy based on competitive exchange rates, independence from foreign capital and long-standing current account surpluses.

This strategy reinforces the need for the developed economies to find a solution for the United States deficit. In this respect, the focus is on continental Europe. In the euro area, macroeconomic policy constraints introduce a bias towards suboptimal growth performance and raise the possibility of further revaluation. Policy-makers' focus on "reform of the welfare State" and their neglect of macroeconomic stimuli has not paid dividends so far. That exports have recently benefited from the global upswing, despite the strong euro, only underlines the fact that the underlying problem is related to weak domestic demand and not to a loss of competitiveness among the mature high-wage countries of the region. The United Kingdom demonstrates that successful short-term management of the economy is possible if domestic demand is taken as the main pillar of growth and job creation.

Another cause for concern is the fact that the pace of recovery has not been uniform among developing countries. The improvement in the global economy in 2003 has been the result of exceptionally good performances of only a handful of countries, with great variation in the spillover effects on other economies. China has been the lynchpin – its particularly strong growth has, to a large extent, contributed to the acceleration of growth across Asia. Its trade deficits with regional partners have been growing, with particularly beneficial effects for the Republic of Korea, Malaysia and Thailand. India has also continued to see an improved performance, while maintaining a positive external balance. Some smaller East Asian economies that had previously been lagging behind the best performers, caught up and are returning to high growth rates in 2004.

The benefits of rapid Asian growth have also been felt outside the region. The recovery under way in Latin America can be traced to strong Asian demand, resulting in an increase in primary commodity prices and volumes of exports. Cyclical rebounds have been particularly pronounced where growing external demand has coincided with an end to financial and/or political crises, as in Argentina, and huge currency devaluations that improved the overall competitiveness of these countries. Despite the fact that devaluation of its currency considerably improved the export performance of Brazil, the largest economy in the region, the country is struggling to avoid an overvaluation by intervening in the currency market. But at the same time, the central bank is keeping the domestic interest rate high because it

Table 1.2

GDP GROWTH IN SELECTED DEVELOPING AND TRANSITION ECONOMIES, 1990–2004[a]

(Percentage change over previous year)

	1990–2000[b]	1998	1999	2000	2001	2002	2003[c]	2004[d]
Developing economies	**4.9**	**1.3**	**3.6**	**5.6**	**2.4**	**3.5**	**4.5**	**5.8**
Latin America	3.3	2.1	0.2	3.5	0.4	-0.6	1.6	4.3
of which:								
Argentina	4.0	3.8	-3.4	-0.8	-4.4	-10.8	8.8	7.0
Bolivia	4.0	5.0	0.3	2.3	1.6	2.7	2.4	2.5
Brazil	2.9	0.1	1.0	4.0	1.5	1.9	-0.2	3.5
Chile	6.1	3.3	-0.5	4.2	3.2	2.1	3.2	4.5
Colombia	2.8	0.8	-3.8	2.4	1.4	1.7	3.6	3.5
Ecuador	2.3	2.2	-5.7	0.9	5.5	3.8	2.7	5.0
Mexico	3.1	5.1	3.6	6.7	-0.3	0.8	1.3	3.5
Paraguay	2.0	-0.6	-0.1	-0.6	2.4	-2.5	2.5	3.0
Peru	4.6	-0.6	0.9	2.8	0.3	4.8	4.0	4.0
Uruguay	3.2	4.4	-3.4	-1.9	-3.5	-10.7	2.5	9.0
Venezuela	1.8	0.6	-5.5	3.8	3.5	-9.0	-9.2	12.0
Africa	2.5	3.1	2.8	3.2	3.6	2.9	3.5	3.9
of which:								
Algeria	1.9	5.1	3.2	2.4	2.6	4.1	6.7	6.5
Cameroon	1.7	5.0	4.4	4.2	5.3	4.4	4.2	4.5
Côte d'Ivoire	3.3	4.7	1.6	-2.5	0.4	-1.8	-3.8	0.0
Democratic Republic of the Congo	-4.9	-1.6	-4.4	-7.0	-2.0	3.0	5.0	7.0
Egypt	4.5	4.5	6.3	5.1	3.5	3.0	3.1	3.0
Ethiopia	4.3	-1.9	6.2	5.7	8.9	2.7	-3.8	6.5
Ghana	4.3	4.7	4.4	3.7	4.2	4.5	4.7	5.0
Kenya	2.1	1.6	1.3	-0.2	1.1	1.0	1.5	2.5
Morocco	2.3	7.7	-0.1	1.0	6.3	3.2	5.5	4.5
Nigeria	2.5	1.9	1.1	4.2	2.9	-0.9	6.0	3.5
South Africa	2.1	0.7	2.0	3.5	2.8	3.0	1.9	2.5
Tunisia	4.7	4.8	6.0	4.7	4.9	1.7	6.1	6.0
Zimbabwe	2.5	2.9	-0.7	-4.9	-8.4	-5.6	-13.2	-9.0
Asia	6.2	0.7	5.4	6.9	3.2	5.4	5.9	6.6
Asia, excluding China	5.1	-1.4	4.8	6.6	1.7	4.5	4.8	5.9
West Asia	3.6	2.9	-0.8	6.4	-0.3	4.3	5.9	4.9
of which:								
Iran, Islamic Republic of	3.6	2.0	2.5	5.9	4.8	6.7	5.9	5.5
Jordan	5.0	3.0	3.0	4.2	4.3	4.9	3.2	5.0
Lebanon	6.0	3.0	1.0	0.0	1.3	1.0	3.0	3.0
Saudi Arabia	2.1	2.8	-0.7	4.9	1.3	1.0	6.4	2.5
Turkey	3.8	3.1	-4.7	7.4	-7.5	7.9	5.8	6.5
United Arab Emirates	3.9	1.4	4.4	12.3	3.5	1.8	7.0	5.0
Yemen	6.1	6.5	2.7	6.5	4.7	3.6	3.8	3.5
East and South Asia	6.7	0.3	6.5	7.0	3.8	5.6	6.0	6.9
of which:								
China	10.3	7.8	7.1	8.0	7.5	8.0	9.1	8.5
Hong Kong (China)	4.1	-5.0	3.4	10.2	0.5	2.3	3.3	6.5
India	6.0	6.0	7.1	4.0	5.5	4.6	7.4	6.5
Indonesia	4.2	-13.1	0.8	4.9	3.4	3.7	4.1	4.5
Malaysia	7.0	-7.4	6.1	8.5	0.3	4.1	5.2	7.0
Pakistan	3.8	2.5	3.7	4.3	2.5	2.9	5.5	5.5
Philippines	3.3	-0.6	3.4	4.0	3.4	4.4	4.5	5.0
Republic of Korea	5.8	-6.7	10.9	9.3	3.1	6.4	3.1	6.5
Singapore	7.7	-0.9	6.4	9.4	-2.4	2.3	1.1	7.5
Taiwan Province of China	6.4	4.6	5.4	5.9	-2.2	3.6	3.2	5.5
Thailand	4.2	-10.5	4.4	4.6	1.8	5.4	6.7	6.5
Viet Nam	7.9	5.8	4.8	6.8	6.9	7.0	6.0	7.0

Table 1.2 (concluded)

GDP GROWTH IN SELECTED DEVELOPING AND TRANSITION ECONOMIES, 1990–2004[a]

(Percentage change over previous year)

	1990–2000[b]	1998	1999	2000	2001	2002	2003[c]	2004[d]
Transition economies	**-2.5**	**-0.8**	**3.6**	**6.8**	**4.5**	**3.9**	**5.9**	**5.9**
CIS	..	-4.1	5.3	9.3	5.9	4.8	7.7	7.1
of which:								
Belarus	-1.6	8.4	3.4	5.8	4.7	4.7	6.8	5.5
Kazakhstan	-4.1	-1.9	2.7	9.8	13.5	9.8	9.5	8.5
Russian Federation	-4.7	-5.3	6.4	10.0	5.0	4.3	7.3	7.0
Ukraine	-9.3	-1.9	-0.2	5.8	9.2	4.8	9.3	7.5
Central and Eastern Europe	..	2.9	1.7	4.0	3.0	3.0	3.8	4.4
of which:								
Bulgaria	-1.8	4.0	2.3	5.4	4.1	4.8	4.3	4.5
Croatia	0.6	2.5	-0.9	2.9	3.8	5.2	4.4	3.5
Czech Republic	1.0	-1.0	0.5	3.2	3.1	2.0	2.9	3.5
Estonia	-0.5	4.6	-0.6	7.3	6.5	6.0	4.7	5.5
Hungary	1.5	4.9	4.1	5.2	3.9	3.5	2.9	3.5
Latvia	-3.4	3.9	1.1	6.8	7.9	6.1	7.5	6.0
Lithuania	-2.7	7.3	-1.8	4.0	6.5	6.7	9.0	7.0
Poland	4.6	4.8	4.1	4.0	1.0	1.4	3.7	5.0
Romania	-0.6	-4.8	-1.1	2.2	5.7	4.8	4.9	5.0
Slovakia	1.9	4.2	1.5	2.0	3.8	4.4	4.2	4.5
Slovenia	2.7	3.9	5.1	4.5	2.9	3.0	2.2	3.5

Source: See table 1.1.

   a Calculations are based on GDP in constant 1995 dollars.

   b Average.

   c Preliminary.

   d Forecasts.

fears a revival of inflation should this incentive for foreign investors be removed too soon.

The structure of demand in the fastest growing economies explains the rise in demand in several commodity markets and the bottoming out of the terms of trade of most developing countries. However, the rise in commodity prices, expressed in dollars, has not substantially improved the terms of trade for all developing countries, as the dollar price of manufactures exported by developed countries has increased at a similar rate. Consequently, even if the growth of the volume of trade continues unabated, the prospects for the terms of trade and the real income of developing countries are less favourable than most commodity prices may indicate. Given that the prices of manufactures exported by developing countries have tended to decrease relative to those of manufactures exported by developed countries, the overall income effect from improved terms of trade is likely to be relatively small.

Figure 1.1

INDUSTRIAL PRODUCTION IN THE G-3 AND EMERGING-MARKET ECONOMIES, 1991–2004

(12-month moving average of percentage changes over same period in the previous year)

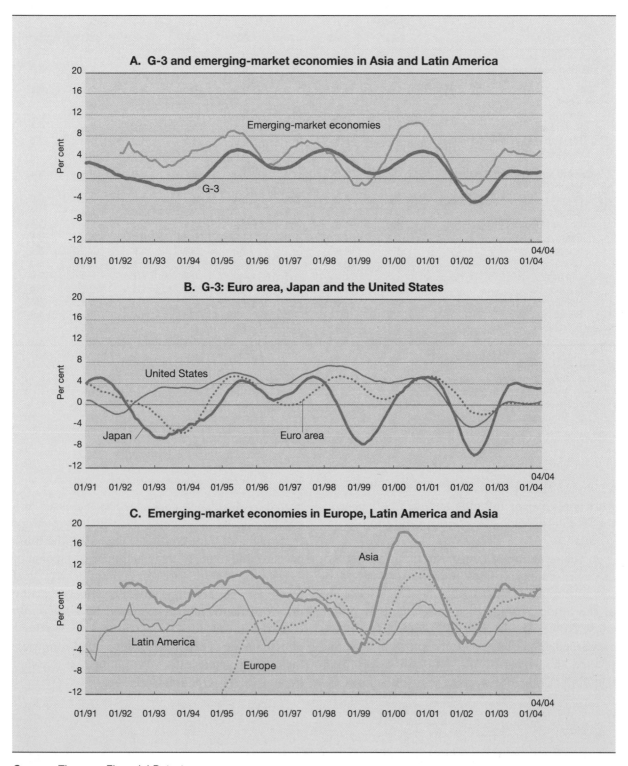

Source: Thomson Financial Datastream.

Note: G-3 comprises the euro area, Japan and the United States. For the purpose of this analysis, emerging-market economies include: the Czech Republic, Hungary, Poland, the Russian Federation and Turkey in Europe; Malaysia, the
Republic of Korea, Singapore, Taiwan Province of China, and Thailand in Asia; and Argentina, Brazil, Chile, Mexico
and Peru in Latin America.

B. Developed economies

1. Economic policy stimuli have boosted domestic demand and output recovery in the United States

The United States economy in 2003 slipped out of a phase of economic weakness that had begun in 2000. An expansionary monetary policy stance, complemented by an aggressive fiscal policy, substantially improved economic conditions, with real GDP expanding at an annual rate of more than 3 per cent (table 1.1).

The higher growth rate in 2003 was, to a large extent, the result of a recovery in household consumption and a surge in company profits that stimulated investment in equipment and software. Investment in real estate remained buoyant due to low mortgage rates.

A sharp turnaround of fiscal and monetary policies was mainly responsible for the upturn in economic activity. The traditional demand-side stimulus eventually yielded the expected results. In 2003, growth in household consumption was mainly fuelled by a stimulus package involving tax cuts and one-time transfers, designed to increase consumer spending. Part of the growth of domestic demand was due to higher government expenditures, notably a surge in defence spending. The recovery in private consumption, reaching a peak rate of more than 8 per cent in the third quarter of the year, encouraged companies to increase capital investment, particularly in information technology, in the second half of the year.

Although there had been signs of a revival of business confidence and of demand for capital goods, the current economic upswing has been the weakest on record in terms of job growth. The last recession and the present recovery have been unique in some ways. Output decline was shorter and milder than in previous recessions, due to the resilience of private consumption and an increase in real estate investment and public expenditures. But the recovery has been slower than previous ones, especially with respect to fixed investment by the business sector and employment (fig. 1.2). The delay in resumption of fixed investment by firms until the second half of 2003 was probably due to overinvestment during the long economic expansion of the 1990s. As for employment, this has been lagging behind output for a much longer period than after previous recessions, even that of 1990–1991 which was marked by a "jobless recovery".

Companies continued to maintain a hiring freeze because of their low expectations concerning the stability and sustainability of the recovery. Since end 2003, however, non-farm payroll employment has been gradually recovering, accelerating substantially only in the first months of 2004. Unemployment has started to decline since its peak in June 2003, but this decline is partly due to an increase in the number of discouraged workers.

The weak labour market performance since 2002 depressed wage growth at least as much as in other G-7 countries. The nominal growth rate of per capita wages in the private sector fell from 6.5 per cent in the peak year 2000 to 2.4 per cent

Figure 1.2

TOTAL NON-FARM EMPLOYMENT IN THE UNITED STATES

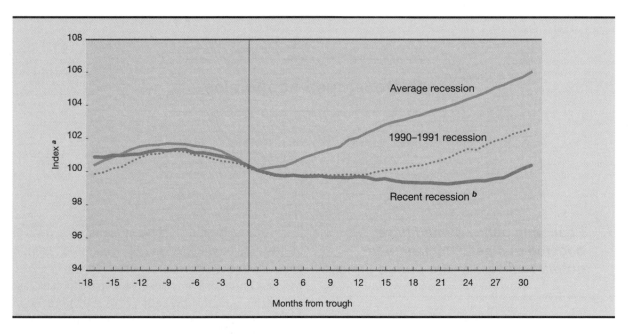

Source: UNCTAD secretariat calculations, based on United States Bureau of Labor Statistics database and information of the
National Bureau of Economic Research's Business Cycle Dating Committee.

a   Level at business cycle trough = 100.

b   The most recent trough in business activity in the United States economy occurred in November 2001.

in 2003 (OECD, 2004). Especially for middle- and low-wage earners, wages fell in real terms during the period of slow growth. This cyclical weakness of real income growth, which would have weakened consumption growth, was, however, compensated to a large extent by fiscal policy.

A comparison of pre-tax and post-tax personal incomes in the United States reveals the strong impact of fiscal expansion between 2001 and 2004 (fig. 1.3). Whereas growth in personal income and disposable personal income had previously moved in parallel, since the beginning of 2001, tax cuts and other counter-cyclical measures fuelled the growth rate of disposable personal income over that of personal income.

In the course of 2003, wage growth, in particular the so-called supplements to wages and salaries, started picking up; this, along with increasing working hours and, more recently, employment, spurred private consumption. Moreover, the increase in wages and the end of a period of

falling unit labour costs led the central bank, the Federal Reserve, to conclude that the period of a deflationary threat had come to an end and the normal cyclical pattern of rising unit labour costs had resumed. Consequently, the Federal Reserve returned to a policy of less aggressive stimulation, increasing its lending rate by 0.25 per cent at the end of June 2004.

Overall, the strong policy stimulus has succeeded in generating growth of domestic demand and profits. Although it could be argued that increased government spending might have boosted domestic demand even more than the tax cuts and investment incentives, the sheer size of the government stimulus seems to have done the job. However, it has created a huge fiscal deficit. The Government aims to reduce the deficit "in the medium term", but further tax cuts in the course of the year will not allow the process of budget consolidation before 2005. The federal deficit is therefore expected to continue to rise during 2004. As a consequence, achieving the announced

Figure 1.3

PRE- AND POST-TAX PERSONAL INCOMES IN THE UNITED STATES, 2000–2004

(Percentage growth rate over same period of previous year)

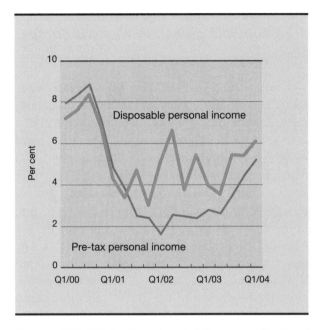

Source: United States Department of Commerce, Bureau of Economic Analysis database.

ing their exposure to currencies, which allows them to keep prices low for a while. But successful hedging only delays the effect of exchange rate changes on a country's trade position. The same is true for firms not yet passing the effect of a falling dollar onto consumer prices. A profit squeeze is unavoidable but it cannot be maintained over a long period. Moreover, the demand for imports in response to a weak dollar may not decrease as much as expected due to increasing relocation by United States firms. The sharp increase in import values is also a consequence of a surge in imports of oil and other commodities.

Therefore, the trade balance is expected to deteriorate further in 2004 and the current account balance is likely to remain in substantial deficit, at over 5 per cent of GDP, well into 2005. This will keep a downward pressure on the dollar de-

Figure 1.4

budget goal for fiscal year 2005 of bringing down the deficit to 3 per cent of GDP from an expected 6 per cent in 2004 would need a sharp reduction in discretionary public spending.

On the external side, the United States economy did not receive much of a stimulus, despite the continued weakening of the dollar, which depreciated vis-à-vis the euro and the yen by 20 per cent and 11 per cent respectively, in 2003 (IMF, 2004a). Indeed, the trade deficit (as shown in figure 1.4) remains a major concern; in the short term, the surge in imports as a result of domestic recovery and weak exports due to slack demand in the EU (i.e. income effect) has more than compensated for the weaker dollar (i.e. price effect). However, in the medium term, the price effect is expected to dominate and the trade deficit to narrow.

In the short term, the effect of a falling exchange rate on the external balance is likely to remain weak, as more foreign companies are hedg-

TRADE BALANCE, REAL EFFECTIVE EXCHANGE RATE AND GDP GROWTH IN THE UNITED STATES, 1994–2003

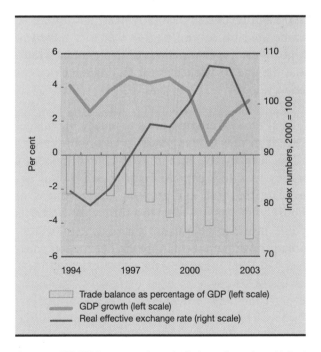

Source: UNCTAD secretariat calculations, based on United States Department of Commerce, Bureau of Economic Analysis database; and IMF, *Balance of Payments Statistics* database and *International Financial Statistics* database.

spite the improved growth performance of the United States economy.

Foreign demand for United States products will be mainly affected by economic developments in Europe (its second largest export market after Canada) and China. On the one hand, European economies are likely to remain relatively weak and only a further rise of the euro could stimulate United States exports. One possible scenario would be higher growth in Europe, which would calm the upward pressure on the euro. On the other hand, China's economy remains strong and imports are surging, but the exchange rate is pegged to the dollar at a level which might at some point discourage the import of United States products (China accounted for over 20 per cent of United States export growth in 2003). In particular, as United States manufactured exports to China are composed mainly of capital goods and industrial supplies (45 per cent and 34 per cent respectively in 2003 (United Nations, 2004)), any slowdown in capital formation in China would have a visible effect on United States external demand growth.

The outlook for 2004 points to a GDP growth rate of close to 4 per cent. Domestic demand benefited from a further round of tax cuts in April 2004 and recovery in employment, but it may be moderated by several negative factors linked to high oil prices, expectations of rising interest rates and the end of fiscal stimuli that have helped recovery so far.

If the Government aims to reduce the budget deficit in due course, fiscal policy will have to adopt a restrictive stance. A switch of monetary policy to a less expansionary stance would aggravate the high and growing indebtedness of households, mainly due to mortgages, and this could prove to be a major obstacle to a sustainable growth path. So far, the higher indebtedness has had little impact on the overall debt burden, as interest rates have been extremely low. However, rising long-term interest rates and a very low savings rate would cause private consumption to become more volatile than in previous cycles. With fiscal and trade deficits close to 5 per cent of GDP, and moderate but visible inflationary pressures, fiscal and monetary policies are likely to become less expansionary from the second half

of 2004, and growth may slow down. This would reduce the export opportunities of many developed and developing countries that are heavily dependent on the United States market.

2. Weak domestic demand hampers economic growth in Western Europe[1]

After three years of slow growth and quasi-stagnation in 2003, most of the European economies, and the euro area[2] in particular, are still at a low level of economic activity. Unemployment remains very high and the outlook is poor. The real appreciation of the euro, by some 20 per cent since the end of 2001, brought weak export growth in volume terms in 2003, although this recovered in the first half of 2004. Investment growth was negative and private consumption growth flat. The major bright spot in Europe has been the United Kingdom, which has managed to avoid recession since the beginning of the global economic slowdown in 2000 and continues to keep unemployment low.

While the outlook for exporters in the euro area has begun to improve in 2004 thanks to an upturn in the world economy and the stabilization of the exchange rate of the euro, overall economic growth is expected to continue to lag behind the United States, Japan and developing Asia, as domestic investment and private consumption remain weak. It is obvious now that domestic demand is the Achilles heel of the large, relatively closed economy of the euro area, due to the inability of economic policy to lift the income expectations of consumers in the three biggest economies.

A common feature of most countries in the euro area has been the persistent weakness in private consumption, which, more than any other aggregate, was influenced by a shift in economic policy in the mid-1990s. Its aim was to strengthen penetration in foreign markets while, in the largest countries, it was to reform the welfare State. However, macroeconomic fine-tuning was not part of the policy package.

Comparing the development of the main demand-side components from 1996 to 2003 between the euro area, the United States and the United Kingdom reveals mixed results of this policy change. While the euro area has succeeded in its external objective, it has failed to stimulate the domestic economy by restructuring the labour market, and to reform the government sector.

Export performance of the large continental European countries, fuelled by the low value of the euro, was impressive in the second half of the 1990s compared to the United Kingdom and the United States. Germany, the largest and most successful competitor in international markets, increased its real exports in seven years by more than 50 per cent, compared with 20 per cent for the United States (fig. 1.5). By contrast, private consumption in the euro area lagged substantially behind that of the United States and the United Kingdom, where in the seven years up to 2003 it grew by nearly 30 per cent. In the euro area, households expenditure increased by only 15 per cent, and in Germany by less than 10 per cent (fig. 1.6). Since the beginning of the global slowdown in 2000, the expansion of private expenditure has come close to a standstill in the euro area. Germany even recorded falls in private consumption in both

Figure 1.6

PRIVATE FINAL CONSUMPTION EXPENDITURE, SELECTED DEVELOPED ECONOMIES, 1996–2003

(1995 prices)

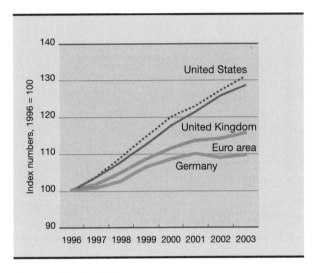

Source: See fig. 1.5.

2002 and 2003, while the other two major economies, France and Italy, saw at least minor growth in consumption. The only exception among the more important members of the euro area was Spain, where a strong increase in real estate prices boosted private wealth, construction and consumption.

The main reasons for the dismal consumer demand in the euro area are slow growth of private disposable incomes in most countries, the absence of stimulating macroeconomic policy and the persistence of a high rate of private savings. After the short period of export-driven recovery in 1999 and 2000, the sudden end to employment growth in Europe hit consumer spending much more, and more directly, than in the United States and the United Kingdom, because real wages (real compensation of employees per head) had already begun to stagnate from the mid-1990s onwards (fig. 1.7). Faced with competition from low-wage Eastern European and developing economies and the threat of a massive outflow of jobs, and in order to stimulate employment directly via less capital-intensive production, most Western European economies came under increasing govern-

Figure 1.5

EXPORTS OF GOODS AND SERVICES, SELECTED DEVELOPED ECONOMIES, 1996–2003

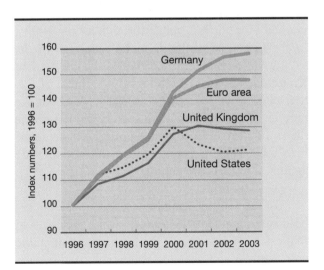

Source: UNCTAD secretariat calculations, based on European Commission, AMECO database.

Figure 1.7

**REAL COMPENSATION OF EMPLOYEES,
SELECTED DEVELOPED ECONOMIES,
1996–2003**

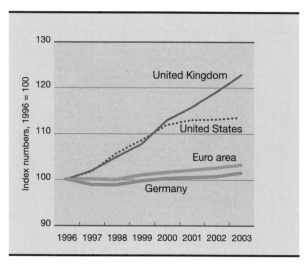

Source: See fig. 1.5.
Note: Compensation per employee of full-time equivalent
deflated by private consumption deflator.

ment pressure to maintain real wage growth below productivity growth.

However, this policy had a negative impact
on domestic demand, and not much of a positive
impact on employment. Companies hesitated to
hire new workers, despite lower wage costs, due
to falling or stagnating private consumption. Germany, the country that pioneered this approach,
had both the lowest increase in real wages and
the worst job and growth performance. By contrast, in the United Kingdom and the United States,
real wages rose without a visible negative impact
on employment. In particular, the United Kingdom has experienced the highest growth rate of
nominal and real wages since the mid-1990s and
the best employment performance. In the United
States, as discussed earlier, the Government has
taken positive steps to stabilize household disposable incomes since the beginning of the slowdown,
thereby bridging the period of slack in employment and wage growth.

In countries with the lowest wage increases,
the negative impact of low nominal wage increases
on private consumption was somewhat alleviated

by low inflation rates or even slight deflation.
However, this relief came at a price, namely relatively high real interest rates. In the euro area,
countries still have slightly differing inflation
rates, but exactly the same nominal interest rates.
Germany, the country with the lowest nominal
wage increases, also recorded the lowest inflation
rate. Hence, in addition to the negative impact of
slow domestic demand, the country faces relatively high real interest rates and the concomitant
disincentive to invest.

Countries such as Ireland and Spain, on the
other hand, which saw both wage and price increases, experienced not only more robust consumption growth, but also lower real interest rates; they
were therefore able to sustain a relatively stable
growth of private investment. In addition, in these
countries, real estate markets still profited from
the aftermath of the fall in real interest rates, which
was a condition for forming the European Economic and Monetary Union (EMU) in 1999.

Overall, the positive effect of improved competitiveness through small wage and unit-labour-
cost increases in a large and relatively closed
economy like the euro area does not compensate
for the loss of domestic demand resulting from
the diminished income expectations of households.
Even more so, if the low-wage approach coincides
with rather high real interest rates and a revaluation of the currency.

In the larger countries of the euro area, households did not accelerate their spending by eating
into their savings. Indeed, the savings rate remained more or less stable throughout the 1990s,
in stark contrast to the dramatic reduction of the
savings rate in the United States and the United
Kingdom. The fear of job losses, the threat of further cuts in wages as well as warnings about the
income effects of an ageing society did not create
the right climate to convince households to sacrifice what they perceive to be their insurance
against a less secure future.

In the United Kingdom, a fall in the household savings rate, triggered by strong increases in
real estate prices against the background of stable
employment and growing wages, boosted private
consumption. This impulse helped the country to
get through the period of global economic slow-

Figure 1.8

REAL SHORT- AND LONG-TERM INTEREST RATES IN THE EURO AREA AND THE UNITED STATES,[a] 1996–2004

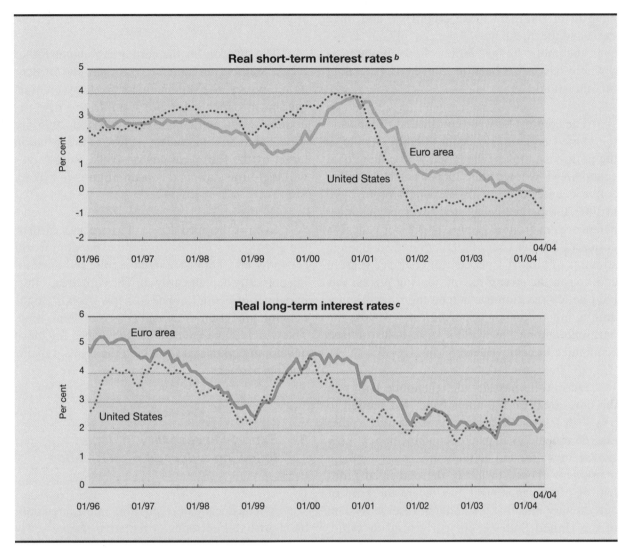

Source: UNCTAD secretariat calculations, based on Thomson Financial Datastream.

   a Deflated by core consumer price index.

   b *United States*: Federal Funds middle rate. *Euro area*: one-month euro offered rate (Datastream synthetic).

   c *United States*: 10-year Treasury bond yields. *Euro area*: 10-year benchmark government bond yields.

down after 2000 without sinking into recession. However, the elevated housing prices in the United Kingdom and the high level of private indebtedness have increased the vulnerability of the economy, especially in the light of monetary tightening by the Bank of England since the end of 2003.

Policy reactions in the euro area concentrated on tackling the "structural" deficits rather than ad-dressing macroeconomic disequilibria by means of expansionary policies. Monetary authorities considered the interest rate to be adequate and appeared to be keeping a margin for manoeuvre should the economic situation worsen. In recent years, real short-term interest rates in Europe have been consistently higher than in the United States (fig. 1.8), despite much higher income growth in the latter. Pro-growth action by the fiscal authorities remains blocked by the regulations of the Stability and Growth Pact. Attempts in some of the larger countries to reduce public budget deficits have added to the weakness of domestic demand and investment. Paradoxically, deficits have been rising in those countries, and have exceeded the threshold of 3 per cent of GDP. However, the public budget deficit of the euro area as a whole has never been in danger of exceeding this threshold.

The contrast between continental Europe and the United Kingdom is again strongly visible in the policy reaction of the latter, where the global economic slowdown after 2000 was tackled by an active counter-cyclical fiscal policy. From 2000 to 2003, the cyclically adjusted government budget balance went from a surplus of 0.8 per cent to a deficit of 2.8 per cent of GDP, giving an average stimulus of almost 1 per cent of GDP per year. In addition to the strong rise in housing prices, this bold policy reaction has helped the United Kingdom avoid recession since the early 1990s, the only one among the world's large industrialized economies to achieve this.

During the past decade, economic policy in the euro area, on the other hand, has tended to treat "structural" measures as substitutes rather than complements to macroeconomic policy. Low growth in wages and unit labour costs is the main instrument chosen to tackle the perceived problem of high wages. This has led to the kind of deflationary bias that the Federal Reserve System of the United States has eagerly tried to avoid. Measures to curb government expenditure, and many other attempts to "reform" the welfare State, have sought to give room to more private incentives and induce more investment. Cost-cutting is the core aim of such a policy approach, complementing firms' attempts to cut production costs in a period of persistent weakness. In a low-inflation environment, this can quickly cross the barrier from disinflation to deflation, as, for the overall economy, the cost of one agent is always the revenue of another. Economic policy that focuses exclusively on the cost side faces a fallacy of composition. Widespread cost-cutting can only be successful if at least one sector accepts running higher deficits. If households save, and private investors inside or outside the country cannot be convinced by low interest rates to spend more, a government that also opts out can only end up with higher deficits. Cost-cutting, without government intervention to stabilize real income, endangers the stability of the whole system and provokes a deflationary trend, even if inflation rates are still slightly positive.

The outlook for the euro area remains rather bleak. Without an aggressive turnaround of economic policy, the stalemate cannot be overcome. Income prospects for households are dim, as nominal wage settlements in 2004 and 2005 are expected to remain modest – close to the inflation target of the European central bank. Real wages will therefore stall, and consumption is not likely to grow.

Even if the euro does not appreciate further, the additional stimulus from the expanding world economy may not be enough to ignite self-sustaining domestic demand growth. The euro area is thus in danger of being trapped in a low-growth, high-unemployment environment for quite some time. This would have adverse consequences for those developing countries for which the EU is a major trading partner.

3. Export-led recovery in Japan following a decade of stagnation

After a decade of stagnation, interrupted only by short-lived episodes of tentative recovery, Japan experienced considerable economic expansion in the second half of 2003, which lifted the annual real growth rate to 2.5 per cent (table 1.1). This performance, compared to the short-lived recoveries in the second half of the 1990s, was more balanced. It was based largely on exports (which had already started recovering in the second quarter of 2002), rather than on government spending, and also on an upsurge of investment in the business sector, as well as a recovery in private consumption since late 2003.

A major determinant of the export drive has been strong demand from China that increased by over 40 per cent in 2003 (33 per cent in current yens (Ministry of Finance, Japan, 2004)). Much of the increase in Japanese exports to China is due

Figure 1.9

to demand from Japanese firms based there for intermediate goods used as inputs in products destined both for export and for the domestic market. Exports to the United States (still the most important market for Japanese exports), fell by 6 per cent in 2003 (IMF, 2004b). A significant proportion of Japanese exports to China is ultimately destined for the United States via Japanese affiliates in China. This suggests that a change in trade patterns is under way, with a decrease in direct exports from Japan and an increase in exports from China to the United States by Japanese firms. Therefore, although China has been gaining in importance as an export market for the country, the United States market is likely to continue influencing significantly the Japanese export performance in the near future.

On the domestic side, gross fixed capital formation also contributed significantly to growth. As a result of the rapid expansion of exports, firms were able to use up their entire production capacity, and eventually started to increase investment to keep up with higher manufacturing production. This recovery in business investment has been funded by larger corporate profits and less recourse to bank lending, since companies have improved their balance sheet positions.

The recovery in consumer spending was mainly due to a rebound in the disposable income of households. This ultimately put an end to the long-lasting deflationary bias on wages and unit labour costs experienced by Japan during the 1990s. In 2003, investment recovered in those manufacturing sectors that mostly benefited from the upswing in import demand from emerging Asia, and so did manufacturing wages; although in other industries wages were still falling in early 2004. Following the recovery in investment, as well as an increase in government transfers, the real disposable income of households rose in 2003, encouraging an increase in private consumption (fig. 1.9).

The boom in China and the recovery in the United States, together with a low valuation of the yen in real terms, have contributed significantly to the long-awaited turnaround. Net exports were a considerable source of output growth in 2003 and have continued to grow in the favourable regional and global environment. As the real exchange rate of the yen has fallen by 20 per cent

REAL WAGE INDICES AND REAL HOUSEHOLD DISPOSABLE INCOME IN JAPAN, 2000–2003

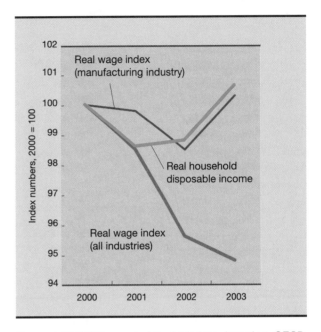

Source: UNCTAD secretariat calculations, based on OECD, *Economic Outlook No. 75*, 2004; and Ministry of Health, Labour and Welfare of Japan, database, where all industries include services and commerce.

since the end of the 1990s, Japanese exports are more competitive. Consequently, the trade surplus has been growing since 2001, and is expected to grow further in 2004 (to over 3 per cent of GDP) (fig. 1.10).

Although reliance on foreign demand is not the sole element, it does make the export-led recovery of GDP rather vulnerable to external conditions, particularly to currency fluctuations. The threat of losing its competitive advantage vis-à-vis China and the United States at the same time has loomed large over Japan's domestic recovery. This is why the Japanese monetary authorities intervened aggressively to fight upward pressures on the yen in 2003, although they could not prevent a slight real appreciation of the yen at the end of that year.

As in the past, the sustainability of the recovery hinges on the ability of economic policy to foster growth over the medium term, and not to fall back into counter-cyclical action at too early

Figure 1.10

TRADE BALANCE AND REAL EFFECTIVE EXCHANGE RATE IN JAPAN, 1999–2004

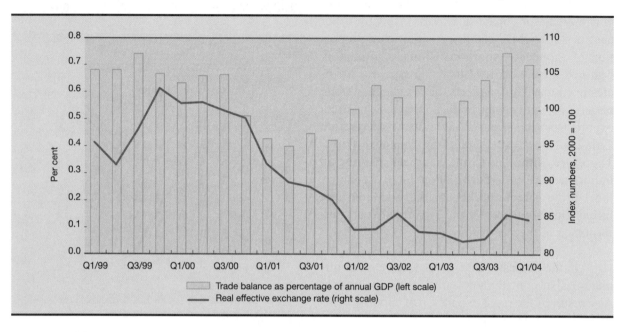

Source: UNCTAD secretariat calculations, based on IMF, *Balance of Payments Statistics* database; OECD, *Main Economic Indicators* database, June 2004; and JP Morgan, *Effective Exchange Rate Indices* database.

a stage. So far, economic expansion has relied only modestly on government consumption; government investment even decreased rather significantly. However, the Government has begun to pursue fiscal consolidation in order to reduce a budget deficit of 8 per cent of GDP, and a central government debt stock that was close to 140 per cent of GDP in 2003 (Bank of Japan, 2004). The strategy followed to reduce the debt will have a significant impact on the sustainability of economic growth. In particular, the official goal of achieving a primary fiscal equilibrium by the beginning of the next decade will require significant tax increases or spending cuts, which could undermine the positive income expectations of households.

Unlike fiscal policy, which could become more restrictive to reduce the budget deficit, mon-

etary policy is not likely to tighten in the near future. The Bank of Japan's commitment to maintaining an expansionary policy until consumer prices have stopped falling is credible and sustainable, as the very low long-term interest rate amply shows. The Bank's attempts to arrest deflation by increasing money supply growth seem to have stabilized deflation, but prices continued falling throughout 2003 (consumer prices by 0.3 per cent and production prices by 1.3 per cent), and there are still no clear signs that this will come to an end in 2004 and 2005.

On the whole, the momentum gained from the positive juncture in East and South Asia is continuing in 2004. With exports and investment expanding at a rapid pace in Japan, and private consumption picking up in early 2004, GDP growth is expected to exceed 4 per cent in 2004.

C. Developing and transition economies

1. Dynamic performance in East and South Asia, largely driven by Chinese economic expansion

Following a moderate slowdown in 2001, East and South Asia have returned to an impressive growth performance since 2002. Regional GDP, which grew by about 6 per cent in 2003 (table 1.2) as a result of strong domestic and external demand, is forecast to accelerate in 2004.

The outstanding performance of East and South Asia has been fostered by supportive fiscal and monetary policies, and by a stable and competitive real exchange rate. Fiscal policy generally maintained an expansionary stance, through both public consumption and investment. Several countries recorded budget deficits of 3 to 6 per cent of GDP in 2003, including Bangladesh, China, India, Malaysia, Pakistan, the Philippines and Viet Nam (ESCAP, 2004). In some countries, such as Malaysia in 2002 and the Republic of Korea in 2003, public expenditure was explicitly used to stabilize the economy in face of slackening private consumption and/or investment. Moreover, economic policy has continued to play a central role in developing infrastructure and providing a favourable monetary environment to the business sector of these rapidly growing countries.

Despite first signs of overheating in China and high investment ratios in the region, interest rates remained at the very low levels they had reached after the Asian crisis of 1997–1998, and some fell even below. Central banks substantially reduced their discount rates, and nominal prime lending rates fell to between 5 and 8 per cent in China, Malaysia, the Republic of Korea, Singapore, Taiwan Province of China, and Thailand. In China, India, Pakistan and Viet Nam, attempts to stabilize exchange rates led to buoyant credit expansion and money supply growth. The central banks of China, India, Malaysia, the Republic of Korea, Singapore and Taiwan Province of China purchased huge amounts of foreign currency, and overall reserves in the region increased from around $970 billion to about $1250 billion during 2003 (IMF, 2004a). As a result, the real effective exchange rate (REER) was fairly stable; it even decreased slightly during 2003 and early 2004 in those countries that had pegged their currency to the dollar, so that, like the dollar, their currencies depreciated vis-à-vis the euro and the yen (fig. 1.11)

The booming economies in East and South Asia, the recovery in the United States and the stability of exchange rates within the region have spurred rapid growth of both exports and imports. Together with the strong investment dynamics, this has favoured a high degree of specialization, thereby promoting intraregional trade. Although the developed countries remain the largest market for developing Asia, during the 1990s and early 2000s there was a major change in Asia's trade patterns. A growing share of intraregional trade has improved the export performance of all the major economies in the region, despite recent overall weakness in the world economy.

China has been playing a central role in these transformations. In 2003 and the beginning of

Figure 1.11

**REAL EFFECTIVE EXCHANGE RATE FOR
SELECTED ASIAN COUNTRIES, 1997–2004**

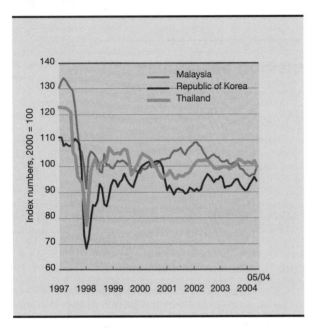

Source: JP Morgan, *Effective Exchange Rate Indices* database.

2004, China was a major engine of growth for most of the economies in the region. The country's imports accelerated even more than its exports, with a large proportion of them coming from the rest of Asia. China's exploding import demand value, which registered a 40 per cent increase in 2003 (WTO, 2004a), provided a substantial impetus to some of its important trading partners in Asia, notably Japan and the Republic of Korea.

In China, GDP grew by more than 9 per cent in 2003, driven mainly by the industrial sector. With policy eager to avoid any sharp turnaround, the momentum of that output surge is expected to be maintained in 2004 and well into 2005. Private consumption increased at a rate of nearly 8 per cent, based on the rapidly rising disposable income of households, and reached almost 45 per cent of GDP in 2003. However, a booming investment in fixed capital is at present the main engine of growth (fig. 1.12). The 26 per cent increase in fixed investment in real terms last year was encouraged by easy access to credit (EIU, 2004a). In 2003, there was rapid capacity expansion in

some industries, especially steel, aluminium and cement, partly as a result of rocketing domestic demand for private housing. In order to prevent overinvestment, the Government, in April 2004, resolved to freeze new investment in those sectors.

With a rate of growth of about 30 per cent for the second consecutive year (at constant values), exports were a major source of growth in 2003. Part of this expansion was the result of a rush to benefit from export tax rebates, which expired at the end of 2003. Nevertheless, the growth of imports outpaced that of exports, thereby reducing the trade surplus for the second consecutive year, as well as the contribution of net exports to economic growth. In the first half of 2004, the trade balance has turned negative.

Worrisome indications of possible bottlenecks in some sectors and overinvestment in others have emerged since the end of 2003 (see box 1.1). The beginning of 2004 seems to have marked a significant shift in the overall direction of the Chinese Government's economic policy, from an emphasis in growth[3] to a more balanced approach taking into account the risks and benefits of extremely high growth rates. Its growth targets for 2004 are: 7 per cent for GDP, 8 per cent for foreign trade volume and 17 per cent for broad money supply growth (State Council of the People's Republic of China, 2004). The Government also announced its intention to slow fiscal spending (which has steadily increased since 1999 and exceeded 21 per cent of GDP in 2003), in order to reduce the budget deficit of around 3 per cent of GDP in 2003. A mix of additional monetary measures and administrative restrictions to curb overinvestment, such as credit tightening, is complementing macroeconomic policy.

The Republic of Korea, Singapore and Taiwan Province of China experienced relatively low growth rates in 2003, as a consequence of weak domestic demand. Exports were the major factor of growth. A resumption of consumption and investment (largely linked to export activities) is expected to lead to a substantial recovery of growth in 2004.

In the Republic of Korea, private consumption contracted in 2003, partly due to the sharp reduction of consumer credit by credit card insti-

Figure 1.12

**FACTORS CONTRIBUTING TO GDP GROWTH IN CHINA, INDIA AND
THE REPUBLIC OF KOREA, 2000–2003**

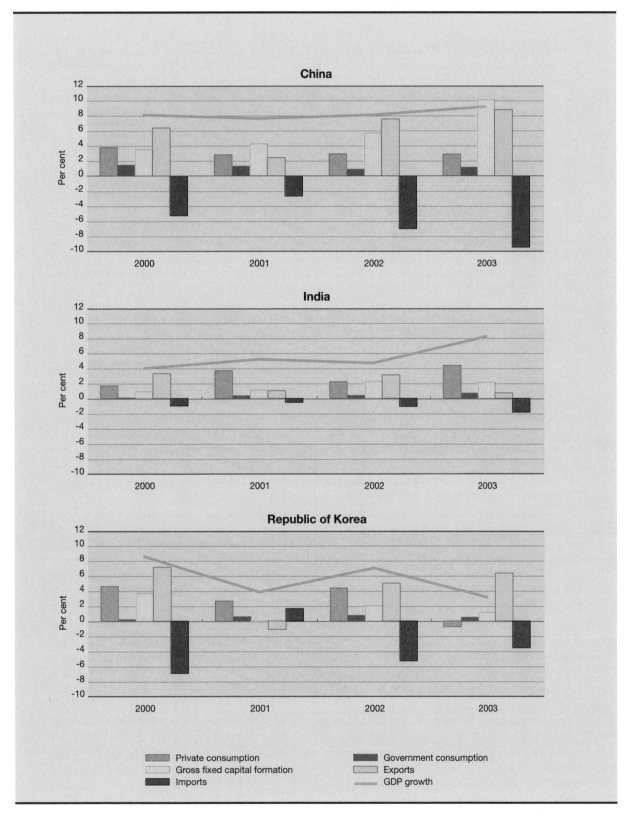

Source: UNCTAD secretariat calculations, based on Economist Intelligence Unit (EIU), *Country Forecast*, June 2004.

Box 1.1

OVERINVESTMENT AND POLICY CONSTRAINTS IN CHINA

China's policy objective of keeping the exchange rate of the yuan stable had to be put in the context of the objective of controlling domestic credit and investment boom. While the rapid growth of investment normally would have called for a significant tightening of monetary conditions, speculation about an imminent appreciation of the yuan has induced huge private capital inflows fuelling a liquidity balloon and relaxed credit conditions.

The growth of investment in fixed assets, by 26 per cent in 2003, and even further acceleration in early 2004, has become a major concern for policy-makers. Easy availability of credit, together with local government officials' zeal to deliver economic growth, triggered another wave of fixed capacity formation in private and, increasingly, in public investment. In 2003, some industries, especially steel, aluminium and cement, undertook rapid capacity expansion, in some cases doubling their capacity. Given the build-up of capacity under way, China will be able to produce 330 million tons of steel annually in 2005, but, according to many observers, domestic demand will not reach that level until 2010. To fully utilize these capacities, China would therefore have to switch from being a net importer of steel (of about 60 millions tons per year in 2002) to exporting some 30 million tons in 2005. The electrolytic aluminium industries face a similar problem; aluminium factories with a production capacity of 3.1 million tons are under construction, which will lift the country's annual supply of electrolytic aluminium to 10 million tons in 2005, but domestic demand may absorb only half that quantity (China Economic Information Network, 2004; Roach, 2004a).

The danger of such a development is that much of the investment undertaken at present could eventually turn out to be unprofitable, as prices for the goods produced in the new plants might fall well below the prices now obtained in the global and Chinese markets. This would lead to new non-performing loans and exacerbate the problems in the banking sector – a well-known phenomenon of credit-led overinvestment. Chinese officials are especially cautious, in light of their experience of similar overinvestment from 1992 to 1994. Even though the investment bubble then was smaller than the current one, it ended with several years of deflation and left a legacy of non-performing loans. Thus, cooling the overheating economy so as to contain financial losses from a future bursting of the bubble has become top priority for the Government.

However, attempts to subdue the credit boom have been complicated by the de facto fixed exchange rate regime. With United States interest rates having fallen to historic lows in 2003, investors have grown increasingly interested in Chinese assets. This has resulted in immense gross inflows of private portfolio capital, based on investors speculating on an imminent appreciation of the yuan. According to Standard & Poor's estimates, $40 to $50 billion of "hot money" flowed into China in 2003. In the absence of full liberalization of capital account, the main players were Chinese investors repatriating their offshore holdings. Conversion of domestically held foreign currency deposits into yuan-denominated deposits also intensified. As the monetary authorities were determined to defend the exchange rate, they were forced to buy a large proportion of this capital and to emit yuan in exchange. This policy increased liquidity in the banking sector and made it possible for commercial banks to hand out more new loans than the central bank would have wanted.

The central bank only partially succeeded in sterilizing this increase in liquidity by the sale of central bank bills. The monetary authorities also tried to dampen loan growth by increasing the banks' reserve ratio and by requiring commercial banks to become more strict in issuing new loans. However, results have been slow to materialize. Credit growth reached 21 per cent in 2003 – nearly double the 12 per cent average annual growth rate in 1997–2002 (Roach, 2004b). A slowdown in

/...

Box 1.1 (concluded)

credit growth in early 2004 proved to be only temporary. Further credit tightening measures were unveiled by the central bank in April 2004, including a further raising of the deposit reserve requirement and closer scrutiny of corporate borrowing. In order to alleviate the liquidity build-up from the inflow of hot money, the central bank has also announced its aim to tighten enforcement of measures restricting capital inflows.

So far, the central bank has been reluctant to raise interest rates in order to cool down the economy, for many reasons. First, this might accelerate the inflow of hot money, as higher interest rates in China would make yuan-denominated deposits even more attractive relative to United States assets. Second, it could make house purchases more costly, thus triggering a sudden fall in real estate prices, which would increase the risk of a hard-landing of the economy. Third, as lending rates and distribution of loans are not yet fully market-determined, part of the credit boom seems to be very inelastic to changes in the interest rate. This is especially true for loans handed out at the request of local governments in an attempt to stimulate growth in their region.

Abandoning the fixed exchange rate and letting the currency appreciate in order to bring liquidity under control does not seem to be an attractive option for the Chinese authorities either, even though they have long considered a possible floating of the yuan. One fear is that a small revaluation at this juncture could attract even more hot money into China, owing to speculation of further appreciations to come. A large appreciation, on the other hand, might substantially hurt Chinese competitiveness in international markets, and it probably would not succeed in curtailing the build-up of capacities aimed at the domestic market, especially overcapacity in steel, aluminium and office space.

With the trade surplus turning into a deficit in the first quarter of 2004, and domestic inflation increasing, pressure for an appreciation of the yuan is abating. In the mid-1990s, China's central bank managed to slow down the economy, without drastic interest rate hikes, by reducing credit growth through other channels such as higher reserve requirement ratios. Even though the increasing openness of the Chinese capital markets has made this task more complicated over the past decade, there is still a good chance that China will be able to manage a soft landing.

tutions, which ended a period of several years of rapid consumer credit expansion. Fiscal policy played a compensatory role, with an increase in government spending and tax reductions. In 2004, two fiscal stimulus packages have been introduced, which should encourage private consumption. Investment spending was very weak in 2003, but should improve in 2004 as a result of growing exports, a fiscal stimulus to expand construction and an expected increase in investment by many of the largest corporations, mainly in the information and communications technology sector. Despite these positive trends in domestic demand, high levels of indebtedness of households and the corporate sector may impose some limits to economic expansion in the near future.

The main driving force of growth in the Republic of Korea in 2003 and 2004 was exports (fig. 1.12). These are highly oriented to China, Japan and the United States, which accounted for nearly 50 per cent of the increase in that country's export revenues in 2003. The central bank, as in China, tried to prevent an appreciation of the won by heavy intervention in the currency market. International reserves grew from $121 billion at the end of 2002 to $156 billion by the end of 2003 (IMF, 2004a).

Exports were also the main determinant of growth in Taiwan Province of China, based on strong demand from Hong Kong (China) and mainland China. Merchandise exports, by value, grew rapidly during most of 2003, reaching a rate of about 23 per cent in early 2004 (Central Bank, Taiwan Province of China, 2004). The expansion of new high-tech production (such as liquid crystal displays), in particular, benefited from a surge in world demand. The sharp increase in investment in these sectors suggests that a new investment cycle might start to reverse the downward trend in the growth of capital formation witnessed since 2001.

Relatively strong economic growth in most countries of the Association of South-East Asian Nations (ASEAN) was largely due to a supportive policy environment that stimulated domestic demand. In Indonesia, Malaysia, the Philippines, Thailand and Viet Nam, it was mainly private consumption that drove economic growth in 2003. The expansion of economic activity and regional trade increased disposable incomes and improved labour market conditions. Personal disposable income was further stimulated by an increase in workers' remittances from abroad (as in the Philippines and Viet Nam) and higher salaries for civil servants, especially in Malaysia and Viet Nam. An expansionary monetary stance, with low interest rates, as well as greater public investment in infrastructure also created conducive conditions for domestic demand.

In most ASEAN countries, private investment has been expanding only moderately and production capacities are still sufficiently large after the strong accumulation of the recent past. Nevertheless, with rising utilization rates, the outlook for private investment is bright. Corporate profitability has increased in the region, and some countries have adopted specific incentives to stimulate private investment.

As these economies have the highest degree of openness in the region (with an export/GDP ratio ranging from 31 per cent in Indonesia to 115 per cent in Malaysia in 2003 (Bank of Indonesia, 2004; EIU, 2004b)), the performance of the external sector usually has a major impact on economic growth. The export performance in 2004 and beyond should be sustained by exports, not only to China, but also, increasingly, to the United

States (especially from Indonesia and Malaysia) and Japan (mainly from Indonesia, the Philippines and Thailand).

India recorded a surge in economic growth in 2003, at a rate of more than 7 per cent. This good performance was mainly driven by a sharp increase in private consumption (fig. 1.12), owing partly to strong growth in the agricultural sector. In addition to its direct contribution to growth (agriculture still represents more than 20 per cent of GDP), the good agricultural year increased the incomes of nearly two-thirds of the population. Low interest rates, high liquidity and falling inflation also encouraged domestic demand and accelerated growth in manufacturing and services, especially domestic trade, transport and communications.

Investment in the services sector also contributed substantially to the strong growth performance. This sector – mainly in IT and IT-enabled services – has been given a boost by the shift of back-office functions from developed-country firms to lower cost locations in India with its huge supply of highly skilled professionals in this field. The upward trend in investment and increasing private consumption provide solid internal sources of growth for India over the next few years, complemented by a modest reliance on the external sector.

Other South Asian countries, such as Bangladesh, Pakistan and Sri Lanka also have growth rates of over 5 per cent. In Pakistan, the increase in exports of goods and services has been one of the major growth driving forces, with exports of textiles stimulating manufacturing output. As in India, the recovery of the agricultural sector contributed to growth in 2003, following two years of bad crops. The balance of payments has been showing a surplus in its current account since 2001, resulting from the expansion of exports and current and capital transfers (workers' remittances from abroad and foreign aid). To stimulate production, the monetary authority has pursued a policy of low interest rates, higher credit to the private sector (especially the manufacturing sector) and a stable exchange rate.

Prospects for 2004 indicate continued strong growth in East and South Asia. The two largest countries, namely China and India, will continue growing at a fairly rapid pace thanks to dynamic domestic and foreign demand. While there might be a slight deceleration of growth in China, owing to recently adopted restrictive measures, there will be an acceleration of growth in other economies, notably the Republic of Korea and Taiwan Province of China, which are recovering from their weak performance in the first half of 2003.

The economic outlook for the ASEAN countries in 2004 and the next few years will also depend on their ability to sustain the growth of domestic demand through an appropriate policy stance. So far, fiscal expansion has played an important role in stimulating economic growth and has offset the negative impact of the recent slowdown of global demand. Monetary expansion has also contributed to encouraging domestic demand, in a context of low interest rates and moderate inflation. In an effort to support economic growth, policy-makers have accepted the necessity of budget deficits in the short term owing to the need for fiscal stimulus.

2. Economic performance in West Asia still deeply shaped by the oil sector and political instability

Economic growth in most countries of West Asia has remained considerably unstable, influenced largely by world oil markets, global economic growth and regional conflicts. In 2003, growth rates picked up in the main Arab oil-producing countries, and stayed high in the Islamic Republic of Iran and Turkey. As a result, the region as a whole (excluding Iraq and the occupied Palestinian territory) grew by almost 6 per cent in 2003. In 2004, oil revenues are higher than expected due to high oil prices. However, since regional oil production growth has been slowing down, overall GDP growth may range between 4.5 and 5 per cent.

From a longer term perspective, recent growth has been insufficient to reverse the poor economic performance of the past 25 years. Even excluding war-torn Iraq and the occupied Palestinian territory, real per capita GDP in 2003 was only 6 per cent higher than in 1980. Moreover, this figure

hides an even more disappointing trend in several countries. Excluding Turkey, per capita income actually fell by 13 per cent between 1980 and 2003, notably in the oil-exporting economies of Kuwait, Saudi Arabia and the United Arab Emirates, where the decline in per capita GDP ranged from one third to one half. Among the main reasons for this were the downward trend in real oil prices since 1980 and insufficient diversification of production. Investment ratios have been low, except in the Islamic Republic of Iran. In the Arab countries, it plunged from 29 per cent of GDP in 1978 to 16 per cent in 2002. Unemployment is another serious problem in this region of rapid demographic growth; according to estimates of the Economic and Social Commission for Western Asia (ESCWA, 2004), it currently affects 16 per cent of the active population, with the youth unemployment rate close to 30 per cent.

Insufficient investment, growth and job creation are not due to a lack of resources; on the contrary, the region as a whole could be characterized as a "savings exporter". West Asia consistently recorded current account surpluses, which led to the accumulation of international reserves and gave rise to private capital outflows. If investment is scarce, this is largely because of the weakness in domestic markets caused by income inequality, and, in oil-exporting countries, to a high proportion of foreign workers who tend to maximize the remittances they send to their home countries. High wages in the oil sector spill over into the non-oil sectors, thereby hampering their international competitiveness. As a consequence, investment is mainly directed towards hydrocarbons and construction.

Persistent political instability and armed conflicts are also taking a heavy toll on these countries. They inhibit investment, cause a disproportionate allocation of resources for defence purposes and affect fiscal balances.[4] This trend has worsened in recent years. A long period of economic sanctions against Iraq, the subsequent military conflict in that country and the intensification of the crisis in the occupied Palestinian territory have had a negative impact on the performance of almost all the economies in the region.

Countries of the Gulf Cooperation Council (GCC) – Bahrain, Kuwait, Oman, Qatar, Saudi

Arabia and the United Arab Emirates – have benefited from recent increases in oil revenues. In these economies, the contribution of the oil sector to GDP is substantial: it represents 32 per cent of GDP in the United Arab Emirates, 38 per cent in Saudi Arabia and 45 per cent in Kuwait. Moreover, as government revenue comes mainly from the oil sector (80 per cent in Saudi Arabia and 90 per cent in Kuwait), government expenditure tends to follow trends in the oil market (Central Bank of the United Arab Emirates, 2003; Saudi Arabian Monetary Agency, 2004; Central Bank of Kuwait, 2004).

In 2003, oil production quotas of the members of the Organization of the Petroleum Exporting Countries (OPEC) were increased in response to strong global demand. However, oil production in GCC countries increased even more, in order to compensate for supply disruption in other OPEC countries (Iraq, Nigeria and Venezuela), especially during the first half of 2003. As a result, GCC oil production expanded by approximately 15 per cent during 2003. Moreover, the average price per barrel of crude oil (OPEC basket) rose in 2003 by roughly 15 per cent, to an annual average of $28.1, boosting revenue in the GCC countries. These two factors pushed GDP growth in the GCC countries to rates not seen since the global economic boom of 1999–2000. The group's GDP rose by 6.5 per cent in 2003, with that of Saudi Arabia, the largest GCC member, rising by 6.4 per cent. The increase in oil revenue also helped significantly to improve the fiscal and external balances of the GCC countries.

In early 2004, both oil production and prices in the GCC countries had been expected to decline. In the first quarter, with production from Iraq, Nigeria and Venezuela substantially recovered, the GCC countries cut back their own production slightly in comparison to their 2003 average level. Moreover, in February 2004, OPEC decided to reduce production quotas by one million barrels a day (equivalent to 4 per cent), effective as of April 2004. Contrary to expectations, oil prices actually rose during the first half of 2004: between January and May, average oil prices exceeded their 2003 level by about 16 per cent (International Energy Agency, various). Consequently, at its extraordinary meeting in June 2004, OPEC decided to increase its production target by 2 million bar-

rels a day in July and by another 500,000 barrels in August. The effective increase in production will probably be more modest, since actual supply already exceeds official OPEC quotas. In any case, the prospects for oil production and prices are quite different in mid-2004 than they had seemed earlier in the year. Average prices in 2004 will probably be higher than the previous year, even if they decline somewhat in the second half, and oil production by GCC countries will probably remain at its 2003 level, or may even increase slightly if new production quotas are not fully respected.

With oil revenues substantially exceeding budgetary forecasts, governments may increase public expenditure in 2004 (as they already did in 2003) and still obtain a fiscal surplus. Their balances of payments are also likely to show a substantial surplus, with further accumulation of international reserves. Consequently, current macroeconomic variables will probably remain stable, with exchange rates pegged to the dollar, low inflation, monetary expansion and low interest rates. These general conditions could encourage private activity, especially in construction, financial services, trade and communications. Thus, even if oil production were to stagnate, GDP growth in the GCC countries is projected to exceed 3 per cent in 2004. However, this growth in itself is insufficient to solve social problems and reduce unemployment.

Other countries in the region were harder hit by the Iraq conflict than the oil-exporting GCC countries. The more diversified economies[5] were seriously affected by the deterioration in the investment climate and disruption of regional trade. In 2003, growth rates remained relatively low (and close to zero in per capita terms) in Jordan, Lebanon, the Syrian Arab Republic and Yemen. In contrast, GDP growth remained high in the Islamic Republic of Iran, at 5.9 per cent.

The regional conflicts had the greatest negative impact on the economy of the Syrian Arab Republic. Not only was its oil trade with Iraq interrupted, but also difficulties arising from its proximity to that country deterred private investment. Jordan similarly suffered from the uncertainty and trade disruptions wrought by the conflicts, but some of the negative effects were offset by an increase in exports and higher defence spending, partly financed by the United States.

The more diversified economies profited largely from the weak dollar. As Jordan, Lebanon and the Syrian Arab Republic have pegged their currency to the dollar, but trade mostly with the European Union (EU) and other non-dollar economies, their export industries have become more competitive with the devaluation of the dollar against the euro and the yen. This has benefited their non-oil exports outside the region and helped them improve their external balance. Another stabilizing element for both growth and the external balance in the more diversified economies was the increase in workers' remittances due to higher GDP growth in the GCC countries. Nonetheless, not all these economies have had a sustainable current account position in the past few years. Lebanon managed to narrow the gap in its external balance slightly; however, the estimated deficit of roughly 15 per cent of GDP in 2004 still remains significant.

In the Islamic Republic of Iran, the economy has been growing, on average, by almost 6 per cent since 2000, driven by a mix of supportive monetary and fiscal policy measures and external factors. Moreover, the reform of the foreign-exchange regime and a real depreciation of nearly 40 per cent between 1999 and 2003 boosted non-oil exports. Other positive developments have been a pick-up in the agriculture sector owing to favourable weather conditions and an increase in oil production and revenue. Agricultural growth has been important for private consumption, since almost 40 per cent of the population still lives in rural areas, and higher oil revenues have expanded both government consumption and capital spending. As in other OPEC countries, growth in oil production is likely to slow down in 2004, with an estimated increase of 3 per cent compared to 11 per cent in 2003 (International Energy Agency, various). Oil revenue will, nonetheless, remain at a relatively high level. GDP growth is expected to decelerate only moderately owing to continuing growth in public and private consumption and investment. The current account balance showed a surplus in 2003. Although imports expanded following a reduction in import taxes, a loosening of import controls and growing domestic demand, they did not pose a problem for the external balance because they were matched by higher export revenues.

The political and security situation will continue to have an important impact in the more diversified economies in the region. If conditions in Iraq stabilize, the neighbouring countries can be expected to profit from increased trade with that country and from possible involvement in reconstruction activities. An additional impulse could also come from the stronger global GDP growth projected in 2004, that could somewhat push up their growth rates.

In Turkey, the largest economy in West Asia in terms of population and GDP, there has been a considerable decoupling from the rest of the region's conjuncture in recent years. While the rest of the region still heavily depends on the ups and downs of the oil market – either by direct reliance on oil revenue or by workers' remittances – Turkey's economic development has been more closely linked with the economic performance of its main trading partners (the Western European countries, which account for about 60 per cent of its trade) and the repercussions of its 2001 financial crisis.

The Turkish economy has experienced sharp swings in recent years, with severe contractions in 1999 and 2001 followed by rapid recoveries (fig. 1.13). After suffering a banking crisis, a strong nominal depreciation of its currency and a contraction of GDP by 7.5 per cent in 2001, the Turkish economy rebounded by 7.9 per cent in 2002 and 5.8 per cent in 2003 (table 1.2). While the 2002 recovery was primarily driven by exports and government spending, in 2003 private consumption picked up and became the main factor behind growth. Exports of manufactures also expanded, despite the real appreciation of the Turkish lira, but total imports increased even faster. The traditional surplus in the trade in services (mainly tourism) could not balance the widening deficit in the goods trade and the interest paid on the external debt. As a result, the current account deficit was 2.8 per cent of GDP in 2003, and continued to grow rapidly in the first quarter of 2004 (Central Bank of the Republic of Turkey, 2004a). So far, capital inflows, attracted by high interest rates, have enabled the financing of this deficit and the accumulation of international reserves ($45 bil-

Figure 1.13

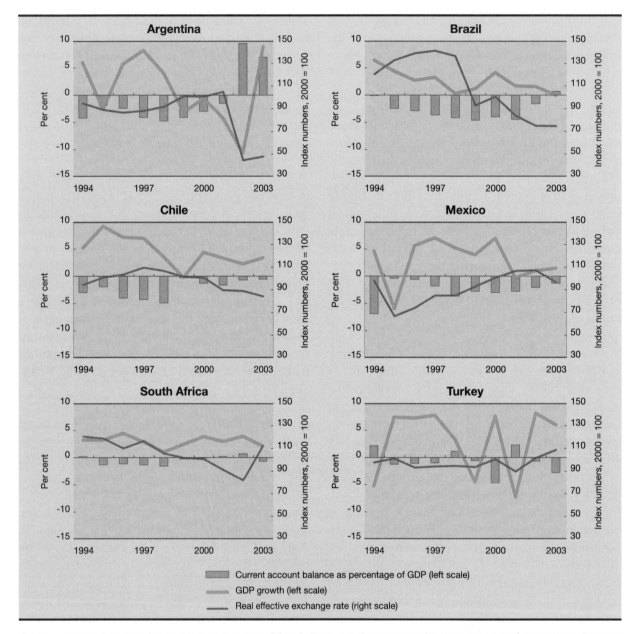

CURRENT ACCOUNT BALANCE, REAL EFFECTIVE EXCHANGE RATE AND GDP GROWTH, SELECTED DEVELOPING COUNTRIES, 1994–2003

Current account balance as percentage of GDP (left scale)
GDP growth (left scale)
Real effective exchange rate (right scale)

Source: UNCTAD secretariat calculations, based on ECLAC, Economic Development Division database; South African Reserve Bank, *Statistics South Africa*, database; IMF, *Word Economic Outlook*, April 2004; and JP Morgan, *Effective Exchange Rate Indices* database.

lion in December 2003, compared with $38 billion one year earlier (IMF, 2004a)). Furthermore, the United States has approved a $8.5-billion loan related to the conflict in Iraq. However, the large external debt (equivalent to 62 per cent of GDP) and the reliance of Turkey on short-term private capital inflows to finance the external deficit make the country vulnerable to volatility in the capital markets.

The monetary authorities have kept interest rates high in order to achieve price stability. The inflation rate went down from 29.7 per cent in 2002 to 18.4 per cent in 2003, and to 8.9 per cent in June 2004 (compared with the consumption price index (CPI) level of June 2003). Hence, even though the central bank's overnight interest rates fell from 36 per cent in 2003 to 24.5 per cent in mid-2004, real interest rates remained high. Domestic interest rates have been even higher in dollar terms, because of the nominal appreciation of the Turkish lira between mid-2002 and early 2004. The strengthening of the lira has also helped stabilize prices, but this has resulted in the real effective exchange rate rising significantly above its pre-crisis level, thereby widening the external deficit. In addition, high interest rates have had a negative impact on the fiscal balance. Even with a primary surplus equivalent to 5.3 per cent of Gross National Product (GNP), Turkey faces an overall fiscal deficit exceeding 11 per cent of GNP in 2003 (Central Bank of the Republic of Turkey, 2004b). Reducing interest rates would alleviate the burden of public domestic debt, but if accompanied by currency depreciation, it could increase that of the public external debt. Although GDP growth is gathering momentum in early 2004, in the medium term, external and fiscal imbalances, that are related to heavy indebtedness, high interest rates and real currency appreciation, represent a challenge to sustained growth.

3. Export growth helps economic recovery in Latin America, but sustainable growth remains elusive

In 2003, GDP in Latin America grew at the same rate as the population, by 1.6 per cent, following two years of negative per capita growth. Economic recession had progressively spread to practically all the Latin American countries since mid-1998, marking almost a quarter of a century of subdued economic growth. In 2003, per capita GDP in the region as a whole was only 3.3 per cent higher than in 1980, the investment ratio dropped to a historical low, the unemployment rate reached an unprecedented high, and public discontent with the economic and social results of the reforms of the previous years became an almost general feature of the region (Latinobarómetro, 2003).

Nevertheless, in several respects, the economic situation improved in 2003 and early 2004. The region now faces more favourable external conditions than in previous years, with improved competitiveness, better commodity prices and lower interest rates. Several countries have gained room for manoeuvre in their macroeconomic management, following the shift away from overvalued currencies. Exceptions to this rule are Ecuador and El Salvador, that have adopted the dollar as their legal currency.

However, Latin American countries have not necessarily adopted more supportive policy stances; in some cases, stringent targets related to inflation or primary fiscal balances have received more attention than growth. Moreover, obstacles to substantial and sustainable economic improvement persist: all Latin American countries, in varying degrees, have to deal with weak domestic demand, a high public debt burden, external vulnerability and insufficient linkages between exports and the rest of the economy. The economic recovery under way in 2004 opens a window of opportunity for more proactive economic policies to support recovery of investment and growth and deal with the legacy of a long period of low dynamism, instability and income concentration. Regional growth in 2004 will probably exceed 4 per cent.

During the first half of the 1990s, several governments in the region pegged their exchange rates to hard currencies to fight inflation. Their success with price stabilization, however, came at a high price: it led to real currency appreciation, a loss of competitiveness for manufactures and severe current account imbalances. At the end of the 1990s, when international financial conditions tightened and terms of trade deteriorated for most Latin American countries, an economic slowdown was inevitable. It turned into a severe recession because several governments, fearing the revival of inflation, tried to prevent currency depreciation at any price. They opted for higher interest rates, fiscal restraint and even outright deflation to avoid the unavoidable. Eventually, a majority of countries adopted more flexible exchange rate regimes and depreciated their currencies.

Remarkably, currency depreciations changed relative prices without triggering a revival of inflation. In the months following devaluations, there was an increase in domestic prices, especially those of tradable goods. But price increases were consistently lower than devaluations, and stabilized quite soon at single-digit rates. For instance, in 1999, the value of the dollar rose 54 per cent in Brazil, while the wholesale price index (WPI) increased by 29 per cent and the consumer price index (CPI) by 9.3 per cent, falling to only 6 per cent in 2000. In Argentina, the value of the dollar surged by 244 per cent in 2002, WPI rose by 114 per cent and CPI by 41 per cent, and in 2003, the increase in consumer prices was as low as 3.7 per cent. There was nothing like the vicious circle of depreciation, inflation and a new depreciation the region had known in the 1980s and early 1990s. Partly, this reflects the fact that, after several years of low inflation, indexation mechanisms were much less stringent than in former devaluation episodes, when more or less all prices tended to be rapidly adjusted to the new value of the dollar. Moreover, nominal wages were quite rigid, due to the prolonged slack in the labour market and a high and rising level of unemployment. Real wages declined, especially in Argentina, Brazil, Uruguay and Venezuela. In Mexico, real wages have been increasing since 1998, but have not yet recovered their pre-crisis (and pre-devaluation) level of 1994 (ECLAC, 2003).

Furthermore, recent devaluations did not lead to unbearable fiscal deficits, as had occurred in past crises. Previously, fiscal and financial crises had provoked uncontrolled monetary expansion and speculative behaviour, which in turn fed further devaluations and inflation, aggravating the fiscal deficit and resulting in a highly inflationary process.

The change in relative prices favoured tradable over non-tradable activities. This was a key element in the substantial improvement of the current account balance of several countries in the region. Simultaneous devaluations and economic contraction or slowdown led to near-balance or even surplus in their current accounts in Mexico (1995), Ecuador (1999), Chile (1999), Colombia (1999), Argentina (2002), Brazil (2002–2003), Uruguay (2002) and the Dominican Republic (2003) (fig. 1.13).

An immediate response to the real devaluations came from imports. In 1999, imports contracted by 15 per cent in Brazil, by 26 in Chile,

and by 45 per cent in Ecuador. In 2002, imports in Argentina, Uruguay and Venezuela fell by 56 per cent, 30 per cent and 29 per cent, respectively. Exports were less quick to react, but eventually picked up in 2003. As a result, Latin America passed from having a trade deficit of $23 billion in 2001 to a surplus of $28 billion in 2003, posting a positive current account of its balance of payments for the first time in decades (ECLAC, 2003).

The move towards more flexible exchange rate regimes in Latin America restored the ability to use the exchange rate as a tool of economic policy. It also enlarged the scope of monetary policies, which were previously committed to defending clearly overvalued exchange rates. As a consequence, it was possible to substantially reduce domestic interest rates, despite some volatility following the abandonment of exchange rate anchors or crawling bands in countries such as Argentina, Brazil, Chile, Colombia and Venezuela. However, this has not yet led to any substantial recovery in credit to the private sector, because of a low demand for credit and the conservative behaviour of banks.

Despite low growth rates, fiscal policy in most Latin American countries in recent years has been aimed at reducing imbalances rather than stimulating economic activity. Several governments sought to curb public indebtedness, which had increased dramatically as a result of diverse factors: slow economic growth, high interests rates and the costs of financial crisis and of changes to the pension system. In addition, devaluations had increased the value, in national currencies, of public debts denominated in foreign currencies.[6]

Confronted with a growing public debt and, in some cases, observing the conditions set by IMF-backed adjustment programmes, several countries adopted ambitious fiscal primary surplus goals for 2004: 3 per cent of GDP in Argentina, 3.2 per cent in Uruguay, 4.25 per cent in Brazil and 6.4 per cent in Ecuador. As a result, overall fiscal balances improved, narrowing the deficit from 3 per cent of GDP in 2002 to 2.4 per cent in 2003. This represented, in terms of the primary fiscal balance, almost 1 per cent of regional GDP, resulting in a shift from a deficit of 0.3 per cent of GDP in 2002 to a surplus of 0.6 per cent in 2003 (ECLAC, 2003).

Fiscal adjustments were facilitated by the public sector capturing part of the large increase in earnings (in local currencies) from exports due to the currency devaluations and the rise in commodity prices. In Argentina, a 20-per-cent tax was imposed on primary exports and 5 per cent on exports of manufactures, while in the Andean countries and Mexico, the public sector received windfall revenues from State-owned export firms. However, an improvement in the primary balance also required, in most countries, restrictive fiscal policies, that restrained investment and public wages and prompted tax hikes. Fiscal policy in Latin America, unlike Asia, has tended to be procyclical, tightening its stance during recessions. One exception is Chile, where the Government followed a medium-term surplus target, accepting a deficit when economic growth was below average, as in 2002 and 2003. Another exception is Argentina, after it abandoned the currency board in 2002.

In 2000 and 2001, fiscal adjustment was seen in Argentina as the precondition for capital inflows, which in turn were considered the key factor for economic recovery. In fact, draconian cuts in public spending deepened economic recession and fiscal imbalances and precipitated what they intended to avoid: debt default. After the collapse of the currency board, policy orientation changed radically; improvement of the fiscal balance is now seen as the result, not the prerequisite, of economic recovery. In fact, tax receipts in real terms increased by 25 per cent in 2003 and by 45 per cent over the corresponding period in the previous year in the first five months of 2004, making possible a gradual recovery of non-financial public expenditures and a substantial improvement of the primary surplus.

Another basic change in Argentinean economic policy was in the exchange rate regime. The devaluation was stronger than expected, and took place in the midst of an economic and political crisis. Nonetheless, the economy bottomed out less than six months after the devaluation, ending a four-year recession. While import substitution played an important role in 2002, the rapid recovery of 2003 (with GDP growing at 8.8 per cent) was due mainly to an increase in investment and private consumption (fig. 1.14). Industry and agriculture have been leading the recovery: in 2003,

Figure 1.14

FACTORS CONTRIBUTING TO GDP GROWTH, SELECTED LATIN AMERICAN COUNTRIES, 2000–2003

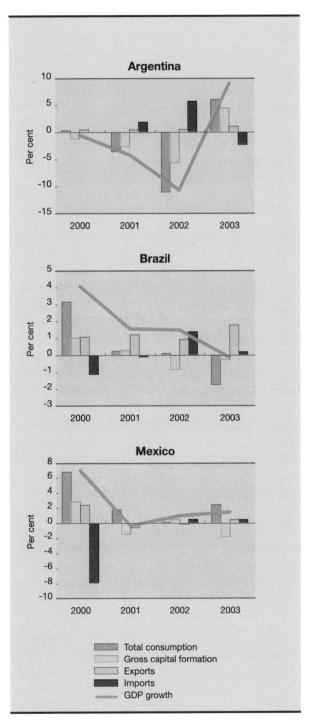

Source: UNCTAD secretariat calculations, based on Instituto Nacional de Estadística y Censos de la República Argentina database for Argentina; Instituto Brasileiro de Geografia e Estatística database for Brazil; and Instituto Nacional de Estadística, Geografia e Informática database for Mexico.

Note: Gross capital formation in the case of Argentina refers to gross fixed capital formation.

manufacturing expanded by 16 per cent, construction by 34 per cent and agriculture by 7 per cent, while services grew only by 4 per cent. This is a radical change from the 1990s, when the services sector was the most dynamic. With regard to job creation, during the growth episodes in the 1990s, the employment/GDP elasticity was between 0.2 and 0.3; by contrast, in 2003 and 2004 this elasticity was close to 1, which means that employment has grown as fast as GDP. As a result, the unemployment rate fell from 21.5 per cent in May 2002 to 14.5 per cent in the last quarter of 2003. Real wages, which fell significantly in 2002, are recovering gradually both in the private and public sector (Ministerio de Economía y Producción de la República Argentina, 2004).

The revival of domestic demand, an accommodating monetary policy, restored competitiveness and a substantial trade surplus should allow for continued recovery in 2004, with a growth rate of about 7 per cent. Two possible obstacles may slow down growth: bottlenecks in energy supply (due to low investments in recent years) and a possible debt settlement that may require large payments. The Government aims to maintain a primary fiscal surplus of 3 per cent of GDP, as it believes that exceeding this may halt recovery. In any case, the achievement of sustained growth will require greater investment, both public and private, which will have to be financed mainly with domestic resources (public current surplus, private profits and domestic credit), as has been the case since 2003.

As in Argentina, changes in the real effective exchange rate (REER) in Brazil had a strong impact on trade and on the composition of growth. Brazil's volume of exports in 2003 was 64 per cent higher than its pre-devaluation level of 1998 (during the five previous years, the export volume had increased by only 11 per cent). The volume of imports contracted by 15 per cent between 1998 and 2003, resulting in a switch from a trade deficit of $7 billion in 1998 to a surplus of $25 billion in 2003, and the current account also shifted from a deficit of 4.3 per cent of GDP to a surplus of 0.6 per cent (fig. 1.13).

However, the contribution of external trade to growth has not been complemented by domestic demand (fig. 1.14). Private consumption was affected by a substantial fall in real wages between 2000 and 2003, and a high unemployment rate that reached a record high, of over 13 per cent, in April 2004 (IBGE, 2004). Investment also contracted in 2002 and 2003, partly due to low domestic demand, and partly to the high real interest rate. After the 1999 devaluation, the interest rate set by the central bank (Selic rate) fell sharply, although never below 15 per cent. However, the central bank raised it again in late 2002 and early 2003 in response to a speculative attack against the currency and the threat of inflation. High interest rates attracted short-term capital flows. As a result, the central bank intervened in the foreign exchange market during much of 2003 in order to prevent a strong real appreciation of its currency. This has come at a high cost, since the interest obtained by the central bank on international reserves is much lower than that paid on the public debt issued in order to sterilize the monetary effect of reserves accumulation. More recently, there has been another gradual reduction of the Selic rate, from 26.5 per cent in May 2003 to 16 per cent in April 2004, which is still close to 10 per cent in real terms (Banco Central do Brasil, 2004b). High real interest rates not only weaken domestic demand, but also represent a heavy burden for public accounts; by January 2004, the public domestic debt was over 48 per cent of GDP. Thus fiscal policy has not been directed to providing incentives to economic activity but to generating high primary surpluses in order to assure the servicing of the public debt.

The Brazilian economy is recovering in 2004, with a growth rate forecast of 3.5 per cent. Even if the country were to show an encouraging trade performance in 2004, more substantial economic growth will require a significant recovery of investment and private consumption. This would be in line with the 2004–2007 national plan, *Plano Plurianual,* that includes investment in infrastructure, social projects and "mass consumption", along with an increase in employment and wages.[7] From a macroeconomic point of view, however, this will also require further cuts in interest rates.

In contrast to the success of Argentina and Brazil in export markets was Mexico's slowdown in export performance. The downturn of the United States economy explains the sudden stagnation of Mexican exports in 2001 and 2002; but while the growth of United States imports resumed in 2003, those originating from Mexico did not recover, most probably due to a real appreciation of the Mexican peso between 1995 and 2002 (fig. 1.13). Mexico has suffered a loss of competitiveness in manufacturing exports vis-à-vis other developing countries whose exports to the United States boomed in 2003. The slowdown of exports, together with weak domestic consumption, caused a drop in manufacturing production and in capital formation (excluding construction) (fig. 1.14). Trade figures for the first months of 2004 showed a strong recovery of Mexican exports, as a result of the United States economy gaining momentum, as well as high oil prices, and GDP is expected to grow 3.5 per cent in 2004. However, the experience of the last few years shows that for sustained growth in Mexico there needs to be a recovery in domestic demand, which requires more growth-oriented monetary and fiscal policies.

In Bolivia, Chile, Ecuador and Peru, exports have been increasing both in value and volume in 2003 and 2004, despite relatively stable real effective exchange rates in those countries in the last couple of years, and even an appreciation in Ecuador. This is the result of a long-term investment process in the primary sector, especially in hydrocarbons and mining. These investments, and an amelioration in the terms of trade, have contributed to the moderate growth of most Andean economies in 2003 (between 2 and 4 per cent), which is continuing in 2004. Higher exports (mainly of oil, gas, copper and gold) have provided supplementary revenues to the governments. However, this relief does not solve the more structural problem posed by the high public and external indebtedness of Bolivia, Colombia, Ecuador and Peru; this could lead to more restrictive macroeconomic policy stances, especially if prices of export commodities return to lower levels. The contrast between growing primary exports and structural fiscal difficulties has raised questions about the taxes paid by transnational corporations (TNCs) operating in those sectors, as these are significantly lower than what they pay in developed

countries and other developing regions (ECLAC, 2001). Another factor that has inhibited economic growth, despite export dynamism, is related to stagnant wages and persistent unemployment, which have subdued domestic demand.

Among the Andean countries, Venezuela is likely to post the highest growth rate (well above 10 per cent) as a result of the normalization of oil production, following the strike between December 2002 and February 2003; this growth would represent a partial recovery from steep GDP contractions in 2002 and 2003. Ecuador should also improve its growth rate in 2004, due to the operation of a new pipeline that permits an increase in oil production and exports. However, the jump in oil production is to some extent a one-off event (further expansion will need new investments), and non-oil sectors are lagging behind. In Chile, low interest rates and a renewed credit supply are encouraging private consumption, and the government is launching several infrastructure projects, mostly based on the build-operate-transfer scheme. These domestic demand factors will give added momentum to an already dynamic export sector, raising GDP growth to around 4.5 per cent in 2004.

All in all, the shift of most Latin American economies towards more flexible exchange rate regimes has helped restore competitiveness in several of them and provided more room for macroeconomic policy. The projected increase in growth rates from 1.6 per cent in 2003 to more than 4 per cent in 2004 would be a significant improvement. However, resuming a sustained growth path requires more fundamental policy changes in order to stimulate domestic demand. Revival of domestic investment and of private consumption requires less restrictive financial and monetary conditions, and in some cases an easing of the public debt burden, reform of the fiscal structure and enhancing the supply of domestic credit. Additionally, a pro-growth environment over a number of years will only be possible if measures aimed at a more equitable distribution of income are implemented.

4. Growth remains subdued in Africa, despite improvement in commodity prices

With real GDP growing at 3.5 per cent in 2003, Africa's economic performance improved slightly compared to 2002, when the overall growth rate did not exceed 3 per cent (table 1.2). In sub-Saharan Africa (SSA), however, real GDP remained sluggish, at about 2.5 per cent. The moderately improved growth in Africa appears to have been influenced mainly by higher prices of fuel and most non-fuel commodities and non-ferrous base metals although, in the case of many non-fuel commodities of interest for Africa, prices were still significantly below their more recent peaks of 1996–1997, just prior to the onset of the Asian crisis.[8] Much of the continent also experienced better weather conditions during the year, and significant progress was made in restoring and/or maintaining political stability in several countries including the Democratic Republic of the Congo, Liberia, Madagascar and Sierra Leone.

Nevertheless, continuing political instability in a few countries has undermined economic growth by disrupting existing economic activities and discouraging new investments, not only in the countries concerned but also in neighbouring countries, through negative regional spillover effects. For example, the economic downturn, due to political instability for the third consecutive year, in Côte d'Ivoire, the largest West African economy of the Communauté financière africaine (CFA), had a negative impact on its landlocked neighbours. The economic slowdown in East Africa, due to the drought in Ethiopia, also adversely affected economic growth in the region. Indeed, overall growth rates in Africa mask wide country or regional differences, with the oil-producing regions registering far stronger growth in 2003 than the non-oil producing ones.

With low investment rates and insufficient economic diversification, the region continues to perform below its economic potential. The majority of the population in many countries still depends on the huge informal sector for jobs and livelihoods. While this implies that measuring economic wealth in the formal sector alone almost certainly under-records the level of real income

in the whole economy, the growth impact of the informal sector is much less clear-cut.

North Africa, with a real GDP growth of 5 per cent in 2003, recorded the best subregional performance of the region, partly because of improved weather conditions that contributed to strong growth in agriculture. Higher oil prices benefited the economies of Algeria, Egypt and the Libyan Arab Jamahiriya. A reversal of economic policy in Egypt and Tunisia (a loose monetary policy combined with real currency depreciations), and the recovery of tourism after a slump following the September 11 attacks in the United States also helped to improve the conditions for growth. Overall production in the region has also been stimulated by the expansion of telecommunication services. In 2004, the relatively high growth rate is probably set to continue. With average oil prices expected to remain high, the oil-exporting countries should benefit, while the recovery of global demand should have a positive impact on the more competitive economies.

In East Africa, real GDP growth did not exceed 2.5 per cent in 2003, despite an economic rebound in Madagascar, following a severe contraction in 2002, and continuing good performance in Uganda and the United Republic of Tanzania. Economic recovery in Uganda was supported by the injection of considerable foreign aid for improving infrastructure, health and education. Macroeconomic stabilization policies had to grapple with the problem of sterilizing the impact of official development assistance (ODA) flows on the exchange rate. These inflows have increased more or less steadily in recent years, from a gross total of $208 million in 1986 to a net total of about $1 billion. The main sources are the International Development Association of the World Bank, the EU, and bilateral donors such as Denmark, the United Kingdom and the United States. The construction and mining sectors remained robust in the United Republic of Tanzania, but real GDP growth dipped by almost one percentage point to about 5.5 per cent, most probably because of the adverse effects of erratic rainfall on the agricultural sector during much of the year. The economy of the Seychelles performed poorly for the third consecutive year, due to a decline in tourism. Output contracted by almost 4 per cent in Ethiopia, where a severe drought affected agricultural output (which accounts for 40 per cent of GDP) and raised food prices. Weather conditions in 2004 augur well for harvests, which should lead to a substantial recovery of GDP growth. Recovery in Ethiopia is likely to account for much of the expected growth at the subregional level, of about 5 per cent in 2004.

Central Africa posted a decline in real GDP growth by one percentage point from the 2002 rate, to 3.5 per cent. A nascent economic recovery in the Democratic Republic of the Congo, resulting from the signing of a peace agreement by warring factions, brought to an end a long period of economic contraction (of almost 40 per cent between 1990 and 2001). The subsequent resumption of lending by the World Bank and the IMF has paved the way for financing by other multilateral institutions as well as bilateral donors. In Chad and Equatorial Guinea, real output growth was extraordinarily high (10 per cent or more) because of new investments in the petroleum sector, but remained subdued in several other countries (Burundi, Central African Republic, Congo and Rwanda), which are at different stages of post-conflict reconstruction.

In West Africa, the real growth rate in 2003 averaged 4.4 per cent, a marked improvement from 1.0 per cent in 2002. The rebound occurred in almost all countries, led by Nigeria – the largest economy in the region – where GDP growth recovered strongly from a slight contraction in 2002. This reflected higher oil prices, increased oil production and relatively strong growth in the agricultural sector. Ghana recorded a slight improvement in cocoa production thanks to the mass cocoa-spraying programme launched by the Government in 2001. This was accompanied by a sharp growth in mining, because of an increase in production and in the price of gold; real output growth was about 5 per cent in 2003. In Mali, despite better cereal and cotton harvests and higher gold prices, real GDP growth declined from 4.4 per cent in 2002 to 3.2 per cent in 2003. Economic growth in the subregion could have been higher had the economy of Côte d'Ivoire not experienced a steady contraction since 2000. This mirrors mounting economic problems stemming from political upheavals in the country since late 1999, which resulted in, among other things, falling export revenues. The crisis in Côte d'Ivoire has had a negative economic impact on landlocked countries, such as Burkina Faso, Mali and Niger, which had to use longer trading routes to alternative ports in Ghana and Togo. Likewise, cross-border trade was disrupted.

Economic growth in the Southern African subregion has been weak, owing largely to drought, which triggered an economic downturn in Zimbabwe (real GDP declined by 13.2 per cent in 2003), and a sharp drop in the growth rate of Angola (from 15.3 per cent in 2002 to 3.0 per cent in 2003). In South Africa – the region's largest economy – the weak performance of the agricultural sector owing to bad weather, and of the manufacturing sector due to the appreciation of the rand and weak global demand, adversely affected real GDP growth. This was exacerbated by the tight monetary and fiscal policies adopted to curb inflationary pressures. The real appreciation of the rand left its mark on exports, which contracted in 2003, leading to a current account deficit (fig. 1.13). The central bank intervened in the currency market to stem the appreciation of the rand, but hesitated to cut interest rates for fear of reviving high inflation in an environment of rapidly rising nominal wages. Real GDP growth declined from 3 per cent in 2002 to 1.9 per cent in 2003, but there was a slight improvement in the unemployment situation.

Overall macroeconomic conditions in Africa have improved. Fiscal deficits (excluding grants) as a proportion of GDP have been reduced to single digits in most countries since the mid-1990s. In 2003, inflation averaged 8 per cent for Africa as a whole, for the fifth consecutive year. Indeed, a few countries, including most in the CFA franc zone of West Africa, as well as Egypt, Rwanda, Tunisia and Uganda, have recorded inflation rates below 5 per cent per annum since the late 1990s.[9] Inflation has generally been on a downward trend, with the exception of Zimbabwe. In Ghana, inflation has been erratic, partly because of the massive depreciation of the cedi and heavy government domestic borrowing requirements.

Current account deficits have remained high in almost all African countries owing to relatively inelastic import demand, debt overhang and high dependence on commodities. In particular, in some countries that recorded trade surpluses, the net import of invisibles (services) and interest payments resulted in negative current account balances.

The depreciation of the real effective exchange rate in Algeria, Egypt, Tunisia, Uganda and, to some extent, Nigeria, should help boost exports in an improving global economic environment (as mentioned earlier, South Africa bucked the trend in this regard with a renewed appreciation of the REER since the end of 2001). However, the success of the depreciation strategies depends largely on the quality of the supply response in these countries. Sometimes this response is beyond the control of governments, particularly for countries that are highly dependent on primary commodities, due to some exogenous factors such as weather.

The region continues to face daunting challenges, which undermine its macroeconomic stability, and its short- and long-term growth potential. These need to be addressed at the national and international levels, as well as within the context of the New Partnership for Africa's Development (NEPAD).[10] Growth prospects are contingent on ensuring expansionary macroeconomic policies without compromising longer term economic expansion. This also means dealing with sources of economic instability, which, for much of Africa, are related to non-economic factors and to external conditions. Critical to increasing the long-term growth potential would be policies, which, *inter alia*, promote human resource development and institution building, improve productivity of the labour force and increase employment, strengthen infrastructure and provide an overall policy environment to facilitate diversification of the economic base, and encourage intraregional trade through a reduction of physical and non-physical barriers to trade. An important contribution from the international community would be to support these policies with enhanced ODA flows (including debt relief) that have a higher grant element within a more flexible framework. This would enable African countries to utilize the flows more effectively and efficiently in order to strengthen their domestic productive capacities to take advantage of existing market access opportunities. This should be complemented by greater market access in the developed countries, including through a reduction of agricultural subsidies within the framework of the Doha Round of the World Trade Organization (WTO).

Prospects for growth also depend upon maintaining political stability and further improving the environment for conflict resolution and prevention, as well as on policies to contain and control the spread of HIV/AIDS, and tropical and communicable diseases, and limit their long-term impact. Real income growth in Africa remains too low for the continent to meet the Millennium Development Goals (MDGs), in particular that of halving poverty by 2015. For most countries, growth would need to be doubled and sustained over a decade in order to meet these targets.

5. EU enlargement and rising oil prices support resilient growth in transition economies[11]

The transition economies of Central and Eastern Europe and the Commonwealth of Independent States (CIS), which were relatively unaffected by the global economic slowdown in 2001 and 2002, continued to register growth rates well above the world average in 2003. The Central and Eastern European countries (CEECs) saw an average GDP growth of 3.8 per cent in 2003 (table 1.2), much higher than that of the EU, their major trading partner. However, the economic performance of different groups of countries was mixed. The Baltic States remained the fastest growing area in this subregion. Among the Central European countries, Slovakia registered the highest GDP growth for the second consecutive year, benefiting from FDI-induced exports, particularly in the automotive sector. Growth was also high in those Southern European countries that received higher FDI flows, such as Bulgaria, Croatia and Romania, while countries in the Balkans were recovering slowly in the aftermath of conflicts.

In general, economic growth was mainly driven by domestic demand, particularly by strong private consumption resulting from higher wages and credit availability. Investment growth was modest and government consumption was contained as a result of progress in fiscal consolidation. Only in Poland and Slovakia did net exports contribute positively to economic growth in 2003. Nevertheless, external conditions are playing an increasingly important role in many countries as global economic activity regains momentum. In addition, in spite of sluggish recovery in the EU, the countries that have recently acceded to the Union appear to be expanding exports and gaining market shares in the EU as a result of the integration process.

The acceleration of growth in the CEECs was mainly due to the strong economic performance of Poland, the most important country in terms of GDP. The country had been suffering from a very high real exchange rate and low export demand stemming from weak growth in Western Europe. After the turnaround of the real exchange rate, expansion of exports became the major driving force behind the strengthening of the Polish economy. However, there was only moderate growth in domestic demand; investment growth, in particular, although improving, remained negative.

The Polish zloty, which had experienced a long period of real appreciation that caused deterioration in Poland's balance of payments, has been floating freely since 2000. It was only due to a sharp slowdown of growth that the current account balance recovered slightly in 2001 and 2002. The strong depreciation, in real terms, of about 20 per cent between mid-2001 and early 2004 restored competitiveness and led to robust export growth in 2003. The recent revival of foreign demand, through increasing market shares in the EU, has contributed to a narrowing of the current account deficit (fig. 1.15). In addition, monetary policy lowered short-term interest rates in line with the inflation differential with the euro area to the point that this differential almost disappeared between 2000 and 2002, and was negative in 2003 (fig. 1.16). On the fiscal policy side, the budget deficit of 4.5 per cent of GDP in 2003 (Ministry of Economy, Labour and Social Policy, Poland, 2004) may not leave much room for manoeuvre in the near future. Output growth has not helped to reduce unemployment so far; Poland still registers one of the highest unemployment rates in the region, at about 20 per cent. Nevertheless, steady economic growth in 2004, mostly based on booming exports, is expected to translate into increased investment and employment in the medium term.

In contrast with Poland, a significant deceleration of GDP growth took place in Hungary,

Figure 1.15

CURRENT ACCOUNT BALANCE, REAL EFFECTIVE EXCHANGE RATE AND GDP GROWTH IN POLAND AND HUNGARY, 1995–2003

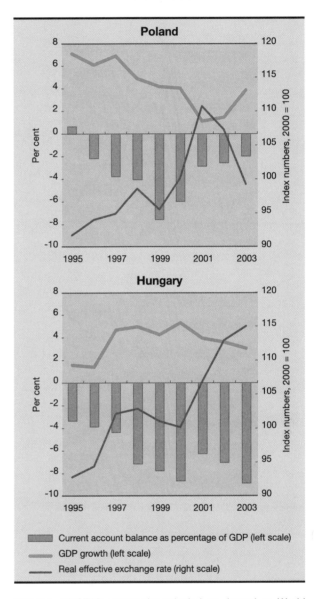

Source: UNCTAD secretariat calculations, based on World Bank, *World Development Indicators, 2004*; OECD, *Quarterly National Accounts* database, June 2004; OECD, *Economic Outlook No. 75*, 2004; and JP Morgan, *Effective Exchange Rate Indices* database.

where a floating currency and the attempt of the central bank to prevent a sudden drop in the exchange rate ended in financial turmoil. Hungary, until recently, had been regarded as one of the most successful transition economies in terms of export

Figure 1.16

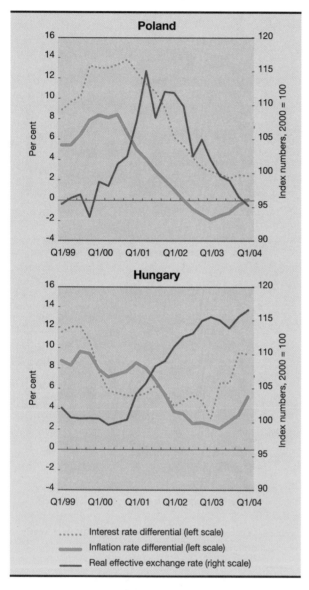

**NOMINAL INTEREST RATE AND INFLATION
DIFFERENTIALS OF POLAND AND HUNGARY
WITH THE EURO AREA AND REAL EFFECTIVE
EXCHANGE RATE, 1999–2004**

..... Interest rate differential (left scale)

─── Inflation rate differential (left scale)

─── Real effective exchange rate (right scale)

Source: UNCTAD secretariat calculations, based on IMF,
International Financial Statistics database; Thomson
Financial Datastream; and JP Morgan, *Effective
Exchange Rate Indices* database.

competitiveness and economic growth. But after
the policy of keeping the Hungarian forint in a
crawling peg with the euro was abandoned in
2001, and the narrow band was replaced by a fluc-
tuation band of ±15 per cent around the euro, the
currency began to steadily appreciate. Together

with excessive wage increases that outpaced productivity growth, the nominal appreciation led to
a substantial loss of competitiveness of Hungarian exports. This caused a worsening of the current
account deficit, which had already badly deteriorated due to a consumption-induced surge in
imports (fig. 1.15). At the same time, fiscal policy
had to rein in government spending after the public budget deficit reached 9.3 per cent of GDP in
2002 (Magyar Nemzeti Bank, 2004).

Speculative attacks against the Hungarian
forint in early 2003 led to increasing exchange
rate volatility. After the central rate of the parity
band was devalued in June of that year, a tightening of monetary policy raised the reference rate
of interest to 12.5 per cent – the highest in the
region – at the end of the year, and increased
the interest rate differential with the euro area
(fig. 1.16). This response of the monetary authorities reflected conflicting objectives relating to
inflation and exchange rates, and created a loss of
investor confidence and credibility. Consequently,
the positive effects of the devaluation on growth
may have been neutralized, as the high interest
rates have harmed the domestic economy, particularly investment. In addition, as FDI inflows into
Hungary have weakened, the greater dependence
of the economy on portfolio investment to finance
the current account deficit has increased its vulnerability to external shocks.

The accession to the EU in May 2004 of eight
CEECs (the Czech Republic, Estonia, Hungary,
Latvia, Lithuania, Poland, Slovakia and Slovenia),
together with Cyprus and Malta, represents the
most significant enlargement, in terms of mem-
bership, in the history of the EU. Even though
economic integration of the acceding countries
with the EU in terms of trade and investment flows
is already high, the enlargement is expected to
enhance these links and their beneficial effects in
the medium term.

The EU enlargement is exceptional not only
in terms of the number of countries included, but
also in the heterogeneity of their economies. According to Eurostat, the population of the new
member States represents 16 per cent of the total
population of the EU-25 (455 million) and their
area is 19 per cent of the enlarged EU area, while
they contribute to only 5 per cent of the total GDP.

Whereas in the acceding countries productivity and GDP have been growing at significantly higher rates than in the EU since the second half of the 1990s, it is estimated that catching up with the EU-15 countries will take several decades, given their low point of departure and, thereby, high potential for productivity gains. In 2002, GDP per capita in Purchasing Power Standards of the acceding countries was only 47 per cent of that of the EU-15, although, compared with the most advanced countries in the EU, the difference is clearly much larger. For the eight acceding CEECs, this figure ranged from 35 per cent in Latvia to 69 per cent in Slovenia. Unemployment rates in 2003 were generally higher in the acceding countries than those of the EU-15 (an average of 14.3 per cent compared to 8 per cent) and employment creation remained subdued (Eurostat, 2004).

While most CEECs have made significant progress with disinflation policies, inflation rates remain well above the euro area rate for a number of them. Short-term nominal interest rates are still much higher than those of the euro, which may put pressure on them to appreciate their currencies, and this may negatively affect their competitiveness. In addition, current account deficits, resulting from high domestic demand that encourages imports, are quite large, and in some cases increasing. These deficits have been mainly financed by the significant amounts of FDI flows attracted to these countries during their period of transition to market economies, and more recently, by the positive expectations resulting from EU enlargement. However, FDI actually declined in the acceding countries in 2003, partly due to the phasing out of the privatization process. Moreover, there is increasing competition for FDI among CEECs. In fact, the pattern of FDI flows in the region is changing. As labour costs increase in the more advanced acceding countries, some of the low-skill activities are moving into the cheaper locations in Southern Europe, where labour costs are much lower. The other CEECs, on the other hand, attract FDI in more knowledge-intensive and higher value-added activities owing to the better skills available in these countries.

Prospects for Central and Eastern Europe in 2004 are for continued solid growth, based on higher domestic demand and expectations of more dynamic export growth deriving from a global economic upturn and accession to the EU, even if the outlook for recovery in the EU remains relatively bleak. However, the need for these countries to address macroeconomic imbalances, associated, in a number of cases, with a twin deficit problem (i.e. current account and fiscal deficits), may lead to a tightening of monetary and fiscal policies. In fact, in 2003 some countries had already seen a reversal of the expansionary stance of the macro-economic policies they had been pursuing in 2001 and 2002 as a response to the global slowdown. In the medium term, as the acceding countries are expected to adopt the euro, compliance with Maastricht criteria, relating to inflation, interest rates, public deficit and public debt, may impose additional restrictions on macroeconomic policies.

The CIS was among the fastest growing regions in the world in 2003. It registered an average GDP growth rate of 7.7 per cent (table 1.2), as a result of strong economic activity in the largest countries of the subregion. Favourable external conditions in the natural resources sector, particularly high oil prices, which increased the value of exports and encouraged record fuel production, were the main factors contributing to robust growth.

Developments in the CIS were greatly influenced by strong growth in the Russian economy, where increasing domestic demand provided additional stimulus to their exports. In 2003, GDP growth in the Russian Federation was 7.3 per cent, showing very positive indicators in all its components. Domestic demand was high due to rising consumer demand sustained by increasing wages, while investment soared, although mainly in the natural-resources-related industries. Currently, oil and gas exports account for more than half of total exports and about one fifth of GDP, while about one third of the federal budget revenues are directly linked to oil. As a result of higher international commodity prices, the economy registered surpluses in its current and fiscal accounts. An oil stabilization fund was established to support fiscal policy and act as a buffer against adverse exchange rate fluctuations.

Meanwhile, the rouble has been experiencing a real appreciation since 1999 under pressure of a huge current account surplus, which reached levels of above 8 per cent of GDP in 2002 and

Figure 1.17

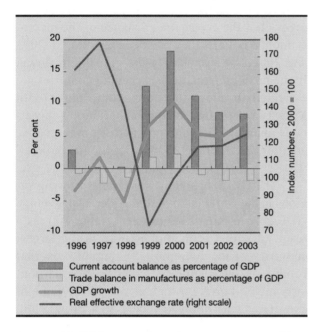

CURRENT ACCOUNT BALANCE, TRADE BALANCE IN MANUFACTURES, REAL EFFECTIVE EXCHANGE RATE AND GDP GROWTH IN THE RUSSIAN FEDERATION, 1996–2003

Source: UNCTAD secretariat calculations, based on World Bank, *World Development Indicators, 2004*; IMF, *World Economic Outlook*, April 2004; OECD, *Main Economic Indicators* database, May 2004; JP Morgan, *Effective Exchange Rate Indices* database; and UN-COMTRADE database.

However, the total capital account was negative due to repayment of the public external debt. The Russian central bank applied an expansionary monetary policy, while purchasing foreign currency to prevent an excessive appreciation.

Recovery of the Russian economy in the aftermath of the 1998 crisis was mainly based on the strong depreciation of the exchange rate of its currency – which boosted competitiveness – and on higher oil prices. As the rouble is recovering its value, the gains from that depreciation are eroding, with negative effects in the external competitiveness of the non-fuel-related sectors of the economy. In fact, the balance of trade in manufactures has been deteriorating in recent years, while the share of manufactured exports in the Russian Federation's total merchandise exports has been declining. This situation raises concerns about the vulnerability of the Russian model of growth: it is strongly based on the natural resources sector, and is therefore extremely dependent on the evolution of highly volatile commodity prices.

Unless the country makes significant progress in shifting its export structure towards a more diversified pattern, with a higher share of manufactures, it seems unlikely that the Government's objective of doubling its GDP in 10 years will be met, as the high oil prices registered in 2003 and early 2004 cannot be guaranteed to remain at the same levels. Indeed, although the outlook for the CIS region in 2004 is positive due to the persistently high oil prices, growth is likely to be less rapid in the medium term, if those prices decline. Additionally, the outlook for the Russian economy may be negatively affected by banking liquidity problems that emerged in mid-2004. ■

2003 (fig 1.17). Private capital outflows, extremely important in previous years, ground to a halt, and even showed a reversal, with increased corporate borrowing from abroad, thereby reinforcing the tendency to currency appreciation.

Notes

1 As the analysis in part one of this report covers mainly 2003 and the first months of 2004, countries which acceded to the European Union (EU) in May 2004 are not included in this section, which is concerned primarily with the EU.

2 Austria, Belgium, Finland, France, Germany, Greece, Ireland, Italy, Luxembourg, the Netherlands, Portugal and Spain.

3 Rapid and sustained GDP growth had been considered necessary for enabling the Chinese economy to tackle several challenges, especially in the labour and fiscal areas. The sharp increase of the labour force in the cities (mainly due to rural migration) and a relatively high unemployment rate put pressure for the creation of urban jobs. In the fiscal area, the Government needs to increase resources for financing the social security system and capitalizing the banking system.

4 For instance, since 1985, defence expenditures have absorbed, on average, 35 per cent of annual current public expenditures in Saudi Arabia.

5 These include the Islamic Republic of Iran, Iraq, Jordan, Lebanon, the Syrian Arab Republic, Yemen and the occupied Palestinian territory. The conflicts in Iraq and the occupied Palestinian territory render any reliable assessment of their economic situation difficult; they are therefore excluded in this section's analysis.

6 In Colombia, the debt of the non-financial public sector increased from 25.4 per cent of GDP in December 1996 to 60.6 per cent in December 2003 (Banco de la República, Colombia, 2004). In Brazil, the public sector debt almost doubled between 1996 (30 per cent of GDP) and 2003 (58 per cent) (Banco Central do Brasil, 2004a). In Argentina,

public debt represented 29 per cent of GDP in 1994, 51 per cent in 2001 and 158 per cent in December 2003; this sharp increase left no choice but to suspend payments on part of the debt (Ministerio de Economía y Producción de la República Argentina, 2004).

7 In the long run, the *Plano Plurianual 2004–2007* is aimed at launching a growth process based on the expansion of the mass-consumption market, which includes gradual access of working families to goods and services provided by modern firms. This mass-consumption-led growth would be sustained by large productivity gains, based on scale economies linked to the size of the domestic market and increased exports, as well as on the process of learning and innovation embedded in investment that is aimed at expanding the production capacity of mass consumption goods in modern sectors (Ministério do Planejamento, Orçamento e Gestão, 2003).

8 However, the gains in Africa's terms of trade seem small, in particular considering the increase in the manufactured import price index and the weakness of the dollar, in which commodity prices are quoted (see chapter II, section on commodity prices).

9 In most countries, however, considering the high weight of food in the price index, inflation is generally sensitive to availability of food, which in turn depends on weather conditions.

10 NEPAD was established in 2001 by the Organization of African Unity to develop an integrated socioeconomic framework for Africa.

11 As the analysis in this report covers 2003 and the first few months of 2004, Eastern European countries which acceded to the EU in May 2004 are included in this section.

Chapter II

INTERNATIONAL TRADE AND FINANCE

A. International trade

---

1. Global trade recovery: developing and transition economies play a major role

---

Global trade increased significantly in 2003, after sluggish growth in 2002 and a slight contraction in 2001. Total merchandise exports grew by 15.5 per cent in current dollar prices. However, unlike the trade expansion of the second half of the 1990s, which was mainly the result of high export volumes, the growth rate in 2003 was characterized by a surge in the unit value of exports (denominated in dollars). This concerned manufactures as well as commodities, and put an end to the downward trend in prices that had begun in 1995. One important reason for these price increases was the depreciation of the dollar vis-à-vis other major currencies. By contrast, total export volume expanded at the more modest pace of 4.9 per cent, compared to the average annual growth rate of the 1990s of 6 per cent, approximately three times the world's average GDP growth in that decade (fig. 2.1). The ratio of export growth to GDP growth fell to the more moderate pre-1990 levels, before trade liberalization and integration processes in developing countries ac-

celerated world trade growth in relation to that of world GDP (*TDR 2003*: 44–49).

Not only was growth in export volume in 2003 slower than in the 1990s, but the origins have also changed. Between 1990 and 2000, developed countries accounted for most of the world's export growth. This was not due to exports rising faster in developed than in developing countries (actually the converse was true, as can be seen in table 2.1), but to the fact that, on average, 70 per cent of total exports originated in developed countries (including intra-EU trade), and only 25 per cent in developing countries during the 1990s. By contrast, the recovery of world trade in 2002 and 2003 was propelled mainly by developing countries: developed countries accounted for about 21 per cent of the increase in the volume of exports in 2003, developing countries for 66 per cent, and transition economies for 12 per cent. This shift is attributable not only to sluggish exports in most developed countries and regions but also to rapid expansion of export volumes in some developing regions (especially East and South Asia) and in the transition economies of Central and Eastern Europe and the Commonwealth of Independent States (CIS).

Figure 2.1

WORLD GDP AND EXPORT VOLUME GROWTH, 1990–2003

(Annual growth rates and ratio of export growth to GDP growth)

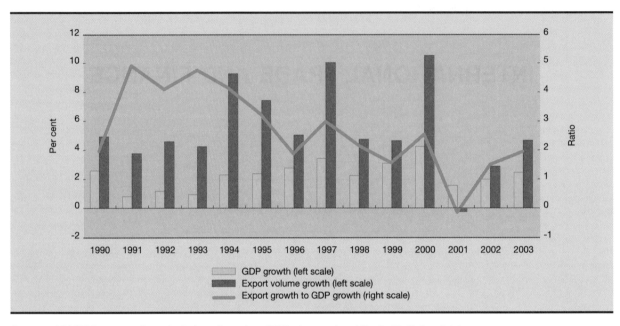

GDP growth (left scale)
Export volume growth (left scale)
Export growth to GDP growth (right scale)

Source: UNCTAD secretariat calculations, based on WTO, *International Trade Statistics* database.

The contribution of developed and developing countries to growth of world imports by volume was more balanced, at around 40 per cent and 50 per cent, respectively, in 2002–2003; transition economies accounted for the remaining 10 per cent. Imports in developed countries remained more dynamic than exports, due to the persistent growth of United States imports. Even with a lower growth rate of imports, the extra imports by developed countries have a significant impact on world trade. For instance, even though United States imports increased by 8.8 per cent in 2003, compared to 40 per cent for Chinese imports, the expansion of imports in absolute value terms was almost the same for the two countries: $105 billion in United States compared to $118 billion in China (WTO, 2004a).

Weak export dynamism in developed countries in recent years has been partly the result of weak GDP growth. In Western Europe, faltering domestic demand within the region explains the low growth of export volumes between 2001 and 2003, since intraregional trade accounts for approximately two thirds of the region's exports. In the United States, the economic downturn in 2001, together with the global slowdown of growth, affected both imports and exports (fig. 2.2). In 2002 and 2003, that country's imports recovered much faster than exports, fuelled by an expansionary economic policy and a strengthening of the dollar until 2002. During the recent recovery, the geographical structure of United States imports changed significantly: imports from China continued to grow – by 52 per cent in current value between 2001 and 2003 – while those from Japan and the ASEAN countries contracted, leaving total imports from Asia almost unchanged. The share of Canada and Mexico in United States imports decreased, while that of the EU increased (USITC, 2004). As for exports, these began to recover in the last quarter of 2003, favoured by the real depreciation of the dollar. So far, however, this has not contained the United States widening trade deficit, equivalent to 5 percentage points of GDP in 2003, up from 2.4 points in 1997 and 4.6 in 2000 (see fig. 1.4).

Table 2.1

EXPORT AND IMPORT VOLUMES OF GOODS, BY REGION AND ECONOMIC GROUPING, 1990–2003

(Percentage change over previous year)

	Export volume				Import volume			
	1990–2000[a]	2001	2002	2003	1990–2000[a]	2001	2002	2003
World	6.0	-0.2	2.6	4.9	6.7	-0.2	2.7	6.0
Developed economies	5.3	-0.9	0.6	1.5	6.2	-1.3	1.4	3.5
of which:								
Japan	2.6	-9.5	7.9	4.9	5.3	-2.0	2.0	7.1
United States	6.7	-5.7	-4.1	2.7	9.1	-2.9	4.6	5.5
Western Europe	5.4	1.8	0.6	0.8	5.0	-0.4	-0.5	2.0
Developing economies	7.6	0.6	6.2	10.8	8.0	0.4	5.3	11.7
of which:								
Africa	3.4	2.2	0.8	7.5	4.2	6.1	2.0	7.9
Latin America	9.3	2.7	0.2	5.2	11.6	1.3	-7.5	2.3
West Asia	5.3	3.3	-5.0	3.3	3.2	7.6	2.7	1.2
East and South Asia	8.1	-0.8	10.5	14.0	7.8	-1.7	9.8	15.9
Transition economies	6.6	8.2	8.1	12.4	6.0	15.0	7.3	11.0

Source: UNCTAD secretariat calculations, based on IMF, *International Financial Statistics* database; WTO, *International Trade Statistics* database; ECLAC, *Statistical Yearbook for Latin America and the Caribbean* database; and Japan Customs and Tariff Bureau database.

   a Average.

Japan's trade surplus continued to grow in 2003, but at a much slower pace than in 2002. Import volumes picked up following an appreciation of the yen and improved domestic economic conditions. Although the United States remains Japan's largest trading partner, bilateral trade between these two countries declined. As Japan's manufacturing has been steadily moving to lower cost locations abroad, especially to China, many of the goods (mainly information technology and electronics products, automobiles and machinery) previously exported directly from Japan to the United States are now finalized and shipped to the United States by Japanese subsidiaries based in China. This would also explain why Japanese exports of capital and intermediate goods to other Asian countries, especially to China, have grown dramatically. In 2003, Japanese exports to China grew by 44 per cent in current dollar terms, much of the increase being driven by demand of intermediate products from Japanese subsidiaries that produce goods destined for both the Chinese market and for exports. As mentioned in chapter I, this expansion gave a major boost to Japan's economic recovery in 2003–2004.

In developing economies, trade volume recovered in 2003, albeit with varying intensity in different regions. East and South Asia experienced the most rapid growth of both imports and exports, continuing their strong growth trend of recent years, except for a slight contraction in 2001. Intraregional trade expanded at an even higher rate, growing more than sixfold over the last three decades. At present, 35 per cent of East Asian exports go to other economies in the region, com-

Figure 2.2

MONTHLY EXPORTS AND IMPORTS OF GOODS AND TRADE BALANCE IN THE UNITED STATES, 1998–2004

(Billions of dollars, 6-month moving averages)

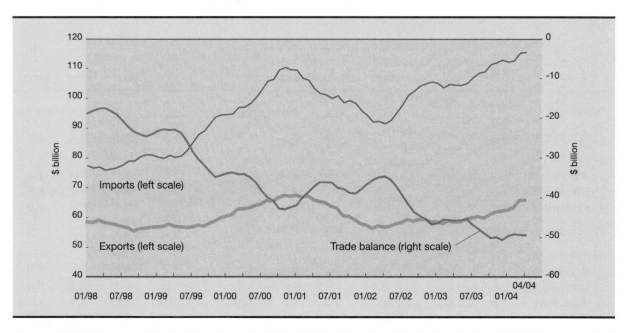

Source: UNCTAD secretariat calculations, based on United States International Trade Commission (USITC), *Interactive Tariff and Trade DataWeb*.

pared to less than 24 per cent in 1985 (United Nations, 2004). This massive increase in intraregional trade has been partly due to higher import demand from within the region, notably from China, but also to a reorganization of production processes into regional production networks, which have resulted in increased trade flows of industrial supplies and intermediate goods. These are produced in the more industrialized countries in the region such as the Republic of Korea and Singapore, and are finalized in countries with low-cost labour, mostly China (*TDR 2002*, chapter III).

The expansion of East Asian trade has occurred together with a substantial change in the destinations of exports. Deeper production-sharing practices within the region have contributed substantially to the rise of intraregional trade flows. In particular, China's emergence as a major production site for labour-intensive stages of production and assembly has exerted a huge impact on such flows, both within Asia and between Asia and the rest of the world. Goods that were

previously processed and exported by other Asian countries are now finalized in China for export. This phenomenon explains, in large part, the increasing bilateral trade imbalances between China and its major trading partners; China has recorded growing trade surpluses with North America and Europe, while widening its trade deficit with the rest of Asia. At the same time, the rapid growth of industrial activity in China is increasing its demand for energy and industrial raw materials, which it imports from other developing countries and transition economies. Consequently, China is playing a fundamental role in international commodity markets, as further discussed in the next subsection.

West Asia (excluding Iraq) saw a large growth of exports in terms of volume and value. Oil-exporting countries benefited from significant increases in oil prices. In 2003, they were, on average, 15.8 per cent above their 2002 level (table 2.2), and rose at a similar rate in the first half of 2004. Furthermore, oil exports of several West

Asian countries expanded significantly in volume during 2003, due to the strong global demand and to the fact that they had to compensate for sharp cuts in supply from Iraq, Nigeria and Venezuela. Imports also registered a significant increase, but much slower than exports, thus enlarging the oil-exporters' external surplus. The largest non-oil-exporting country in the region, Turkey, also experienced strong growth in exports, mainly to Western Europe, but imports grew even faster due to an overvalued lira.

In Africa, both exports and imports rose by almost 8 per cent each in volume, and 22 per cent and 17 per cent respectively in value. Much of the export expansion came from a few oil exporters: Algeria, Angola, Egypt, the Libyan Arab Jamahiriya and Nigeria accounted for almost 60 per cent of the growth in regional export value. However, several other countries in the region also saw higher exports: 23 out of 53 countries recorded an increase in exports of more than 15 per cent, and only six experienced a contraction (WTO, 2004a). This could be attributed largely to higher commodity prices (especially oil, mining and agricultural raw materials) and to improvements in the supply side, with greater crop production in several countries.

Trade in Latin America has been recovering slowly from its downturn of 2001 and 2002, but the situation differs by country and subregion. Between 2001 and 2003, a halt of the buoyant trade growth experienced in Mexico during the nineties, had a major impact on regional figures, since that country accounts for roughly 45 per cent of Latin American exports and 50 per cent of its imports. Due to the United States slowdown and persistent appreciation of the Mexican peso, exports of manufactures were down, and only picked up in 2004, in a delayed reaction to the recovery of United States imports. In 2003, Latin American export growth was mainly due to the solid performance of the Southern Common Market (MERCOSUR) and some Andean countries.

In MERCOSUR, real exchange rate depreciations in previous years and price increases of some important export products restored the profitability of tradables in manufactures and primary commodities, and attracted investments towards them. Moreover, the introduction of new agricultural techniques lowered costs and permitted an expansion of the planted area and of exports, particularly of soybeans. In 2003, the value of exports rose significantly in Argentina (15 per cent), Uruguay (17 per cent), Brazil (21 per cent) and Paraguay (36 per cent) (ECLAC, 2004a). In Brazil, exports have been increasing steadily in volume and value terms following the devaluation: they grew by more than 50 per cent between 1999 and 2003. In several Andean countries, exports grew as a result of several large investments in hydrocarbons and mining, undertaken mainly by transnational corporations (TNCs) as part of their long-term strategies; in these cases, the real exchange rate or other short-term considerations played a minor role. In Bolivia and Ecuador, new pipelines substantially expanded the capacity for transportation of oil and gas, and have already enabled an increase in production and exports. In Chile and Peru, the completion of investment projects in copper- and gold-mines along with rising commodity prices boosted mineral exports in the second half of 2003 and the first quarter of 2004. The increased supply capacity in Latin American primary production matched dynamic demand, especially from China. This country became an important market for Brazil (more than 6 per cent of its total exports), Argentina, Chile, Costa Rica and Peru (around 9 per cent of these countries' exports) in 2003. But even when Chinese demand was not directed at Latin American countries, it nevertheless contributed to the increase in commodity prices, thereby indirectly having a favourable impact on the region's export revenues (see subsection 2 below).

The external trade of the transition economies, which has been very dynamic for more than a decade, was not interrupted even by the 2001 global slowdown. In 2003, both imports and exports expanded by 27 per cent at current values, with almost all countries increasing their exports and imports by more than 20 per cent (WTO, 2004a). For the Central and Eastern European countries (CEECs) that acceded to the EU in May 2004, expectations related to accession prompted an ongoing process of relocation of production and generated additional trade flows between these countries and the EU. This process did not lose momentum even during the period of quasi-stagnation of trade and GDP in Western Europe, mainly the euro area, that began in 2001 (table 2.1).

Table 2.2

WORLD PRIMARY COMMODITY PRICES, 1998–2003

(Percentage change over previous year)

Commodity group	1998	1999	2000	2001	2002	2003
All commodities[a]	**-13.1**	**-13.9**	**2.0**	**-2.9**	**-2.0**	**8.1**
Food and tropical beverages	**-14.9**	**-18.5**	**1.0**	**0.0**	**-2.0**	**1.0**
Tropical beverages	-17.3	-20.9	-13.2	-22.0	8.7	6.0
Coffee	-28.5	-23.2	-16.2	-28.5	0.0	3.2
Cocoa	3.7	-32.1	-22.2	22.7	63.3	-1.3
Tea	4.3	-7.0	6.8	-20.2	-9.5	8.4
Food	-14.1	-18.3	5.3	5.0	-4.0	0.0
Sugar	-21.2	-30.0	30.5	5.6	-20.3	2.9
Beef	-7.0	6.1	5.7	10.0	-0.3	0.5
Maize[b]	-15.0	-11.1	-3.0	1.2	10.5	7.2
Wheat	-19.9	-10.9	3.5	9.2	16.2	-0.7
Rice	1.3	-18.6	-18.1	-15.2	11.0	4.2
Bananas	-3.1	-9.9	-2.3	38.8	-9.6	-28.8
Vegetable oilseeds and oils	**7.1**	**-23.3**	**-22.8**	**-8.5**	**26.2**	**17.1**
Agricultural raw materials	**-10.8**	**-10.3**	**1.9**	**-1.9**	**-6.7**	**17.5**
Hides and skins[b]	-13.1	-5.9	11.2	5.5	-2.9	-16.8
Cotton	-8.3	-22.9	3.5	-20.9	-3.3	38.0
Tobacco	-5.5	-7.0	-3.3	-0.3	-8.2	-3.5
Rubber	-29.8	-12.6	7.9	-14.1	33.1	41.7
Tropical logs	-1.2	-7.2	3.8	6.3	-10.5	20.2
Minerals, ores and metals	**-16.0**	**-1.8**	**12.0**	**-9.9**	**-1.8**	**12.1**
Aluminium	-15.1	0.3	13.8	-6.8	-6.5	6.0
Phosphate rock	2.4	4.6	-0.4	-4.5	-3.3	-5.9
Iron ore	2.8	-9.2	2.6	4.5	-1.0	8.5
Tin	-1.9	-2.5	0.6	-17.5	-9.4	20.6
Copper	-27.3	-4.9	15.3	-13.0	-1.2	14.1
Nickel	-33.2	29.8	43.7	-31.2	13.9	42.2
Tungsten ore	-6.4	-9.3	12.1	45.5	-41.8	18.0
Lead	-15.3	-5.0	-9.7	4.9	-4.9	13.8
Zinc	-22.2	5.1	4.8	-21.5	-12.1	6.3
Crude petroleum	**-31.8**	**38.7**	**55.6**	**-13.3**	**2.0**	**15.8**

Source: UNCTAD, *Commodity Price Bulletin*, various issues.
  a Excluding crude petroleum.
  b These series have been revised from *TDR 2003*.

On the contrary, CEECs actually gained market shares inside the EU in 2003. The trade of CIS countries was no less dynamic in 2003, with higher values and volumes of imports and exports. In this group of countries, commodity exports (particularly oil and gas) have dominated.

World trade in services (transport, travel and other commercial services) grew by 12 per cent in 2003, twice as much as in 2002 (WTO, 2004b). As with trade in goods, however, much of this expansion seems to have been due to an increase in prices of some services. Moreover, transport services accounted for the bulk of the expansion, while travel services (tourism) continued to be subdued. Transport services grew in 2003 in terms of both volume and value as a result of the global recovery of merchandise trade, which required increased shipments of commodities. Once again, the expansion of demand was driven, to a large extent, by China, and partly by the Iraq conflict. Costs of maritime transport increased sharply in 2003 and early 2004, ending the declining trend of previous years. An indication of the increased costs of freight is provided by the Baltic Dry Index: its average level climbed from 1,138 points in 2002 to 2,617 points in 2003 and 4,805 in January–May 2004.[1] A sustained demand of shipping transport services, especially from East Asia, resulted in a supply shortage following several years of relatively little shipbuilding and large-scale decommissioning of ships. Higher freight costs also reflected rising costs of insurance and fuel, in addition to increased costs of using older merchant ships (ECLAC, 2004b).

Travel services, measured by the number of international tourist arrivals, have not recovered from their 2001 downturn. After an annual increase of 4.2 per cent between 1990 and 2000, they declined in 2001 (by 0.5 per cent) and grew only by 2.7 per cent in 2002, before contracting again by 1.2 per cent in 2003 (World Tourism Organization, 2004). The fall in the number of arrivals in 2003 was concentrated in East and South-East Asia (by 11 per cent) and in North America (by 7 per cent). East and South-East Asia and Canada were severely hit by the outbreak of Severe Acute Respiratory Syndrome (SARS) during the second quarter, while security concerns discouraged arrivals to the United States, which fell for the third year in a row. Tourism in Europe stagnated (only Eastern Europe showed an increase), as a result of slow economic growth that hampered intraregional tourism, and of a strong euro. By contrast, in most developing regions, excluding East Asia, arrivals increased significantly in 2003. Tourism in Latin America and the Caribbean grew as a result of devaluations of their currencies (especially vis-à-vis the euro), a reorientation of tourists from the United States to destinations seen as closer and safer, and the recovery of intraregional tourism. Intraregional travel has also been important in the Middle East (including Egypt), where arrivals expanded by 10 per cent.

2. *Commodity prices on the rise, mainly driven by expanding demand in China*

After a long period of decline, commodity prices in current dollar terms have been on the rise since 2002, and for some commodity groups they are approaching their levels of the previous peaks of 1996–1997. Prices have been increasing consistently for all commodity groups, the largest increases being in vegetable oilseeds and oils, agricultural raw materials and minerals, ores and metals groups (table 2.2). Price increases of food and tropical beverages were only very modest (fig. 2.3). For coffee and cotton, price increases have brought some relief to producers in developing countries that have been faced with a critical situation in recent years. However, for some other commodities, such as bananas, producers continue to suffer the negative consequences of an oversupplied market.

In general, recent commodity price increases can be explained by higher demand stemming from global economic recovery and, particularly from the rapidly expanding economic activity in Asian countries, especially China. In addition, supply has adjusted fairly slowly to the increased demand as a result of cutbacks in production that followed previous long-lasting price declines. However, there are some additional factors that may introduce a nuance to the classical supply-and-demand interpretation of a commodity price hike. While a cyclical commodity price upswing is undeniable, a closer look reveals that commodity price increases are not impressive enough to warrant alluding to a commodity boom or a bull market.

Along with commodity price indices, the unit value indices (in dollars) of manufactured goods exported by developed countries also increased by over 9 per cent in 2003 (UN/DESA, 2004). This implies that overall commodity terms of trade did not actually improve, and for some commodity groups they may even have considerably worsened. Likewise, it is important to take into account the impact of the depreciation of the United States dollar. As international commodity prices are usually quoted in that currency, movements in the dollar exchange rate are reflected in these prices.

Figure 2.3

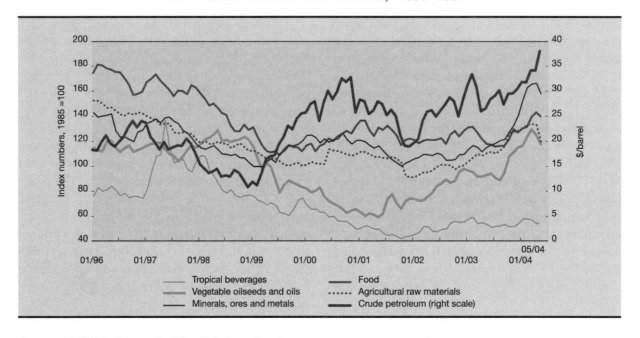

**COMMODITY PRICE INDICES BY COMMODITY GROUP,
AND CRUDE PETROLEUM PRICE,[a] 1996–2004**

Source: UNCTAD, *Commodity Price Bulletin*, various issues.
   a Crude petroleum, average of Dubai/Brent/Texas equally weighted ($/barrel).

Typically, commodity prices move in the opposite direction to the dollar exchange rate. A depreciating dollar means that commodity prices rose much less or fell in terms of other major currencies. As a result, demand for commodities in consuming countries whose currencies are not pegged to the dollar has not fallen with the higher dollar prices, and might even have increased. For many large consumers, the surge in commodity prices has been matched by the sharp depreciation of the dollar in recent years. While the UNCTAD Combined Commodity Price Index in terms of current dollars increased by over 8 per cent in 2003, in terms of Special Drawing Rights (SDRs) it decreased by 1.3 per cent (fig. 2.4). Similarly, IMF (2004c) estimates of non-fuel primary commodity prices showed an increase of 7.1 per cent in terms of dollars in 2003, but a decline of 0.9 in terms of SDRs and of 10.6 per cent in euros.[2] Given these exchange rate movements, the export earnings of African commodity producers in the CFA zone have been negatively affected, as their currencies are pegged to the appreciating euro.

Additionally, the weak dollar, together with the low global interest rates, lifted international investors' demand for commodities. They have been more attracted by expectations of the higher returns that commodities could provide in comparison to other assets. Although this form of speculative investment normally focuses on precious metals, this time it has augmented demand for other metals as well, and even for some soft commodities. The role of these investment funds has thus added to the already considerable volatility of commodity markets, and it may negatively affect the prices of raw materials if international interest rates return to more normal levels. In fact, the upward trend in commodity prices seems to have stopped or even reversed in the second quarter of 2004, which may be partly the result of increasing expectations of higher interest rates. However, in the first half of 2004, commodity price indices remained significantly higher than in the same period of the previous year.

Once account is taken of the above-mentioned factors, which do not directly relate to commodity supply-and-demand fundamentals, the major structural factor that has been pushing up world commodity prices in 2003 is the increasing demand from China. The continued rapid growth of the Chinese economy has necessitated increasing amounts of commodity inputs to meet its industrialization and development requirements. Consequently, in recent years, China has become the world's largest consumer of many commodities and, as Chinese production cannot cope with the pace of demand, it has also become an essential importer. Table 2.3 shows the magnitude of Chinese consumption growth in comparison with global consumption and with consumption growth in other countries for certain commodities. At the same time, as China is also the largest producer and major exporter of several commodities, it has become a key country in international commodity markets, with a critical influence on price levels.

Chinese upward pressure on prices is particularly important in agricultural raw materials and metals and minerals, but it has also been strongly felt in vegetable oilseeds and oils. In the case of soybeans, China's imports more than doubled at a time when they actually declined in the rest of the world. Since China accounts for more than one third of global soybean imports, this could explain why total world imports of soybeans registered an increase of nearly 17 per cent (United States Department of Agriculture, 2004). The increasing importance of China in the global market is partly a reflection of the changing food consumption patterns in the country, including the increased use of soybean residuals as animal feed for meat production. Booming Chinese soybean demand in 2003, combined with reduced production in the United States as a result of negative weather conditions and decreasing stocks, stimulated the agricultural sector in many South American countries, particularly in Argentina, Bolivia, Brazil and Paraguay.

In the raw materials sector, cotton and rubber are outstanding examples of the Chinese effect on demand and prices. Problems in the cotton market, in particular the negative effects of agricultural subsidies in developed countries on prices, have been high on the international agenda; four African cotton-producing countries (Benin, Burkina Faso, Chad and Mali) highlighted this issue at the WTO trade talks in Cancun in September 2003.

Figure 2.4

COMMODITY PRICE INDICES,[a] UNIT VALUE INDICES OF DEVELOPED-COUNTRY MANUFACTURED EXPORTS AND EXCHANGE RATE, 1996–2004

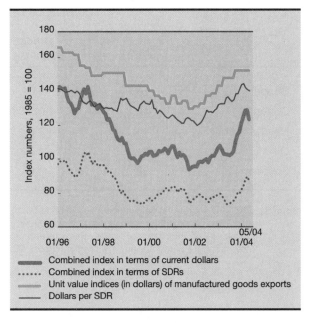

— Combined index in terms of current dollars
...... Combined index in terms of SDRs
— Unit value indices (in dollars) of manufactured goods exports
— Dollars per SDR

Source: UNCTAD secretariat calculations, based on UNCTAD, *Commodity Price Bulletin*, various issues; and United Nations Statistics Division, *Monthly Bulletin of Statistics*, various issues.
a In dollars and SDRs.

However, cotton prices rose considerably in 2003, thanks to increased global demand resulting from the previously low prices relative to competing fibres and to the dynamism of the Chinese textile industry that has encouraged a rapid increase in cotton mill consumption. Even though China is the largest cotton producer, it has had to import raw cotton in the last two years owing to the depletion of its own stocks due to poor weather conditions. China's raw cotton consumption in the 2002–2003 season increased by more than 12 per cent, representing over 30 per cent of total consumption, while demand from the rest of the world stagnated. Thus, thanks mainly to China's imports, global cotton imports grew by nearly 5 per cent, even though imports in other countries fell. Cotton import demand in China in the 2003–2004 season is expected to be about one fifth of world imports, up from only 1.6 per cent in 2001–2002 (International Cotton Advisory Committee, 2004).

Table 2.3

GROWTH IN THE CONSUMPTION OF SELECTED PRIMARY COMMODITIES IN 2003: CHINA AND THE REST OF THE WORLD

(Percentage)

| | Consumption growth | | | Contribution of China to global consumption growth | Share of China in global consumption |
	China	*Other countries*	*World*		
Copper	9.6	1.0	2.6	67.4	19.5
Cotton	12.3	0.3	3.7	93.5	30.5
Natural rubber	11.1	3.6	4.9	39.2	18.5
Oil	11.1	1.5	2.1	34.4	7.0
Soybeans	32.3	0.9	4.9	84.9	16.3

Source: UNCTAD secretariat calculations, based on United States Department of Agriculture (USDA), *Oilseeds: World Markets and Trade,* April 2004; International Cotton Advisory Committee (ICAC), *La volatilité des prix sur le marché mondial du cotton,* 2004; International Rubber Study Group, 2004; International Copper Study Group, *Copper Bulletin,* 2004; and International Energy Agency, *Oil Market Report,* May 2004.

In the case of rubber, growing demand in China, the world's leading consumer country for this commodity (owing to the rapid expansion of the automotive industry) has driven up rubber prices. In 2003, China's natural rubber consumption grew by over 11 per cent, compared to the nearly 5 per cent increase at the global level, and represented 18.5 per cent of global consumption (table 2.3). China currently produces only about one third of its total annual consumption.

Similarly, the booming manufacturing and construction sectors in China have pushed up demand for metals and minerals, resulting in price peaks for some of them such as copper, iron ore and nickel, mostly driven by strong stainless steel consumption and production. In the case of copper, Chinese imports of refined copper have doubled in the past three years, accounting for more than 17 per cent of world imports in 2002. For the near future, even though there are some concerns about overheating of the Chinese economy, leading to capacity bottlenecks and the possibility of growth slowing down, Asian demand for commodities is expected to remain firm, with China playing the leading role followed, in time, by India. In fact, measures announced by the Chi-

nese Government to prevent overheating of the economy may be an additional factor explaining the weakening in the upward trend in commodity prices during the second quarter of 2004. A side-effect of China's high demand for commodities was found in the freight market, where prices exploded partly because of lack of ships, inefficiencies in Chinese ports and high oil prices.

The economic boom in China is also highly energy intensive; the resulting strong demand is therefore playing a fairly decisive role in global markets (particularly for coal and oil). Unlike other commodities, for coal the impact on the global market arises mainly on the export side. As both the largest producer and consumer of coal in the world, China can reasonably satisfy most of its own coal needs. However, strong coal consumption in the domestic market has been reducing the amount of coal available for export, thereby pushing up world coal prices. In the oil sector, the weight of oil in the fuel-energy mix in China is relatively limited due to the importance of coal and the comparatively low use of road transportation and individual automobiles. As a consequence, China's share in world oil demand is fairly low, accounting for only 7 per cent of total demand (table 2.3). Nevertheless, China's growth in demand for oil has doubled in the last decade, which is one of the main reasons for the current tight oil markets. As a result of escalating industry needs and increasing automobile use, China has overtaken Japan to become the second largest oil-consuming country in the world. With net oil imports increasing by 33.4 per cent in 2003, China was responsible for over one third of the growth of global oil demand (IEA, various).

Crude petroleum prices have been growing steadily since May 2003 and during the first half of 2004, reaching, in nominal terms, a record level since the beginning of the 1990s. Apart from growing demand, prompted by China and by the global economic recovery, the oil market is vulnerable to uncertainties surrounding the possibility of supply disruptions, even though the market is not in a structural deficit position and supply could be expanded. One major reason for the tightness is geopolitical tensions in the Middle East, and particularly in Iraq. Although in other important producers, like Nigeria and Venezuela, oil production has recovered after serious cuts in early 2003 due to internal conflicts, these precedents have added to uncertainty in oil markets. In addition, the low level of oil reserves in consuming countries, mainly in the United States, combined with a cold winter and the actions of speculators, increased the pressure on the demand side. Last, but not least, OPEC tried to prevent a decline in prices, even though it increased its production in order to compensate for the reduction or suspension of exports from Iraq, Nigeria and Venezuela in the first half of 2003. This policy of high prices is mainly favouring the production and exports of non-OPEC oil-producing countries, such as the Russian Federation, where oil production is more costly.

Once again, the depreciation of the dollar has had a major influence on oil prices, as OPEC calculates in dollars but has to take into account the increasing costs of its imports from the non-dollar areas. At the beginning of 2004, OPEC was keeping prices in the upper part of the $22–$28/barrel band established in 2000, and even exceeding it. For the second quarter of 2004, it announced a reduction in quotas based on expectations of oversupply in a season of relatively low demand (a previous reduction came into effect in November 2003). However, considering that prices were much higher than expected in the second quarter of 2004, a formal increase of OPEC production was decided in June 2004, effective as of 1 July (two million barrels/day) and 1 August (a supplementary 500,000 barrels/day). It is important to note that OPEC as a whole has been producing above its official target in recent months.

The sustained increase in oil price has raised concerns worldwide about the negative repercussions this may have on global economic recovery.[3] Particularly hard hit are the many developing countries that are highly dependent on oil imports and normally more energy-intensive than developed countries. On the other hand, for oil producers it means higher real income, which can create growing demand for exports from the rest of the world. So far, the dangers stemming from higher oil prices should not be overestimated as long as higher import prices in developed countries do not translate into accelerating inflation and restrictive actions of the major central banks.

Despite the recent commodity price increases described above, viewed over a longer term perspective, and in real terms, they still remain at very low levels and considerably below their levels of the 1970s and early 1980s. This is the case for commodity producers in developing countries as well as for commodity consumers in the developed economies. From the point of view of commodity producers, the result of deflating commodity prices by the unit value indices of manufacturing exports of developed countries (in dollar terms) is usually considered as an approximation of commodity terms of trade. Figure 2.5 shows that the commodity terms of trade have continued their deteriorating trend in the long term. On the other hand, from the point of view of commodity consumers, it confirms that the real value of commodities obtained by deflating their prices with the consumer price index (CPI) of developed countries (using the CPI of the United States as a proxy) is now significantly lower than that of a quarter of a century ago. A clear example is that of oil: the recent dramatic increases in oil prices have provoked much debate, particularly as they reached record levels in current dollar terms. Figure 2.6 shows that in real terms, the oil price for consumers in developed countries is still relatively low compared to the levels recorded at the time of previous sharp oil price hikes in the 1970s.

Figure 2.5

COMMODITY TERMS OF TRADE AND REAL COMMODITY PRICES, EXCLUDING PETROLEUM, 1970–2004

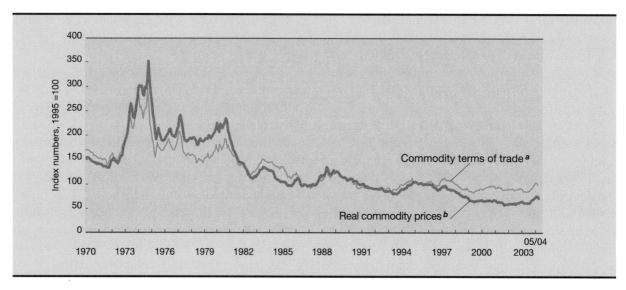

Source: UNCTAD secretariat calculations, based on UNCTAD, *Commodity Price Bulletin*, various issues; United Nations Statistics Division, *Monthly Bulletin of Statistics,* various issues; and IMF, *International Financial Statistics* database.
   a Combined index of commodity prices in terms of current dollars deflated by unit value indices of manufactured goods exports of developed countries.
   b Combined index of commodity prices in terms of current dollars deflated by United States CPI.

Figure 2.6

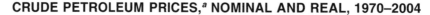

CRUDE PETROLEUM PRICES,*ᵃ* NOMINAL AND REAL, 1970–2004

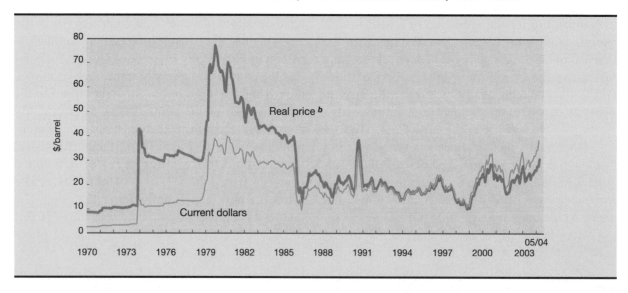

Source: UNCTAD secretariat calculations, based on UNCTAD, *Commodity Price Bulletin*, various issues; and IMF, *International Financial Statistics* database.
   a Crude petroleum, average of Dubai/Brent/Texas equally weighted ($/barrel).
   b Deflated by United States CPI (1995 = 100).

Table 2.4

EXPORT VOLUME, PURCHASING POWER OF EXPORTS AND TERMS OF TRADE OF DEVELOPING COUNTRIES, 1980–2003

(Average annual percentage change)

	1980– 2003	1980– 1985	1986– 1990	1991– 1995	1996– 2003
All developing countries					
Volume indices of exports	10.1	2.1	16.6	14.7	5.3
Terms of trade	-1.3	-3.9	-0.7	0.3	0.5
Purchasing power of exports[a]	8.7	-2.2	15.9	15.2	5.9
Non-oil exporters					
Volume indices of exports	11.9	8.3	18.4	16.5	6.6
Terms of trade	-0.5	-2.8	-0.8	0.9	-0.7
Purchasing power of exports[a]	11.3	4.7	16.7	17.5	5.8
Major exporters of manufactures					
Volume indices of exports	13.7	10.3	21.1	18.6	7.3
Terms of trade	-0.2	-1.5	0.6	0.5	-1.2
Purchasing power of exports[a]	13.5	9.8	22.0	19.3	6.1

Source: UNCTAD, *Handbook of Statistics*, various issues; and table 2.1.
  a The value index of exports deflated by the import unit value index.

Developing countries as a whole experienced a deterioration in their terms of trade between 1980 and 2003, by an average rate of 1.3 per cent per annum (table 2.4). Consequently, although their export volumes rose strongly, the purchasing power of those exports increased much less. The sharpest decline in the terms of trade occurred in the first half of the 1980s which, combined with very slow growth in export volumes, implied a fall in the purchasing power of exports during this period. In the subsequent periods between 1986 and 2003, the terms of trade stabilized, and hence the volume and purchasing power of exports rose broadly in parallel.

If the major oil-exporting countries are excluded, the decline in the terms of trade between 1980 and 2003, on average, has been smaller. But as with the group of developing countries as a whole, the terms of trade of the non-oil exporters declined for all the sub-periods shown in the ta-

ble except for the first half of the 1990s. Consequently, the growth in the purchasing power of exports has almost constantly been below that of export volumes. Nevertheless, as discussed above, world market prices for a number of commodities have been increasing over the past two years.

In this context, the report of the meeting of eminent persons on the impact of commodity problems on the development of commodity-dependent countries, organized by UNCTAD in 2003, offers a wide range of actions that can improve conditions in commodity markets (UNCTAD, 2003). A particularly important action would be diversification into those products for which global market demand is likely to remain strong for a number of years.

The decline in the terms of trade during the period 1996–2003 was strongest for those developing countries for which manufactures have been

Figure 2.7

PRICES OF UNITED STATES IMPORTS OF MANUFACTURES, BY ORIGIN, 1990–2003

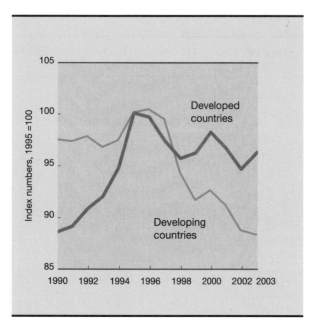

Source: UNCTAD secretariat calculations, based on United States Bureau of Labor Statistics database.

the main source of export earnings. This indicates that the manufactures exported by developing countries may have acquired features in world markets that had traditionally been associated with primary commodities, namely a secular downward trend in the terms of trade and the dilemma of fallacy of composition (*TDR 2002*, chapter IV). Indeed, looking at the evolution of the level of index numbers for major exporters of manufactures over the entire sample period, it was highest in terms of export volumes and lowest for the terms of trade in the most recent years of the sample period (i.e. between 2000 and 2003). The evolution of the price index of United States' imports of manufactures also shows a strong and positive correlation between the evolution of prices and the level of per capita income of exporting countries. Moreover, it shows that, compared to imports from developed countries, the decline in prices of United States imports from developing countries has been strong over the past five years, and that prices are now at their lowest level since 1990 (fig. 2.7)

Summing up, the decline in the terms of trade continues to be a problem for exporters of primary commodities, even though sustained import demand from China may prolong the recent price increase for some commodities. But it appears that it is increasingly becoming a problem for developing-country exporters of manufactures as well. Indeed, as discussed in *TDR 2002* (chapter IV, section B), evidence shows that the degree of deterioration in the terms of trade for developing countries' manufactures vis-à-vis those of developed countries reflects the level of technology embodied in their manufactured exports.

B. Capital flows and finance

1. Capital flows from developing to developed countries

Since 1999, developing and transition economies have experienced sizeable and growing surpluses in the current account of their balance of payments. This is primarily the result of persistent surpluses in their trade of goods and services ($240 billion in 2003) and rising current transfers ($90 billion in 2003, almost twice their 1999 value), while the deficit in net income payments ($122 billion in 2003) increased at a slower pace due to declining international interest rates. As a counterpart to their current account surplus, they recorded a net export of capital of more than $200 billion to the rest of the world in 2003. Thus they further increased their net export of capital to developed countries by 45 per cent from the already high level of 2002 (table 2.5).

East Asia and West Asia continued to have the highest current account surpluses, and some large Latin American countries also registered surpluses. Transition economies as a group had a moderate surplus, though this was concentrated in the members of the Commonwealth of Independent States (CIS), while EU acceding countries continued to receive net capital inflows to finance their current account deficit of $32 billion (IMF, 2004c).

Despite this large overall net capital outflow from the developing to the developed countries, the fact that there was an increase in "net *private*

capital flows" to developing countries, from $13 billion in 2002 to $83 billion in 2003 (table 2.5) was interpreted by many international observers as a positive sign for the developing countries' growth prospects. The World Bank, for example, suggested that "this increase in private capital inflows offers significant opportunities for developing countries to invest in infrastructure and facilitate trade finance to foster a self-reinforcing cycle of sustained capital flows, economic growth and poverty reduction." (World Bank, 2004)

Since the net private capital inflows (in bonds, equities and other capital flows) into developing countries were more than offset by their net accumulation of foreign currency reserves – resulting in total net outflows of $200 billion – this interpretation is misleading. In order to properly assess the role of overall capital flows to developing countries, outflows in terms of rising reserves have to be taken into account. For example, a large proportion of the private gross capital inflows into China has been attracted by expectations of a revaluation of the Chinese currency, despite low interest rates in China. These inflows have, to a large extent, been bought up by the Chinese central bank and invested, at higher interest rates, in United States Treasury bonds, thereby financing the United States budget deficit, but not real investment within China.

But the accumulation of reserves not only puts the figure for net private capital flows in perspective, it also hints at the fact that many national policy-makers were concerned that the

Table 2.5

NET CAPITAL FLOWS AND THE CURRENT ACCOUNT:
DEVELOPING AND TRANSITION ECONOMIES, 1996–2003

(Billions of dollars)

	1996	1997	1998	1999	2000	2001	2002	2003
Developing economies								
Private capital flows	200.1	139.5	45.6	59.7	23.9	27.3	12.9	82.9
Private direct investment	100.7	126.5	129.7	145.6	149.7	161.4	112.0	102.5
Private portfolio investment	83.8	39.8	33.1	64.7	8.5	-86.3	-91.1	-78.1
Other private capital flows[a]	15.6	-26.8	-117.3	-150.5	-134.4	-47.9	-8.0	58.3
Official flows	-16.0	42.6	36.8	8.3	-13.8	23.0	11.6	2.7
Change in reserves[b]	-86.0	-90.2	-32.5	-79.7	-96.6	-108.3	-170.6	-320.9
Current account balance	-79.4	-51.8	-23.5	43.6	114.3	70.3	136.2	199.5
Africa								
Private capital flows	9.1	4.0	9.1	11.8	1.1	6.5	7.2	9.5
Private direct investment	3.6	7.9	6.9	9.8	8.2	23.9	12.3	14.3
Private portfolio investment	2.8	7.0	3.7	8.3	-2.2	-8.8	-0.7	1.8
Other private capital flows[a]	2.7	-10.9	-1.6	-6.3	-4.9	-8.5	-4.4	-6.6
Official flows	-3.0	3.3	4.7	3.5	3.1	1.9	4.2	4.1
Change in reserves[b]	-6.7	-11.2	2.7	-3.4	-13.2	-12.5	-7.6	-14.4
Current account balance	-5.5	-6.5	-19.5	-15.9	5.4	-1.5	-7.4	-3.9
Sub-Saharan Africa								
Private capital flows	6.9	0.7	8.1	10.3	1.5	3.5	6.1	7.6
Official flows	-2.7	4.4	5.2	4.0	4.0	3.0	5.6	5.3
Change in reserves[b]	-4.0	-6.2	1.6	-3.8	-6.5	-2.4	-3.2	-5.7
Current account balance	-6.3	-9.3	-17.8	-15.3	-2.5	-9.3	-12.5	-12.0
East and South Asia								
Private capital flows	118.6	34.0	-50.6	2.7	-4.2	10.1	24.8	84.3
Private direct investment	53.4	56.5	56.1	66.4	67.4	60.5	53.1	49.3
Private portfolio investment	32.0	6.3	8.4	56.6	20.1	-54.4	-57.6	-58.4
Other private capital flows[a]	33.1	-28.8	-115.0	-120.2	-91.7	4.0	29.3	93.4
Official flows	-13.2	25.2	17.5	1.8	4.0	-2.0	-1.9	-8.6
Change in reserves[b]	-46.1	-35.9	-52.6	-87.1	-60.8	-90.7	-157.8	-245.3
Current account balance	-40.8	15.3	113.8	106.5	86.8	90.1	131.7	148.3
China and India								
Private capital flows	48.4	37.9	-4.6	10.3	13.8	43.0	44.7	101.8
Official flows	2.3	1.5	5.6	7.0	-0.5	0.9	2.4	5.7
Change in reserves[b]	-34.4	-40.5	-9.1	-14.6	-16.6	-56.0	-94.3	-148.6
Current account balance	1.2	33.9	24.6	12.4	15.4	16.7	40.2	32.6
First-tier NIEs								
Private capital flows	11.5	-14.8	-23.5	18.5	10.1	-16.2	-10.1	-10.9
Official flows	-11.3	11.2	-3.6	-19.9	-6.9	-7.8	-7.4	-13.7
Change in reserves[b]	-8.8	-7.6	-31.9	-55.9	-43.1	-28.8	-44.4	-75.9
Current account balance	-2.2	6.1	64.9	58.4	41.4	52.0	63.6	86.5
West Asia[c]								
Private capital flows	2.0	9.6	8.4	-7.9	-24.9	-16.3	-27.6	-22.9
Private direct investment	4.1	5.2	5.1	3.9	7.7	8.1	6.9	8.9
Private portfolio investment	1.0	-2.7	-6.2	-4.5	-12.3	-15.8	-19.0	-24.3
Other private capital flows[a]	-3.1	7.2	9.5	-7.3	-20.4	-8.6	-15.4	-7.4
Official flows	7.4	6.7	5.2	6.6	-11.0	-3.2	-5.4	-11.0
Change in reserves[b]	-18.0	-16.6	10.3	-0.2	-27.4	-10.6	-3.1	-25.6
Current account balance	6.0	6.3	-26.6	10.0	68.9	36.3	27.6	51.5

/...

Table 2.5 (concluded)

NET CAPITAL FLOWS AND THE CURRENT ACCOUNT: DEVELOPING AND TRANSITION ECONOMIES, 1996–2003

(Billions of dollars)

	1996	1997	1998	1999	2000	2001	2002	2003
Latin America and the Caribbean								
Private capital flows	70.4	91.9	78.6	53.2	51.9	26.9	8.5	11.8
Private direct investment	39.6	56.9	61.5	65.5	66.4	68.9	39.6	30.0
Private portfolio investment	47.9	29.2	27.2	4.4	2.9	-7.2	-13.7	2.9
Other private capital flows*a*	-17.1	5.8	-10.1	-16.6	-17.4	-34.7	-17.4	-21.1
Official flows	-7.2	7.3	9.5	-3.4	-9.9	26.3	14.6	18.2
Change in reserves*b*	-15.2	-26.5	7.2	11.1	4.8	5.4	-2.0	-35.5
Current account balance	-39.1	-66.8	-91.2	-57.0	-47.0	-54.5	-15.8	3.8
Transition economies								
Private capital flows	17.7	38.1	31.8	26.9	18.3	-6.7	34.1	48.3
Private direct investment	15.3	17.5	23.3	25.6	25.3	27.7	27.3	16.8
Private portfolio investment	1.2	23.0	5.3	1.3	-2.4	-9.4	-7.5	-9.4
Other private capital flows*a*	1.2	-2.4	3.3	-0.1	-4.6	-24.9	14.3	41.0
Official flows	10.9	5.7	10.5	-1.9	-0.7	2.8	-8.3	-9.9
Change in reserves*b*	-5.2	-13.9	-2.1	-13.0	-20.3	-5.2	-25.4	-43.0
Current account balance	-16.0	-29.0	-27.9	-4.8	14.6	17.8	9.6	7.8

Source: UNCTAD secretariat calculations, based on IMF, *World Economic Outlook*, April 2004.

Note: It should be noted that IMF data underlying this table have been substantially revised in 2004. On the basis of IMF data published in spring 2003, the net private capital inflow to developing countries in the United Nations definition amounted to $51.8 billion in 2002. The difference is due in part to the new inclusion of Hong Kong (China) in the aggregate data for 2004, in part by substantial revision of the figure for portfolio investment for other East Asian countries.

a "Other private capital flows" comprises other long- and short-term net investment flows, including private borrowing and residuals not covered under other items; due to limitations in data coverage such residuals may also include some net official flows.

b A minus sign in the lines for change in reserves indicates an increase.

c Including Israel and Egypt, excluding Turkey.

effects of such inflows on the exchange rate would destabilize their economies. This concern is reflected in the decision of some developing countries' monetary authorities to purchase foreign currency to prevent the inflows from triggering an appreciation of their national currencies, as this would have hurt their competitiveness in world markets. Furthermore, private capital is not going primarily to countries that are in need of financing for infrastructure development; rather, it is going mainly to those countries that, at present, do not need foreign capital to finance investment, e.g. China – which has lately shown that as much as 40 per cent of its GDP can be used to finance investment without having to depend on outside capital. In these countries, the national authori-

ties' problem is not a lack of investment, but an excess of it, leading to an overheating of the economy.

2. Regional developments

Changes in net capital flows, including the accumulation of foreign reserves, have differed markedly across regions and countries. In 2003, both the amount of private capital inflows to developing economies and the increase of those flows were concentrated in a few regions and countries. East and South Asia, especially China and India, were the main recipients of net private capital flows to developing economies, accounting for almost all the increase in such flows (table 2.5). Developing Asia and the newly industrializing Asian economies continued to increase their large external surpluses, from $132 billion to $148 billion, due to their favourably competitive position and a pick-up of growth in the United States. Moreover, the main component of the increase in net private capital flows into this region was not foreign direct investment (FDI), which actually fell slightly, but "other private capital flows", which include credit and short-term capital flows. A significant proportion of this increase, however, consisted of speculative investment, based on expectations of a revaluation of the regional currencies. Consequently, governments in the region absorbed a large share of these inflows to prevent a real appreciation of their currencies and a loss of competitiveness.

Recent currency depreciations in many Latin American countries have enabled those countries to increase their competitive position, thus reducing their reliance on external capital to finance their development. The region managed to stage a modest economic recovery in 2003, while at the same time turning the current account from a deficit of $15.8 billion into a surplus of $3.8 billion (table 2.5) – the first surplus in decades. Much of this was the result of external surpluses in Argentina, Brazil and Venezuela, while countries such as Chile, Ecuador and Mexico reduced their current account deficits. However, even if this recovery increases the room for manoeuvre in policy-making, many of these countries still have to resort to international financial markets for refinancing or restructuring the payments of the principal of their external debt. As a result, they are still exposed to the risk of a tightening of the conditions governing access to those markets, even if those operations do not involve net capital movements.

In Brazil and Argentina, the nominal devaluations in 1999 and 2002 contributed to major improvements in competitiveness. Inflationary pressures have been kept in check by low levels of domestic demand in Brazil and by substantial excess capacity in Argentina. Manufacturing exports have picked up, while the improved competitiveness of domestic firms has promoted import

substitution. In Venezuela, high oil prices and low domestic demand led to another year of a huge current account surplus in 2003.

Argentina's improved competitive position allowed the country to stage a strong economic recovery, with an annual GDP growth rate of almost 9 per cent, without running into new current account deficits. This performance is all the more remarkable since many economists had warned that the current lack of access to global capital markets, due to pending negotiations on restructuring the country's foreign debt, would seriously hinder growth prospects. In fact, the only relevant gross capital inflows were debt arrears from the public and private sectors ($10.6 and $2 billion respectively), while the Government made net payments on non-defaulted debt and the private sector continued to export capital, albeit to a much lesser extent than in 2001 and 2002. Approximately half of the $8 billion current account surplus was used to accumulate international reserves, following the national authorities' goal of maintaining the real exchange rate at a competitive level and reducing the economy's vulnerability to external shocks (INDEC, 2004).

The situation in Brazil has not been quite as positive. The positive effects of the devaluation on exports, combined with the negative impact of slow economic growth on imports, led to a current account surplus of $4 billion. FDI fell sharply in 2002 and 2003, and short-term private capital flows displayed high volatility, with successive phases of net outflows and inflows since mid-2002. During much of 2003, there was an accumulation of international reserves through financing by the IMF and by short-term private capital inflows that were attracted by high interest rates. In response, the Government, in an attempt to avoid appreciation of the exchange rate, recycled the capital to the United States at very low yields; at the same time it had to pay the difference between the low United States yield and the high interest on the public debt issued in order to sterilize the monetary effects of accumulated reserves.

In Venezuela, the Government introduced strict exchange controls so as to restrain the massive capital outflows from the private sector, which totalled almost $10 billion per year in 2001 and 2002

(Banco Central de Venezuela, 2004). At the same time, it re-established a fixed exchange rate regime. As a result, the external surplus, fuelled by high oil revenues, led to a rapid accumulation of international reserves.

In Africa, the reduction of the current account deficit has been due to rising prices in commodity markets – especially oil – rather than the result of improved competitiveness. Modest GDP growth, compared to other regions, meant that imports grew slower than exports. The current account deficit for Africa as a whole therefore narrowed, from $7.4 billion to $3.9 billion. For sub-Saharan Africa, the current account deficit fell only slightly (table 2.5). Capital inflows, both official and private, thus remained almost stagnant, at a low level. The most important capital inflow was FDI, much of which was concentrated, as in 2002, in the oil sector of relatively few countries (Algeria, Angola, Chad and Nigeria). In South Africa, where short-term inflows were attracted by high domestic interest rates, the Government and central bank opted for intervention in the currency market, in order to restrain the appreciation of the rand due to the inflow of hot money.

In the Russian Federation and the transition economies of Central and Eastern Europe, conditions continued to diverge markedly. Rising oil prices and export volumes in the Russian Federation increased the current account surplus by almost a third, to $39.5 billion, while the financing requirements of Central and Eastern Europe rose by almost half, to $31.7 billion (or 3.9 per cent of the region's GDP). Bosnia and Herzegovina, Croatia, The former Yugoslav Republic of Macedonia, Serbia and Montenegro, and the Baltic countries, in particular, had to rely heavily on foreign finance. Estonia's current account deficit rose to 13.7 per cent of GDP, thereby remaining above 10 per cent for the second year in a row. Some of the larger EU acceding countries also continued to experience large current account deficits, running at 5.5 per cent of GDP in Hungary and 6.5 per cent in the Czech Republic (IMF, 2004c).

As in the Russian Federation and parts of Africa, West Asian oil producers benefited from rising oil prices and accelerating global economic growth, which increased global oil demand and boosted that region's exports. As a group, these countries almost doubled their current account surplus, from $27.6 billion to $51.5 billion (table 2.5). Since the improvement in the balance-of-payments position in the region stemmed mainly from oil revenues, the largest oil exporters – Saudi Arabia, Kuwait, Qatar and the United Arab Emirates – recorded the biggest increases. As a result, there was a large net export of capital from the region.

3. *Large build-up of reserves*

Developing countries in all the regions have increased their reserve holdings by huge amounts. Their purchase of foreign currency reached a net value of $320.9 billion, with the largest purchases made by Asian countries. China bought $117.1 billion and India $31.7 billion. The Russian Federation came third with purchases of $27.2 billion, followed by Brazil with $11.5 billion and Malaysia with a little more than $10 billion. Turkey, Indonesia and Mexico also bought significant amounts (IMF, 2004a).

This unprecedented accumulation of reserves is part of an attempt by developing countries to adapt to the continuing volatility of private international capital flows. The most recent volatility in 2003 and 2004 has been partly due to increased speculation about a sharp devaluation of the dollar. Since 2002, confidence in the dollar among international investors has been faltering due to the persistently high current account deficit of the United States. As investors began shifting part of their portfolios from United States assets into assets of other – developed, developing or transition – economies, many currencies came under pressure to appreciate.

Monetary authorities in countries with a de facto or formal fixed exchange rate vis-à-vis the dollar were confronted with the decision to either sterilize the net inflows or to abandon their unilateral fixing of the exchange rate. Those countries that decided to maintain their fixed exchange rate regimes consequently accumulated substantial dollar reserves. The most widely debated case is that of China, which has been keeping its currency, the yuan (renminbi), within a narrow band of around 8.28 yuan to the dollar after the 1994 devaluation. Here, investors' distaste for United States assets, amplified by their appetite for Chinese assets, led to an enormous increase in gross foreign private capital flows into China. Speculation of an imminent appreciation of the yuan further augmented the capital flows by adding a stream of "hot", speculative money. This prompted the Chinese central bank to buy large quantities of dollars to defend its currency peg. Malaysia and Hong Kong (China), which belong to the small group of economies in Asia that have a fixed exchange rate pegged to the dollar, also bought United States assets, mainly Treasury bonds, in large quantities (box 2.1).

But even a number of countries that do not have a formal currency peg felt obliged to intervene in the foreign-exchange market to prevent an excessive appreciation of their currency. Hardly any developing country today has a truly free-floating currency. Instead, most of them have attempted to dampen excessive volatility in their exchange rate on the one hand, and to keep their exchange rate at a rather competitive level, on the other. With the dollar depreciating, monetary authorities in all countries, with or without a formal exchange rate arrangement, have been in a similar position. True, "dirty floaters" have not felt as obliged to buy foreign reserves as the official "peggers", but, nevertheless, many of them have considered some form of intervention necessary to avoid being adversely affected by a currency appreciation.

During 2003, the Indian monetary authorities, for example, increased their foreign currency holdings by 46 per cent to prevent short-term speculative inflows from jeopardizing their economic policy goals. In Brazil, the central bank bought dollars in order to keep the real from excessive appreciation, because a loss of competitiveness would have hurt economic recovery in South America's largest economy. In the Russian Federation, the central bank saw in the strong rouble a threat to that part of the economy that is not oil dependent, and also bought dollars in large quantities.

The fear that excessive capital inflows could lead to an overvaluation of developing countries' currencies was not unfounded. Following stabilization policies in the early 1990s, many countries had experienced an overvaluation of their currencies that harmed domestic industries, hurt the international competitiveness of their export-oriented industries and diminished their ability to earn the foreign currency necessary to finance the imports needed for pursuing a balanced growth path. Keeping the exchange rates stable at a convenient level is seen as a strategy that gives them the long-term ability to finance imports of capital goods and consumer goods when faced with volatile capital flows.

The exchange rate stabilization strategy also reflects lessons drawn from the experiences of the currency crises in East and South-East Asia and Latin America, which painfully drew the attention of developing countries to the risks of an overvalued exchange rate and of an over-reliance on foreign capital to finance the resulting current account deficits. While the Asian crisis only hit countries that had some kind of fixed or rigid exchange rate, the capital flight from Brazil in the run-up to the Brazilian presidential elections in 2002 – that was controlled only with a large IMF loan package – has shown that even countries with a flexible exchange rate regime are not immune from currency and financial crises, as long as they depend on a constant inflow of foreign capital to finance their current account deficit or external debt repayments.

However, in some of the countries that have accumulated reserves over the past two years to prevent overvaluation, their unilateral attempts to cope with excessive capital inflows has led to problems in stabilizing the domestic economy. While most countries have succeeded, to a large extent, in sterilizing the inflows, China recently has had problems keeping an investment and credit boom under control. The boom was fuelled by the Government's expansionary policy combined with a liquidity increase resulting from capital inflows and consequent purchases of dollars.

Other countries have been faced with rising fiscal costs stemming from their attempts to sterilize the consequences of their immense purchases of reserves. As mentioned above, buying foreign reserves in the foreign exchange market leads to an increase in liquidity in the domestic money market. In order to reduce the liquidity, central

Box 2.1

ASIA'S SAVINGS AND THE UNITED STATES' EXTERNAL DEFICIT

Given the large trade imbalance between the United States and Asia and the enormous accumulation of United States bonds by Asia's investors and central banks, it has been suggested that the fate of the United States economy is in the hands of Asian investors. According to this argument, if Asia were to stop financing that country's current account deficit, the results could be dramatic: the demand for United States bonds would collapse, the dollar would depreciate, interest rates would soar and the economy would suffer a slowdown. It is further contended that developing Asian countries such as China would then finally have the possibility to use the capital they had exported to the United States in recent years for investment and consumption at home. However, closer inspection shows that these arguments are disputable.

What would happen to Asia if it decided to no longer finance the United States' external deficit?

At present, the United States imports more goods from Asia than it exports to the region. This is only possible because Asian investors (both private investors and central banks) are willing to purchase United States assets in exchange for the goods they export to that country. If this were to slow down, demand in the United States for Asian products would fall, and the price of United States assets relative to Asian assets (that is, the exchange rate of the dollar vis-à-vis the Asian currencies) would also decline. This would affect Asian exporters: their sales prices and volumes would come under pressure. Asian producers for the domestic market would also be hurt as imports into Asia would become relatively cheaper, leading to greater consumption of imported rather than domestically produced goods. Together, these two mechanisms would lead to a falling Asian surplus in its trade (and current account) balance with the United States, which would reflect a diminished net capital flow from Asia to the United States.

In the unlikely event that Asian investors decided to sell existing dollar assets and import American goods from the receipts, while not selling any of their products against fresh United States assets ("repatriating their savings"), the dollar would have to depreciate to an extent that would turn Asian current accounts into deficit. This would reverse the net capital flow from Asia to the United States. As this might imply a further dollar depreciation, the adverse effects on Asian firms would be dramatic.

Thus Asia cannot profit from a "repatriation" of its foreign capital investments. An appreciation of the major Asian currencies – yen, won or yuan – against the dollar would slow down export expansion and dampen profits and economic growth. Only if national economic policy managed to stimulate domestic demand by cutting interest rates, and thereby stabilizing overall monetary conditions, would the Asian countries be able to remain on their high and stable growth path. However, this might prove difficult, since interest rates are very low and a significant proportion of private investment in Asia, particularly in developing countries such as China, is in the export-oriented sector, which would be hurt by an appreciation of the local currency against the dollar. In Asia, if government policies failed to restructure their economies by replacing United States demand for their goods by domestic demand, the region's overall GDP growth would slow down, albeit not as much as its export growth. Moreover, there would be a "net inflow of capital" from the United States only if GDP in these Asian countries were to fall short of what is used up domestically for consumption and investment at the new exchange rate of their currencies to the dollar.

/...

Box 2.1 (continued)

What would happen to the dollar if the Asian central banks stopped buying
United States Treasury bonds?

Recently, Asian countries have experienced large current account surpluses and large gross capital inflows from abroad. The central banks have kept their exchange rates constant by buying United States Treasury bonds, but they have also started to diversify their foreign-exchange reserve holdings. If they were to completely stop buying United States assets, and there were no private Asian investors willing to invest in United States assets, the effect would be much the same as described above: there would be a gap between the goods that United States consumers can buy and the goods and assets they can sell at the current exchange rate. Therefore, the only possible adjustment would be a depreciation of the dollar. Again, this would hurt Asian exporters and undermine economic growth in the region.

However, it is unclear how much the dollar in this case would really depreciate. A significant share of the gross private capital inflows into Asia at present is probably "hot money" from investors betting on an imminent appreciation. If the currencies actually did appreciate, this pressure could ease. This might be the case especially for China, whose former overall trade surplus dipped into deficit at the beginning of 2004.

What would happen if Asian central banks diversified their dollar bonds into
different assets?

Risk considerations might induce Asian central banks to sell United States bonds and to buy other assets, such as European bonds. As long as private investors did not counteract this shift in investments, such a move would increase the demand for European assets at the expense of United States assets. If, at the same time, Asian central banks tried to prevent their own currencies from appreciating against the dollar, as they have done over most of the past two years, the only possible adjustment would be in the exchange rate of the euro. The euro would then appreciate against both the dollar and the Asian currencies, while the exchange rate of the dollar vis-à-vis Asian currencies would remain unaltered.

Would a fall in the exchange rate of the dollar vis-à-vis Asian currencies hurt
the United States?

This question is not easy to answer. However, some theoretical considerations and historical experience suggest that the effects will be far from dramatic, and completely different from what developing countries experienced when their currencies depreciated sharply.

Since United States companies, governments (state and federal) and households are not highly indebted in yen or yuan, a fall in the value of the dollar would not increase their debt service. Consequently their net wealth would not decline and neither would their financing costs increase. Hence, the depreciation would not directly slow down the United States economy.

Further, there is no direct link between the willingness of foreigners to hold United States Treasury bonds and higher domestic interest rates in the United States. An appreciation of the Chinese cur-

.../...

Box 2.1 (concluded)

rency, for example, would significantly reduce investors' expectations of short-term gains, thus leading to a redirection of the flow of some of the short-term funds from China to the United States. This would compensate, at least in part, for the reduced holdings of United States Treasury bonds by foreign investors. Additionally, since investors in the United States usually hold a certain proportion of their gross wealth in foreign assets (denominated in foreign currency), their (net) dollar wealth would increase with the depreciation. This in turn would increase the demand for United States assets (both bonds and stocks). If the drop in demand for United States Treasury bonds from the foreign central banks were bigger than the increase in domestic demand for these bonds, the interest rate might rise. However, the additional demand for equities would put upward pressure on stock prices, thereby counteracting the negative effect of the rising bond yields on companies' investment plans.

Even more important, any interest rate movement as a reaction to a shift in foreign and household demand for United States bonds would be compensated by a shift in the portfolios of financial intermediaries and in the behaviour of the United States' central bank, the Federal Reserve. In the medium and long term, the price of bonds, and thus the long-term interest rate, is determined by the central bank's short-term policy rate and expectations of changes in that rate. The Federal Reserve fixes the short-term interbank interest rate by providing unlimited amounts of liquidity to the federal funds market if it wants to keep the federal fund rate close to its target rate. If domestic banks perceive the current and expected future short-term interest rates as being too low relative to the long-term interest rate, they will borrow from the Federal Reserve in the federal funds market and buy longer running Treasury bonds. This increases the price for this type of Treasury bond, thus lowering the long-term interest rate.

Thus, as long as the dollar depreciation does not provoke a change in the Federal Reserve's monetary policy stance, or changed expectations of banks about the future course of the Federal Reserve's monetary policy, long-term interest rates will not be affected by the change in the rest of the world's willingness to buy Treasury bonds.

Of course, the assumption of the Federal Reserve's monetary policy and corresponding expectations remaining unaffected by a depreciation of the dollar may not be justified. A huge currency appreciation in Asian countries could, theoretically, force the central bank to act. A strong depreciation of the real effective exchange rate of the dollar would dramatically increase the international competitiveness of United States exporting firms. Demand and prices for their products would increase, both through stronger export demand and import substitution. After a certain time lag, this would result in an increase in the profitability of the sector producing tradable goods and a pick-up in investment. At the same time, consumer prices would start to rise due to increased import prices. If the Federal Reserve's monetary policy were to remain unchanged, overall monetary conditions that reflect effects of interest rates and the exchange rate would in fact loosen. Consequently, in order to keep the economy on the targeted growth path, the Federal Reserve would have to react to a depreciation of the dollar by increasing nominal interest rates.

However, this would not necessarily hurt overall United States growth. With the tradable sector booming, production would merely shift from the non-tradable to the tradable sector, without necessarily having a negative impact on GDP growth. However, the composition of growth would alter: with rising import prices, consumer prices would increase and real wages fall. A slower growth in consumption demand would be the consequence. At the same time, export demand would increase.

banks regularly issue stabilization bonds against domestic money. However, if the domestic interest rate is higher than the rate on United States Treasury bonds (which has been the case for most developing countries, but not for China), the monetary authority has to pay the bond-holders more than it can get from recycling the reserves in United States Treasury bonds. The resulting costs then have to be borne by the developing country's general budget, and consequently by the taxpayer. In the spring of 2004, the Republic of Korea, which has also been heavily intervening in the foreign-exchange market, had currency stabilization bonds worth more than 30 trillion won ($27 billion) outstanding. Brazil and South Africa had to face high costs of sterilizing their increased reserves.

While the accumulation of reserves by developing countries slowed slightly in the first months of 2004 compared to late 2003, the basic trend of heavy interventions in the foreign-exchange market and corresponding sterilization has remained intact in 2004. Compared to both the long-term historical average as well as the corresponding figures from the same months in 2003, most developing countries continued to accumulate foreign reserves at a rapid pace. However, with the recovery in the United States gaining hold – and thus that country's assets becoming more attractive for private investors – and the increase in the long-term United States interest rate, the flow of speculative money to developing countries decreased somewhat in the second quarter of 2004. This alleviated the need of developing countries to counteract these inflows with foreign currency purchases. This is a further indication that in most countries, reserves have recently been accumulated as a bulwark against volatile capital flows, and not to set aside resources to pay future imports.

However, there are some exceptions to this general trend, mainly in countries concerned about the medium- and long-term debt sustainability. In Brazil, for example, such concerns led to outflows of short-term capital and increased the cost of external financing; as a result, the Government decided to use international reserves to make debt repayments to the IMF in December 2003 and the first quarter of 2004, and to avoid an excessive depreciation of the real. New purchases of foreign assets by Brazil's central bank would thus at least partly be interpreted as an attempt to rebuild those diminished reserves in order to prepare for new speculative outflows of private capital or impending debt repayments.

4. Financing conditions

The improved balance-of-payments situation of many developing countries has reinforced the fall in the risk premiums of their sovereign bonds. In early 2004, the yield spread on Brazilian bonds fell below 500 basis points for the first time since 1998, down from more than 2,000 basis points in early 2003. The risk premium on Turkish bonds more than halved, to around 300 basis points. Even for the Russian Federation, which defaulted on its debt in 1998, the yield spread fell to roughly 200 basis points. EU acceding countries gained from the prospect of joining the European Economic and Monetary Union (EMU): Hungarian and Polish risk spreads fell to historic lows of around 50 basis points and slightly below 100 basis points respectively (fig. 2.8).

Among the internationally traded developing-country bonds, only Argentinean debt still carries a risk spread of several thousand basis points; this is not surprising, given that the restructuring of its sovereign debt is an issue that is yet to be resolved. However, as Argentina is not borrowing on the international market, the risk premium has little relevance for its domestic economy. Domestic financing conditions in local currency are favourable: short-term real interbank rates are slightly negative and 30-day nominal prime lending rates are at around 10 per cent.

However, the fall in international risk premiums needs to be viewed along with the prospect of increasing interest rates in the United States, as this might reverse Latin American countries ability to refinance their outstanding debt and reduce their interest burdens. In 2003, net interest payments made by Latin American countries fell by $0.5 billion, to $52.1 billion, the lowest level since 1997 (IMF, 2004c). However, the prospect of a tightening of international interest rates may reverse the fall in the risk premiums, as seems to have occurred in Brazil in the second quarter of 2004.

Figure 2.8

YIELD SPREADS OF SELECTED INTERNATIONALLY ISSUED
EMERGING-MARKET BONDS,[a] 1998–2004

(Basis points[b])

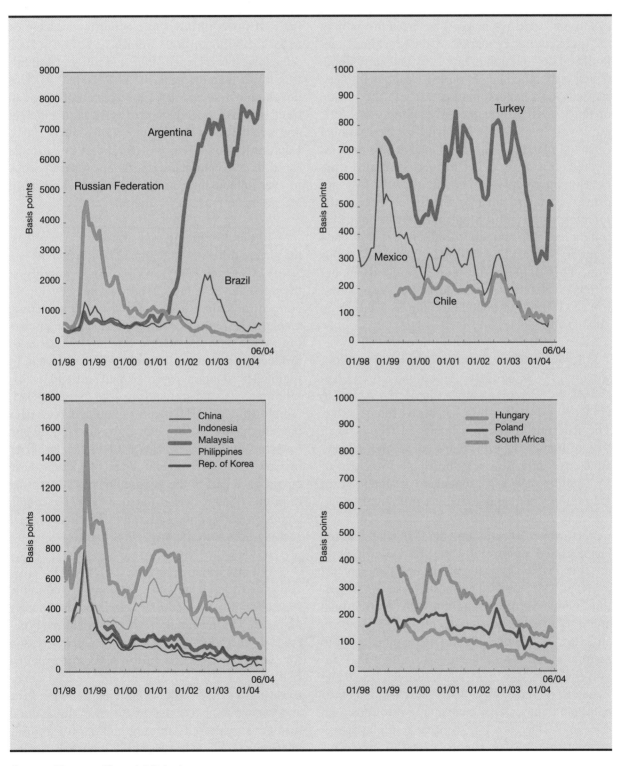

Source: Thomson Financial Datastream.

a Differential between the yield on a representative bond issued by the borrowing country and those of the same maturity issued by the government of the country in whose currency the borrower's bonds are denominated.

b One basis point equals 0.01 per cent.

5. Calm year for financial markets, no major currency crises

Another positive side-effect of the extensive intervention of developing countries' central banks in foreign-exchange markets has been the calm in the global currency market. After Argentina's default and devaluation in late 2001 and early 2002, which also pulled neighbouring Uruguay into crisis, and the financial market scare in the run-up to the Brazilian presidential elections in 2002, 2003 was a remarkably calm year for international financial markets. This development was also reflected in a drop in net official lending to the developing countries. While in 2002 the IMF approved a record loan to Brazil to prevent the looming crisis getting out of control, countries sought less IMF support in 2003: its net credit and loans fell from $13.4 billion in 2002 to $1.8 billion. This explains the significant fall in net official capital flows to the developing economies, from $11.6 billion in 2002 to only $2.7 billion in 2003 (IMF, 2004c).

Even more encouraging is the fact that, worldwide, demand for emergency loans has abated. In all regions other than Latin America, net lending from the IMF has even been negative. The Russian Federation managed to pay back $1.9 billion in net terms thanks to its high oil revenues. In Latin America, the single IMF loan of $5.2 billion to Brazil accounted for almost all of the region's net capital receipts from the Fund.

However, even though the IMF's net lending has declined significantly, several countries rely on new IMF disbursements in order to pay for previous IMF loans. This is the case for Argentina, which is still struggling with international creditors to come to an agreement on how to restructure its defaulted debt. Uruguay managed to restructure its foreign debt, with strong IMF involvement, in May 2003, while Bolivia, Brazil and Ecuador are under close IMF supervision as they continue to have large outstanding positions with the Fund. Thus, the IMF continues to play a significant role in some countries, and the problems of debt crises remain unsolved, even in regions where, overall, economic conditions have recently improved.

6. FDI to developing and transition economies declines

Although FDI remains the major source of foreign financing in developing countries, their net FDI flows (inflows minus outflows) declined to $102.5 billion in 2003 from $112 billion in 2002 – the lowest level since 1996, and roughly $60 billion lower than the peak in 2001 (table 2.5). This development seems to be part of a more general trend linked to the reduction of cross-border merger and acquisition (M&A) operations since 2001.[4] Economic slowdown and financial constraints faced by transnational corporations (TNCs) – due to over indebtedness and declining stock values – are the main reasons for the fall in M&As.

In the developing and transition economies, the picture differs from region to region. In East and South Asia, net FDI flows remained roughly at their 2002 level: some $50 billion, and were highly concentrated in China (including Hong Kong, China). The region's continued success in attracting FDI is partly related to the reorganization of production processes through the development of regional production networks, and partly to its low labour costs and expanding domestic market, which attracted FDI from developed countries outside the region. Net FDI flows for Central and Eastern European countries (CEECs) declined. As in East Asia, a significant share of FDI to these countries is part of the geographical restructuring of production processes, but also the EU acceding countries are becoming attractive locations for FDI seeking access to the larger EU market.

In Latin America and the Caribbean, too, FDI continued to fall in 2003. Prolonged economic stagnation discouraged FDI targeting host-country markets. The termination of privatization processes in several countries was also a major reason for the decline in FDI inflows. Export-oriented FDI showed a mixed picture: the Andean countries (particularly Chile, Colombia, Ecuador, Peru and Venezuela) continued to attract FDI in natural resources (especially mining and hydrocarbons), but Mexico, where the assembly industry oriented to the United States market stagnated, saw a decline in FDI inflows. On the other hand, FDI outflows from the region rose.

A significant proportion of FDI flows to the CIS and West Asia also went to natural-resource extraction. These investments (essentially in oil and gas) seem to be relatively disconnected from local economic conditions, responding, instead, to the long-term strategies of TNCs. In Africa, FDI flows slumped from an exceptional peak of $24 billion in 2001 to about $12 billion in 2002, which appears to be a return to the normal trend considering the size of FDI flows during the period 1997–2000. Net FDI flows during 2003 are estimated to have amounted to about $14 billion. In all, FDI flows to the region are concentrated in a few countries, and in the extractive sectors of oil and minerals, with total flows in any particular year reflecting new investments in these sectors. ■

Notes

1   In early June 2004, this index had fallen to 3,282 points, after reaching a peak of 5,681 points in February (Bloomberg, 2004).

2   The HWWA (Hamburg Institute of International Economics) Index, which tracks world prices of commodities from the perspective of industrialized countries, shows an increase of 14.3 per cent on a dollar basis and a decrease of 4.2 on a euro basis (http://www.hwwa.de/indikatoren/idsp_rohstoffindex. html, accessed June 2004).

3   See, for instance, a recent study of the International Energy Agency (IEA, 2004).

4   The continuing low value and number of cross-border M&As, which had been the main drivers of global FDI flows since the late 1980s, contributed significantly to this performance. For a discussion of FDI flows in 2003 see UNCTAD (2004).

REFERENCES – PART ONE

Banco Central de Venezuela (2004). *Información Estadística*. Database: http://www.bcv.org.ve/c2/indicadores.asp.

Banco Central do Brasil (2004a). *Boletim do Banco Central do Brasil – Relatório Anual 2003*, Volume 39. Brasilia, Junho.

Banco Central do Brasil (2004b). *Indicadores econômicos consolidados*. Database: http://www.bcb.gov.br/?INDECO.

Banco de la República, Colombia (2004). *Estadísticas sobre Deuda Pública*, Boletín n° 7. Bogotá, marzo.

Bank of Indonesia (2004). *Financial Statistics*. Database: http://www.bi.go.id/web/en/Data+Statistik/.

Bank of Japan (2004). *Financial and Economic Statistics Monthly*. Tokyo, July.

Bloomberg (2004). Bloomberg's index database: http://www.bloomberg.com/.

Central Bank of Kuwait (2004). *Quarterly Statistical Bulletin*, January–March. Kuwait City.

Central Bank of the Republic of Turkey (2004a). *Turkish Balance of Payments Statistics*. Ankara.

Central Bank of the Republic of Turkey (2004b). *Quarterly Bulletin I*, January–March. Ankara.

Central Bank of the United Arab Emirates (2003). *Statistical Bulletin Quarterly*, October–December. Abu Dhabi.

Central Bank, Taiwan Province of China (2004). *Balance of Payments Quarterly*, Ist quarter. Taipei.

China Economic Information Network (2004). *Six weaknesses of the Chinese economy*. Accessed in March: www.cei.gov.cn.

ECLAC (2001). *Mining in Latin America in the late 1990s*. United Nations publication, sales no. E.99.II.G.33. New York and Santiago, United Nations Economic Commission for Latin America and the Caribbean.

ECLAC (2003). *Preliminary Overview of the Economies of Latin America and the Caribbean 2003*. United Nations publication, sales no. E.03.II.G.186. New York and Santiago, United Nations Economic Commission for Latin America and the Caribbean.

ECLAC (2004a). *Economic Development Division Database*. Santiago, Economic Commission for Latin America and the Caribbean.

ECLAC (2004b). *Fletes marítimos, precios de construcción y arriendo de buques: sus cambios recientes* (Boletín FAL Edición No. 213, mayo de 2004). New York and Santiago, Economic Commission for Latin America and the Caribbean.

EIU (2004a). *Country Forecast, China*. Hong Kong (China), London and New York, Economist Intelligence Unit, July.

EIU (2004b). *Country Forecast, Malaysia*. Hong Kong (China), London and New York, Economist Intelligence Unit, June.

ESCAP (2004). *Economic and Social Survey of Asia and the Pacific 2004*. United Nations publication, sales no. E.04.II.F.20. New York and Bangkok, United Nations Economic and Social Commission for Asia and the Pacific.

ESCWA (2004). *Survey of Economic and Social Developments in the ESCWA Region 2004: Summary* (E/ESCWA/EAD/2004/3, 7 April). New York and Beirut, United Nations Economic and Social Commission for Western Asia.

Eurostat (2004). *An overview of the economies of the new member states*. Statistics in focus; Economy and Finance, Theme 2 – 17/2004. Luxembourg.

IBGE (2004). *Monthly Employment Survey*. Brasilia, Instituto Brasileiro de Geografía e Estatística, May.

IEA (2004). *Analysis of the Impact of High Oil Prices on the Global Economy*. Paris, International Energy Agency, May.

IEA (various issues). *Oil Market Report*. Paris, International Energy Agency.

IMF (2004a). *International Financial Statistics* (database). Washington, DC, International Monetary Fund.

IMF (2004b). *Direction of Trade Statistics.* Washington, DC, International Monetary Fund.

IMF (2004c). *World Economic Outlook.* Washington, DC, International Monetary Fund, April.

INDEC (2004). *Estimaciones trimestrales del balance de pagos y de activos y pasivos externos de la República Argentina 2002 y 2003.* Buenos Aires, Instituto Nacional de Estadística y Censos, Dirección de cuentas internacionales.

International Cotton Advisory Committee (2004). *La volatilité des prix sur le marché mondial du cotton.* Communication presented at the technical seminar of "Association Cotonnière Africaine" on 5 March 2004 in Dakar, Senegal.

Latinobarómetro (2003). Press Report 2003. Santiago, Corporación Latinobarómetro.

Magyar Nemzeti Bank (2004). *Quarterly Report on Inflation*, Ist quarter. Budapest, May.

Ministerio de Economía y Producción de la República Argentina (2004). *Información Económica al Día.* Database: http://www.mecon.gov.ar/peconomica/basehome/infoeco.html.

Ministério do Planejamento, Orçamento e Gestão (2003). *Plano Plurianual 2004–2007.* Mensagem Presidencial, Brasilia.

Ministry of Economy, Labour and Social Policy, Poland (2004). *A Study of Poland's Economic Performance 2003.* Warsaw, March.

Ministry of Finance, Japan (2004). *Trade Statistics,* Customs and Tariff Bureau. Database: http://www.customs.go.jp/toukei/srch/indexe.htm.

OECD (2004). *Economic Outlook No. 75.* Paris, Organisation for Economic Co-operation and Development, June.

Roach S (2004a). *China – Determined to Slow.* Morgan Stanley, Global Economic Forum, 24 March.

Roach S (2004b). *Global: All Cylinders?* Morgan Stanley, 20 February.

Saudi Arabian Monetary Agency (2004). *Annual Reports (Statistical Tables).* Riyadh.

State Council of the People's Republic of China (2004). *Report on the Work of the Government.* Beijing, March.

UN/DESA (2004). *Monthly Bulletin of Statistics.* New York, United Nations Department of Economic and Social Affairs, Statistics Division, March.

UNCTAD (2003). *Report on the meeting of eminent persons on commodity issues* (TD/B/50/11). Geneva, United Nations Conference on Trade and Development.

UNCTAD (2004). *World Investment Report, 2004.* United Nations publication, sales no. E.04.II.D.33, New York and Geneva.

UNCTAD (various issues). *Trade and Development Report.* United Nations publication, New York and Geneva.

United Nations (2004). *Commodity Trade Statistic Database* (UN Comtrade). New York, United Nations Organization.

United States Department of Agriculture (2004). *Oilseeds: World Markets and Trade.* Washington, DC, April.

USITC (2004). *Interactive Tariff and Trade DataWeb* (http://dataweb.usitc.gov/). Washington, DC, United States International Trade Commission.

World Bank (2004). *Private Capital Flows Return To A Few Developing Countries As Aid Flows To Poorest Rise Only Slightly.* Press Release, 19 April. Washington, DC.

World Tourism Organization (2004). *WTO World Tourism Barometer*, 2(1). Madrid, January.

WTO (2004a). *International Trade Statistics Database.* Geneva, World Trade Organization.

WTO (2004b). *World Trade 2003, Prospects for 2004.* Press Release, April. Geneva, World Trade Organization.

Part Two

POLICY COHERENCE, DEVELOPMENT STRATEGIES AND INTEGRATION INTO THE WORLD ECONOMY

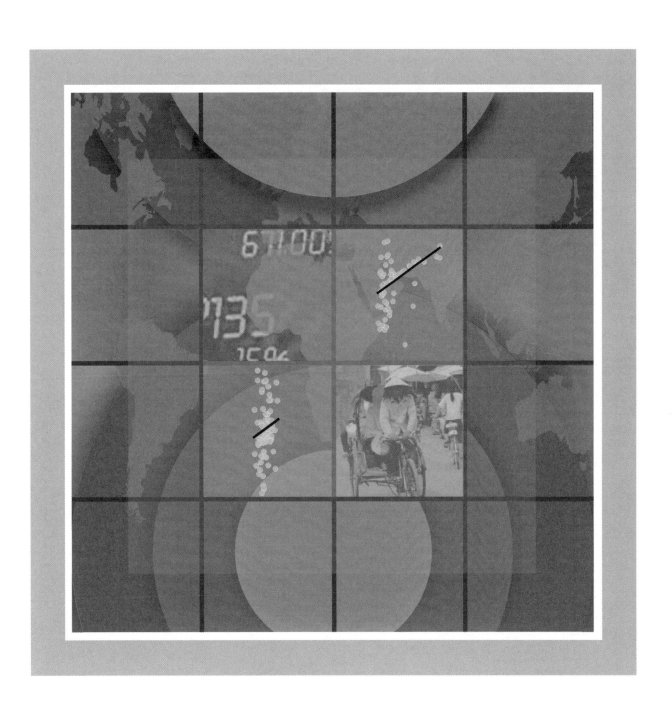

INTRODUCTION

Beginning in the mid-1980s, many developing countries made close integration into the international trading system a pillar of their economic reform agenda. They sought to achieve this not only through active participation in multilateral trade negotiations, but also through rapid unilateral trade liberalization. In many countries, trade liberalization was accompanied by an opening up of their financial sector and capital account. Rapid liberalization and increased exposure to international market forces and competition were expected to boost efficiency and competitiveness, which in turn would underpin a more rapid rate of economic growth and a narrowing of the income gap with developed countries. However, by the early 1990s there were many instances where the outcome of this policy strategy did not live up to expectations.

The prevailing analysis suggests that the often disappointing developmental effects of closer integration into the world economy are due to persistent market access barriers to a number of key developing-country exports. They are also due to the absence in many developing countries, and particularly the poorest among them, of appropriate governance and institutional frameworks and to a lack of productive capacities to respond quickly to export opportunities, even when they benefit from preferential market access conditions.

The disappointing developmental effects of closer integration led to increasing pressure on developed countries to abolish market access barriers to products of export interest to developing countries. At the same time, developing-country policy-makers began to be encouraged to adopt measures designed to strengthen the supply capacity of their economies with a view to building competitive industries and benefiting from improved access to world markets. Increasing attention was given to improving macroeconomic and exchange-rate management; appropriate sequencing of liberalization of the trade, financial and capital-account regimes, underpinned by prudential regulation and financial sector reform; reinforcing domestic institutional capacity; and attracting foreign direct investment (FDI). This policy package was expected to enable developing countries to overcome the constraints they face with regard to fixed investment and technological upgrading, and to raise productivity.

Underlying the advice to adopt this policy package is the assumption that all economies, regardless of their size, institutional histories or level of development, respond in much the same way to a uniform set of price incentives. Further, there is an implicit suggestion that achieving such a uniform set of price incentives and keeping it free from distortions is best guaranteed by allowing international markets to set prices. It is argued that this is in large part because the higher degree of competition in those markets comes closest to an ideal level of "contestability", and because the absence of government interference helps minimize the distortive impact of "rent seeking" or "directly unproductive profit-seeking" activities. Proposing this development strategy – which may be called the "openness model" – implies the view that coherent policy-making is based on a shared understanding of a uniform set of instruments of trade, macroeconomic, financial and development policies. It has also meant, in practice, that developing countries trade discretionary policy measures for the promise of improved access to international markets for their goods, and to finance and technology. On this account, while making this bargain work depends principally on actions taken "at home", it also implies strengthened policy surveillance from, and more effective collaboration among, international economic institutions (Mussa, 1997; Winters, 2001).

To date, adopting this strategy has still not enabled most developing countries to establish the virtuous interaction between international finance, domestic capital formation and export growth, which underpinned the catching-up process of Western Europe after the Second World War and of the East Asian newly industrializing economies (NIEs) during the 1980s and early 1990s. Critics have attributed this to the uniform application of neo-liberal policies, which does not take account of the diversity of economic conditions and challenges found in low and middle-income economies. Others have pointed to growing social tensions accompanying rapid opening up, which have had an adverse impact on efficiency and growth. Moreover, in an increasingly interdependent world, the very idea of a spontaneous economic order in which developing countries, by putting their own house in order through opening up to international market forces can guarantee the kind of stability needed for sustained growth in incomes and employment, appears to many as decidedly "utopian" (Rodrik, 2002: 24).[1]

Part Two of this Report suggests that efforts at designing a feasible development agenda require a more complex analytical and policy framework than that offered by the "openness model". This framework must explore how the virtuous interactions between export activities, domestic capital formation and structural change are established. It should further consider potentially destabilizing interactions between trade and other elements of the integration process, particularly those associated with international finance. And it should explicitly include the legitimate role that economic institutions at the national level play instead of relying on a vision of the world in which indi-

vidual economic agents will react to prices that reflect relative scarcities of goods and production factors at the global level. In this way, it would provide a framework for identifying the combination of domestic policy-making and collective actions at the international level needed to manage the potential adjustment costs and tendencies towards economic divergence that accompany deeper integration, particularly where it brings together countries at very different levels of development.

In what follows it is suggested that a policy package based on the concept of "coherence" will enable better management of contemporary globalization processes in the interest of economic development. It is shown that the "openness" approach, in order to work, requires coherence between national development strategies and global processes and disciplines, as well as policy coherence between and within the various aspects/sectors of the global economy that impact on development prospects of developing countries. All these are lacking to some extent in today's global economy.

A coherent treatment of the interdependence between trade, development and financial issues was an important element in the debate leading to the set-up of the post-war international economic system. This debate arose from the desire to avoid deflationary adjustments and beggar-thy-neighbour policies of the kind that had severely disrupted economies in the inter-war period.

The present institutional set-up has its roots in the arrangements that resulted from the reorganization of international economic relations after the Second World War. The set-up of the post-war international trade regime was predicated on the belief that, in conditions of strictly limited private international capital flows, an international monetary system on an intergovernmental basis with convertible currencies at fixed, but adjustable, exchange rates would provide a stable environment conducive to trade and investment. Under the aegis of the General Agreement on Tariffs and Trade (GATT), this regime considered the tariff as the only legitimate trade policy measure. Other trade measures (i.e. those affecting quantities or the fixing of import prices) were prohibited, except in certain clearly defined circumstances. The convertibility of currencies at fixed, but adjustable, exchange rates supported the GATT approach, as participants in international trade negotiations could predict the full extent to which the competitive position of domestic industries would be affected by tariff cuts without having to be unduly concerned about other exogenous factors or resorting to competitive devaluations to balance unanticipated adverse consequences of trade liberalization.

The rules-based system of trade negotiations in the form of the GATT was all that survived from the initially proposed charter of the International Trade Organization (ITO), whose mandate would also have included to coordinate national economic policies to ensure adequate levels of global demand and employment in support of the development of low-income countries. As such, the specific problems of developing countries participating in the post-war international trading system were largely absent from the mandates of the intergovernmental institutions created immediately after the Second World War. Multilateral efforts to remedy this neglect culminated in the First UNCTAD Conference in 1964. Central to that discussion was the idea that developing countries can base economic development on their own efforts only if they have sufficient policy space to accelerate capital formation, diversify their economic structure and give development a greater "social depth". This discussion also emphasized the interdependence between trade, macroeconomic and financial policy issues.

The need for a coherent treatment of these issues has gained in importance with the abandoning of the system of fixed, but adjustable, exchange rates and the adoption of widespread floating, combined with a return of private international capital flows to levels similar to those that had caused instability in the inter-war period. Indeed, there are growing concerns about the adverse impact on trade of exchange rate instability created by financial factors, in particular, in the context of the financial crises that have hit a number of emerging-market economies over the past decade. The risk of sharp currency depreciations, which, as demonstrated by the Asian crisis, can arise even in countries with sound macroeconomic and external positions, increases the perceived cost and uncertainty of trade, and discourages governments from lifting trade restrictions. In practice, large currency depreciations by some crisis-hit coun-

tries have provoked claims of "unfair trade" from import-sensitive sectors in some of their main trading partners and pressure for a trade policy response. This runs counter the generally recognized principle that trade restrictions should not be used to offset a rise in the international cost competitiveness of competitors resulting from fluctuations in exchange rates.

There is no disputing that trade must continue to occupy a central place in an effective global partnership for development, or that all countries have a mutual interest in the effective functioning of the multilateral trading system. However, trade and financial linkages with the world economy can only complement, but not substitute, for domestic forces of growth. Moreover, these linkages need to be coherent with national development strategies designed to generate virtuous interaction between domestic capital formation and export activities. Establishing such virtuous interactions can be achieved by a national development strategy that is successful in augmenting the existing stock of physical and human capital, enabling the use of more efficient technologies, and shifting resources away from traditional, low-productivity activities towards activities that offer a high potential for productivity growth. Under some circumstances, and particularly when a period of real currency appreciation has hampered export performance, real currency depreciations can improve international cost competitiveness and boost exports. On the other hand, sizeable exchange rate volatility can offset annual gains in domestic productivity and drastically alter international cost competitiveness virtually overnight. Moreover, sharp and abrupt depreciations can make it difficult for exporters to take advantage of the rise in international cost competitiveness resulting from such depreciations. The fact that sizeable exchange rate volatility and major exchange rate depreciations have typically been associated with shifts in the direction of short-term international capital flows shows that insufficient coherence in the international monetary and financial system can jeopardize the successful implementation of national development strategies designed to foster domestic supply capacities.

The following discussion documents the lack of policy coherence in today's global economy and proposes ways to approach the issues of coherence so as to maximize the developmental effects of integration into the world economy.

Chapter III first discusses the issues arising from greater trade and financial integration looked at from the perspective of interdependence between trade, macroeconomic and financial issues as well as between openness and integration in the world economy, and domestic policy space. Chapter IV shifts the focus to the impact of monetary and financial factors on the supply side of developing-country exports. It examines the particular effects caused by sharp and abrupt currency depreciations on the trade performance of developing countries and goes on to analyse monetary policy options with regard to fixed or flexible exchange rates in the context of high volatility of short-term capital flows. The concluding section summarizes the main arguments and discusses policy challenges to enhance coherence between the international trading, monetary and financial systems with a view to establishing a virtuous interaction between international finance, domestic capital formation and export growth and maximizing the developmental effects of integration into the world economy. ■

Note

1   For the evidence on growth performance, see *TDR*s *1997* and *2003* and UNCTAD, 2002; on the problems of applying uniform policy advice, for Africa see *TDR 1998* and UNCTAD, 2001, for Latin America see ECLAC, 2002, and for countries in Central and Eastern Europe see ECE, 1990. On the damaging social impact of these policies see UNDP, 1999; UN-HABITAT, 2003; and ILO, 2004.

Chapter III

OPENNESS, INTEGRATION AND NATIONAL POLICY SPACE

A. Introduction

The move to unrestricted cross-border flows of goods, services and capital has always been one of the principles of globalization. Since the late 1970s, "the propensity to truck, barter and exchange one thing for another" (Adam Smith), unhindered by political boundaries, has been regarded as the cornerstone of a global system that would produce efficiency gains from allowing resources to be directed to their most efficient use, and specialization gains from accessing a greater variety of intermediate and capital goods. If improved institutional quality and technology spillover are added, trade and capital openness should automatically allow for catch-up growth in poorer countries and bring about income convergence at the global level (see, for example, IMF, 2002; WTO, 1998; World Bank, 2002; Winters, 2004). But the empirical evidence supporting this approach has been elusive. In fact, most of the evidence suggests that the impact of trade openness has been highly uneven, and contingent on a variety of institutional factors, and that there is room for discretionary policy measures at the micro and macro level.[1]

A more balanced perspective, also taking its cue from Adam Smith, links a process of success-ful integration back to productivity gains from specialization, gains that are amplified through innovation, the use of better equipment, scale economies at the firm level and by "externalities" such as learning and improvements in human capital. This ties economic success to a heightened degree of economic interdependence through the mutually reinforcing interactions between expanding markets and an increasingly complex division of labour (Young, 1928). Extending and deepening such interactions depends on new investments under conditions of objective uncertainty. To improve and expand existing capacity as well as to introduce new products and processes, a "profit-investment nexus" is needed that requires supporting financial arrangements, including accommodative monetary policy and relatively stable legal institutions.[2] Under the right conditions, high profits will increase the incentive of firms to invest, as well as their capacity to finance new investment; this in turn boosts profits by enhancing the rates of capital utilization and the pace of productivity growth. For most countries, this nexus is closely linked to industrialization, where the presence of scale economies, externalities and an array of indivisibilities and complementarities in production and consumption are strongest, and from where productivity growth feeds into a wider process of structural change as labour shifts out of lower value-added sectors into more capital- and technology-intensive activities and complementary service activities.

At the same time, as the increasingly interdependent nature of industrial activity heightens the gains from specialization, it also exposes more and more individuals, firms and communities to an increased threat from discontinuities and disruptions. Ruptures occur from myriad shocks and coordination failures across imperfectly functioning (or missing) factor and product markets.[3] As a result, a successful and sustained "take-off" requires the evolution of a range of complementary norms, policies and regulations that help discipline and restrain the more destructive and nurture the more creative forces of the emergent industrial economy. A general lesson from history is that "policy space" expands considerably with the transition from a world dominated by agriculture, slow-moving technology and small-scale business to one dominated by manufactured goods, rapidly evolving technology and big firms.[4]

Hence, the potential benefits from participating in a more detailed international division of labour must be weighed against the coordination and adjustment costs arising from the heightened interdependence accompanying further specialization in, and fragmentation of, economic activities. Indeed, the fact that interdependence is now taking place across borders adds new constraints, rivalries and risks to sustained economic progress. However, there remains a basic challenge for economic policy-makers: to decide whether and to what extent market forces can be left alone to ensure that progress is consistent with increased participation in the international economy, and when and what kinds of policies and institutional arrangements might be needed to better manage the process.

> The increasingly interdependent nature of industrial activity exposes more and more individuals, firms and communities to an increased threat from discontinuities and disruptions.

> Integration is not just about the efficient use of given resources, but about extending and reinforcing the cumulative gains of local dynamic growth forces.

The evolving international division of labour is further complicated as large national firms in more advanced economies acquire the capabilities and the possibilities to organize and control their production activities across borders (Hymer, 1976; Dunning, 1981). While the timing and the direction will vary among countries and sectors, the decisive elements in the internationalization of production are firm size, control over rent-creating strategic assets and market penetration. Since large firms tend to have more capital at their disposal and more control over market forces, they will do the most overseas investing.

Finally, the growth of trade and the rise of international firms accelerate the mobility of capital and extend the reach of financial institutions. At the domestic level, these institutions essentially help to channel resources for investment purposes by reconciling the differences between borrowers and lenders in the timing of payments, and transforming short-term liquid liabilities into long-term illiquid assets. The efficiency of the system will be reflected in its ability to minimize the liquidity premium and the risk of erroneous investment decisions (*TDR 1991*). As international trade and production expand, specialized financial institutions are joined by international banks seeking to widen the scope and reach of their services to sovereign and local governments, to local financial institutions and non-bank firms. They concentrate their borrowing in markets with the lowest interest rates and their lending in markets with the highest, with funds moving whenever the differential is greater than the transaction costs.

The resulting cross-border flows of capital can help deepen the international division of labour by offsetting structural weaknesses resulting from persistent trade deficits, and allowing a faster pace of investment than might otherwise be possible from domestic resources. In poorer economies, such flows can thereby reinforce a catch-up growth dynamic. However, these flows are highly information sensitive, and vulnerable to information asymmetries, contract-enforcement problems and macroeconomic risks. They also tend to be more footloose than other cross-border economic flows, in part, because of its openness to innovative techniques in search of the preferred combination of liquidity and returns. Under these conditions, both the direction and the terms of borrowing can become major sources of discontinuity across the international division of labour. Moreover, an expanding international economy presents new and riskier profit opportunities, allowing liquid capital a greater margin to seek out short-term arbitrage positions and speculative gains. As a result, such flows can be extremely volatile and subject to pro-cyclical bandwagon effects; they can cause gyrations in security prices, exchange rates and trade balances, and make financial crisis a "hardy perennial" of the international market economy (Kindleberger, 1975).

Thus, integration is not just, or even most importantly, about the efficient use of given resources, but rather about extending and reinforcing the cumulative gains of local dynamic growth forces through exports and capital flows. However, and as at the domestic level, those forces introduce discontinuities, shocks and potential conflicts of interest, which can generate sizeable adjustment costs for national economies participating in the international division of labour; they may even trigger divergence away from leading economies. From this perspective, the real challenge is not so much about the extent or the sequencing of liberalization, but about finding the particular combination of international market forces, policy space and collective action needed by countries with different institutional and industrial capacities, to ensure that the integration process is welfare-enhancing for all participants in the international division of labour.

Historically, finding that balance has proved difficult, making for an ebbing and flowing of the integration process. The following sections examine a number of episodes where incoherence has arisen as a result of a lopsided emphasis by policymakers on openness, at the expense of policy space and coordinated actions.

B. Unbalanced integration in the 1920s

The inter-war period is often flagged as a warning of what can happen when the virtues of openness are foregone in favour of narrower national and sectoral interests. From this perspective, a series of ill-judged interventionist measures, particularly a retreat into tariff protection, but also misguided monetary interventionism by central banks, excessive social spending and restrictions on labour mobility, have been blamed for plunging the world economy into a destructive pattern of autarkic development (Crucini and Kahn, 1996; World Bank, 2002; Wolf, 2004).

But while there can be no doubting the scale or extent of economic damage from the crisis that engulfed the global economy in the early 1930s, or the political turmoil that followed in its wake, such accounts are often guilty of painting the inter-war economic experience in unduly simple terms. In particular, they downplay the relatively strong recovery in international economic relations in the 1920s, marked by an overall rise in the share of trade in world GDP, as well as a revival of capital flows, notably a boom in sovereign borrowing and some growth in FDI (tables 3.1 and 3.2). They

Table 3.1

MERCHANDISE EXPORTS AS A SHARE OF GDP, 1913 AND 1929

(Per cent)

	1913	1929
Western Europe	16.3	13.3
France	7.8	8.6
Germany	16.1	12.8
Netherlands	17.3	17.2
United Kingdom	17.5	13.3
United States	3.7	3.6
Canada	12.2	15.8
Latin America	9.5	9.7
Asia	2.6	2.8
Japan	2.4	3.5
World	7.9	9.0

Source: O'Rourke (2002: table 2).

Table 3.2

FOREIGN DIRECT INVESTMENT, 1913 AND 1938

(Outward stock of FDI/GDP, per cent)

	1913	1938
Canada	6	14
France	23	21
Germany	11	1
Japan	11	21
Netherlands	82	91
United Kingdom	49	38
United States	7	8

Source: Twomey (2000).

also ignore the general policy direction taken by the international community to reorganize post-war economic relations around the goal of openness, and, consequently, fail to consider how that policy agenda contributed to mismanaging the return to stability.

Although the end of the First World War left Europe in a state of political and moral uncertainty,

economic policy-makers held up the economic order in the period before 1914 – the *belle époque* – as a state of "normalcy" which needed to be restored as quickly as possible (Bayen, 1954). Indeed, this was seen as the most fundamental step to achieving wider peace and stability, and was premised on restoring the pre-war international monetary system, which was expected to guarantee price stability under a system of fixed exchange rates tied to gold.

From this starting point, a policy consensus was forged, which aimed at restoring flexibility at the microeconomic level through the elimination of trade barriers and other market distortions erected during the war, and the establishment of harmonious trade conditions around the principle of non-discrimination (as proposed in Article 3 of the Versailles Peace Accord). It also aimed at recovering stability at the macroeconomic level by first reducing the high level of public debts acquired during the war, through fiscal surpluses achieved by an initial round of expenditure cuts and increased taxes, followed by tight restrictions on any subsequent efforts to expand government spending. At the same time, monetary policy would be put back in the hands of technocrats working through independent central banks, and in accordance with the requirements for freely flowing international capital.

Primary responsibility for implementing this agenda rested with domestic policy-makers. However, it was acknowledged that, as a consequence of the war, privileging international market forces might cause political resistance, and that, consequently, pressure could usefully be brought to bear on policy-makers to push them in the desired direction. The initiative was taken in a series of international economic conferences beginning in Brussels in 1920, and followed up over the next 13 years in Genoa, Portorose, Geneva, Lausanne and London (Pauly, 1997). Efforts were also made to bring about closer central bank cooperation (Eichengreen, 1996). More radically still, in cases where economic imbalances and political uncertainties were particularly pronounced, stabilization would be achieved through adjustment programmes managed by the League of Nations.

By assuming an underlying "natural" state of fully employed resources, adjustments accompanying economic openness were expected to be small in scale and short in duration, allowing international markets to establish the right price incentives, and bringing about a rapid return to growth and stability. With eyes firmly fixed on the past, the sequence of reforms aimed to get long-term capital flowing again before opening up trade, although it was generally accepted that success ultimately hinged on re-creating the mutually supportive pattern of trade and capital flows that existed before 1914.

With economic policy-makers expecting the gold standard to deliver long-term growth and stability, the room for policy action to bring about an orderly adjustment in and across countries was squeezed between measures to regain and maintain the confidence of financial markets and to allow competitive pressures to re-establish external balance. Little attention was given to whether pre-war monetary arrangements were appropriate for the emerging post-war pattern of economic integration, or whether the steps taken by individual countries to regain stability might actually add to the incoherence in international economic relations.

The belief that marginal adjustments through the marketplace would bring global stability clouded the judgement of policy-makers as to the scale of investment, both private and public, needed to rebuild and modernize a European economic space transformed by the dislocations of war, the break-up of old empires and the rising voice of organized labour. In particular, the economic consequences of accumulated wartime debts and German reparations were greatly underestimated. In the absence of their cancellation, highly indebted countries were faced with the onerous task of generating both a fiscal and a trade surplus to meet their international financial obligations, even as they struggled to repair the damage to productive capacity and investment prospects. Moreover, the problem was not just one of managing sovereign debt; in many countries, bank capital, depleted by post-war inflation, had to be shored up by foreign borrowing, and corporate debts accumulated during the war increased further under the post-war restructuring efforts through both foreign bond issues and bank borrowing supported by foreign loans (Kregel, 1996a); in agriculture too, which remained a major source of foreign-exchange earnings and employment for many countries – in-

Table 3.3

AVERAGE TARIFF RATES ON MANUFACTURED PRODUCTS FOR SELECTED COUNTRIES, 1913–1931

(Weighted average in percentage of value)

	1913	1925	1931
Belgium	9	15	14
France	20	21	30
Germany	13	20	21
Italy	18	22	46
Japan	30	..	..
Sweden	20	16	21
Switzerland	9	14	19
United Kingdom	0	5	..
United States	44	37	48

Source: Bairoch (1993).

cluding the United States and France – rising levels of indebtedness anticipated a pattern of instability previously confined to primary exporters on the periphery.[5]

As the constraints on investment were underestimated, so the prospects for strong and rapid export recoveries were overestimated, particularly for the industrial heartland of Europe, where a rapid return to pre-war export performance was essential to meet financial obligations without further damaging the domestic economy. A disappointing trade performance cannot, however, be explained simply as being the result of an unforeseen protectionist wave. In fact, trade policies were broadly re-established along pre-war lines: quantitative controls were quickly abolished, tariff levels returned to earlier levels – which were quite high, particularly for manufactures (table 3.3) – and the commitment to non-discrimination (in the form of most-favoured-nation (MFN) treatment) was generally confirmed.[6] In Germany, a severely weakened manufacturing sector faced added obstacles, as newly independent economies in Eastern Europe looked to support their own infant industries through tariff protection, and the persistence of high tariffs in surplus economies, notably the United States, dampened prospects for an export-led recovery (Chang, 2002). In the case of Britain, the loss of markets in key sectors such as coal, textiles and shipbuilding also reflected the rise of new competitors in its traditional colonial markets. But the real challenge facing these older industrial economies was to respond to the new and strengthened manufacturing capacity that had emerged elsewhere during the war through renewed investment in more dynamic industries.

Under these conditions, the decision of Europe's leading industrial centres to return to the gold standard at the pre-war parity level damaged prospects of a strong export recovery,[7] and the resort to tight macroeconomic policies to defend that decision further compromised efforts to re-establish a dynamic profit-investment nexus. The resulting sharp slowdown of growth in the European industrial heartland was itself an important contributory source of weak trade performance and a major reason why trade levels in 1929 were below what might otherwise have been expected. By contrast, countries that re-entered the gold standard with devalued currencies saw strong growth in trade, persistent surpluses, an earlier recovery in investment and comparatively lower levels of unemployment. This was notably true of France – which was still an industrial laggard – and Belgium, as well as other smaller European countries.

Given these conditions, and with no hope of a coordinated debt write-off, exposure to a series of unfamiliar dangers from rising debt charges, falling prices and the shifting sentiments of financial markets, made policy-makers in the 1920s a good deal more "balance-of-payments conscious" (ECLA, 1965: 15). Effective management of the resulting policy trade-offs was complicated by the shifting interests of leading creditor and debtor countries. Under the gold standard, long-term capital flows and an increasingly complex multilateral trading system were mutually supportive, largely because the United Kingdom's foreign lending was a substitute for its domestic investment. In addition, its deficit on

> By assuming an underlying "natural" state of fully employed resources, adjustments were expected to be small in scale and short in duration.

> The international economy which took shape in the 1920s was very different from the one that had collapsed in 1914.

the trade account was offset by a surplus on the current account due to earnings on foreign investment, which allowed it to maintain open markets, even in the face of rising protectionism abroad. Moreover, a general sense of credibility centred on confidence in the stability of the pound sterling, allowing short-term capital flows to play a complementary stabilizing role, at least in the core countries (Eichengreen, 1996).[8]

With no clear leadership of the financial system and persistent worries about a gold shortage, economic uncertainty was added to the political doubts of the post-war world, thus delaying further any recovery in long-term capital flows. In the absence of policy coordination between surplus and deficit countries, the system relied increasingly on short-term capital, through portfolio flows and bank lending, to maintain a degree of balance and to bolster reserves. Such flows occurred on an unprecedented scale, led by United States investors who were attracted by high returns thanks to tight European monetary policies and minimal exchange rate risks. These flows introduced a much more speculative dimension to the recovery, which had started in the second half of the 1920s following the Dawes Plan and the restoration of the gold standard in the United Kingdom. Indeed, with limits to an export-led recovery, and domestic expansion restricted by high domestic interest rates and persistently high levels of unemployment, capital inflows were used increasingly to meet debt repayments in a Ponzi-type of financing[9] (Bayen, 1954).

Thus, the international economy which took shape in the 1920s was very different from the one that had collapsed in 1914. The combination of exchange rate risk, volatile capital movements and a high and rising debt stock meant that deflationary pressures, financial fragility and the threat of contagion were closely intertwined. Under these circumstances, a country's balance-of-payments position and its reserve situation became much more prominent indicators of economic vulnerability and distress, and triggers for short-term capital movements.[10] The boom in the second half of the 1920s failed to stimulate productive investment or create sufficient jobs in the leading industrial economies; it provided only a temporary cover for these structural problems, even as trade expanded and the openness agenda was given a renewed sense of vigour.

In 1927, with the gold standard back in place, the attention of policy-makers shifted to trade openness. Although the International Economic Conference in Geneva produced few concrete outcomes, it added momentum to extending the principles of the "Manchester School" and the advantages of free competition to the trading system through a "beefed-up" League of Nations secretariat (Pauly, 1997: 55–61). But within six months after that Conference, capital flows from the United States to Europe dropped off sharply following an equity surge on Wall Street, and continued to fall when United States interest rates were hiked in an effort to curb "irrational exuberance". The result was a further tightening of monetary policy in Europe. At the same time, agricultural prices, which had been falling for some years, showed a marked downward fall in 1929, as exporters intensified their efforts to generate foreign exchange in the face of dwindling capital inflows and mount-

ing payment difficulties on outstanding loans. The remaining policy option, of deflationary measures to counter widening imbalances in external payments by cutting imports, simply shifted the problem elsewhere. This made a bust in heavily indebted European economies inevitable, and once it happened, it ensured there was little to stop it spilling over into "twin" banking and currency crises.

With sensible collective responses ruled out by an absence of leadership at the international level, and little thought given to the peculiar circumstances under which the international financial and trading system had operated before the war, the idea of a return to "normalcy" in international economic relations was, from its inception, built on unstable foundations. Still, economists' belief, propagated through international conferences, that the only option was to build the confidence of financial markets as a prelude to the recovery of international capital flows and the reduction of trade barriers, led to an unhealthy restriction on policy space at home, even as it promoted a blind faith in international market forces as a means to regaining stability. Given the size and nature of adjustments to be made, such thinking contributed to a destabilizing mix of deflationary pressures and volatile capital flows, which eventually culminated in the "beggar-thy-neighbour" policies of the 1930s.

C. Recasting multilateralism: development challenges and the origins of UNCTAD

The post-World War II multilateral agenda arose from the desire to avoid deflationary adjustments and beggar-thy-neighbour policies of the kind that had severely disrupted the inter-war economy. It was premised on an expanded policy space which would allow policy-makers to combine a reasonable degree of price stability with

full employment and growth. But, perhaps just as importantly, the inter-war period had confirmed that industrial countries were too specialized and interdependent to achieve economic stability and lasting improvements in economic welfare without the establishment of some kind of new international economic order. Thus, and quite unlike the years following the First World War, policy-makers were not only willing to consider a range of more active international policy instruments and measures – an international currency, provision of international liquidity, multilaterally negotiated trade rules, a managed exchange rate system, controlling of destabilizing capital flows – but to discuss what kinds of international arrangements would be needed to manage these most effectively.

Discussions about these were already under way in the late 1930s, and as plans on the reorganization of post-war international economic relations advanced, the institutional arrangements proposed included:

> The post-war multilateral agenda arose from the desire to avoid deflationary adjustments and beggar-thy-neighbour policies of the kind that had severely disrupted the inter-war economy.

- An international monetary fund to ensure an orderly system of multilateral payments by means of stable but adjustable exchange rates, in conditions of strictly limited private international capital flows;

- An international bank for reconstruction and development to provide long-term capital for post-war reconstruction by encouraging and supplementing private capital flows;

- An international trade organization to provide a rules-based framework to facilitate multilaterally negotiated reductions in trade barriers, as well as to coordinate national economic policies to ensure adequate levels of global demand and employment in support of the development of low-income member countries;

- An international commodity stabilization fund for bringing about stability of prices of raw materials and primary commodities through the creation of international buffer stocks; and

- An international employment agreement which would commit countries to full employment along with the requisite international measures and arrangements to oversee and implement such an obligation.

Common to the proposed mandates of all these institutions was the recognized need for coordinated policy efforts to create an open multilateral trading system that would benefit, rather than threaten, domestic income and employment, and tether unruly capital flows to ensure financial and exchange rate stability (*TDR 1984*). This institutional project was never completed; the final outcome reflected prolonged (and noticeably asymmetric) negotiations between the passing global hegemonic power (the United Kingdom) and the ascendant one (the United States). In the end, only the International Monetary Fund (IMF) was established, on the lines of a stabilization fund proposed by Harry White and the United States delegation, along with the (under funded) International Bank for Reconstruction and Development (IBRD). An international agreement on employment was strongly opposed by the United States (as a purely domestic issue), but was eventually tied to the trade agenda through a proposed charter for an International Trade Organization (ITO). However, this subsequently failed to gain ratification in key countries, notably the United States. A limited portion of the ITO mandate was reworked into the General Agreement on Tariffs and Trade (GATT), but the idea of a Stabilization Fund for commodities was dropped altogether.[11]

The formative years of these multilateral arrangements produced mixed outcomes. The GATT negotiations were primarily concerned with the exchange of tariff concessions extended on a multilateral basis under the unconditional MFN clause. A series of tariff-reducing rounds between 1947 and 1956 saw average tariffs fall, albeit front-loaded on the opening Geneva Round (when the United States reduced its tariffs by an average of 20 per cent on all dutiable imports); while their immediate economic impact was probably not significant, they did help to establish the principle of a tariff-based multilateral system and a commitment to a measured liberalization process (*TDR 1984*: 63). By contrast, the scale of the reconstruction challenge, and the transition back to a situation where the IMF could begin to fulfil its

Table 3.4

**ECONOMIC PERFORMANCE BEFORE THE FIRST WORLD WAR AND
AFTER THE SECOND WORLD WAR IN SELECTED COUNTRIES**

(Average annual growth rates)

	1870–1913			1950–1973		
	Investment	*Export*	*GDP*	*Investment*	*Export*	*GDP*
Canada	..	3.1	3.8	5.5	7.0	5.2
France	..	2.8	1.7	4.5	8.2	5.1
Germany	3.1	4.1	2.8	6.1	12.4	6.0
Italy	2.5	2.2	1.5	5.1	11.7	5.5
Japan	2.7	8.5	2.5	9.2	15.4	9.7
United Kingdom	1.4	2.8	1.9	3.9	3.9	3.0
United States	4.7	4.9	4.1	4.0	6.3	3.7

Source: Maddison (1982: tables 3.2, 3.7 and 5.4).

responsibility to promote exchange rate stability and manage orderly balance-of-payments adjustments, were greatly underestimated, and transitional arrangements were required to manage the process. However, the predicted return of economic stagnation did not materialize, so that the problems of short-term adjustment were easier to solve, and United States authorities and financial institutions were able to assume a pivotal role in managing the system.[12]

While the reliance of the system on the economic fortunes of the dominant economic power was inevitable in the short run, it left a series of weaknesses and shortcomings; some of these would only become fully apparent once post-war economic relations stabilized in the late 1950s (Panic, 1995; Eichengreen, 2004). The arrangements were, nevertheless, successful in bringing together a club of similar economies that had been converging on each other for some time (Baumol, 1986), and their economic closeness made the task of learning to work together easier. The combination of favourable economic conditions, a consensus on policy objectives with sufficient policy space, and supportive multilateral institutions provided a climate of predictability and stability

in an increasingly interdependent international economy. It also allowed the building of a strong nexus between investment and exports. Recovery led to rapid and sustained growth, which ensured that the adjustment costs associated with closer trade integration were contained and the benefits broadly shared (*TDR 1997*). The result was a quarter of a century of unprecedented economic growth and stability (table 3.4).

For those outside this club, the kind of export-based profit-investment nexus underpinning growth in the more advanced economies appeared to be weak or absent. Moreover, while the obstacles to growth facing developing countries had surfaced in the context of wartime military and political alliances, these remained marginal in the Bretton Woods negotiations.[13] A truly development *problématique* did not begin to take shape in the World Bank until the mid-1950s, and was not really completed until the early 1960s when the International Development Association (IDA) was established. Moreover, the World Bank's original mandate as a guarantor of medium- and long-term loans meant it lacked an independent capacity to create development finance, and its dependence on funds raised from the main capital markets hampered its ability to meet the emerging structural needs of developing countries (Akyüz, 2004).[14] Perhaps more damaging still, in this respect, was the failure to adopt the Havana Charter, which contained a number of elements of more immediate interest to poorer countries.

Consequently, the first real strides in development policy analysis occurred outside the Bretton Woods institutions. They drew heavily on the newly emerging discipline of growth theory, but were conceived more broadly in the context of a transition from industrial "backwardness". The resulting development strategy was built around two main challenges facing low-income economies: the shortage of capital was seen as the biggest constraint on the structural transformation needed in poorer countries to sustain faster growth; and it was believed that breaking that constraint could not rely on market forces alone. Given low private domestic savings rates, along with low income, a non-inflationary way to close the gap between domestic savings and investment was found in external flows of capital from rich to poor countries in the form of private investment, loans and development assistance. But the scale of the challenge was underestimated. While early estimates by the United Nations put the resource requirements of developing countries from foreign sources at $15 billion a year, World Bank loans averaged between $200 million and $400 million annually during the 1950s, with bilateral flows averaging $2 billion annually from 1950 to 1955, rising to over $4 billion by the end of the decade (*TDR 1984*: 90).[15] Private capital flows were even more limited, and almost exclusively took the form of direct investments in the commodity sector. Moreover, as economic thinking on development grew in sophistication, and was deepened and refined by academics and policy-makers from the developing countries themselves, efforts to

> The combination of favourable economic conditions, a consensus on policy objectives and supportive multilateral institutions provided a climate of predictability and stability.

> The point in the international trading system where asymmetries between centre and periphery appeared in sharpest focus was in the terms of trade for primary exports.

measure the size of the resource gap revealed developing countries to be net exporters of capital, once the repayment of loans, terms-of-trade losses and capital flight were included in the calculation.[16]

With international private capital flows constrained and development assistance still limited (and often tied), increasing attention was focused on the role of international trade as a more dependable means of removing the resource constraints on economic growth in poorer countries. This marked something of a break with the trade pessimism which had been a powerful current both before and after the war (Rayment, 1983), particularly in developing countries, where the collapse of the trading system in the 1930s had forced a greater reliance on the domestic market. However, neither the multilateral trading arrangements, where the GATT had become a largely technical instrument for managing trade between rich countries, nor the most dynamic regional trading arrangements, notably the evolving European Common Market (*TDR 2003*), were appropriate venues for improving developing-country participation. Between 1950 and 1960, the share of developing countries in world trade fell from 31 per cent to 21 per cent, and even in primary commodities, their share fell from 41 per cent to 29 per cent. As a result, the kind of export-based profit-investment nexus that was underpinning the successful pattern of interdependence among advanced economies, appeared to be weak or missing altogether in the developing world.

An examination of the comparative trade performance of rich and poor countries published by the GATT in 1958 and prepared by the noted economist Gottfried Haberler, confirmed that tariff and other barriers, particularly against food-exporting developing countries, was one source of the problem.[17] Still, the Haberler Report reflected conventional thinking on the trade openness model, "based on the classic concept that the free play of international economic forces by itself leads to the optimum expansion of trade and the most efficient utilization of the world's productive resources" (UNCTAD, 1964: 18); its assumption of near equality of initial conditions leading to convergence and common trading interests was inconsistent with the burgeoning literature on economic development. As Nurkse (1959: 26) noted at the time,

> In a world in which (outside the Soviet area) over nine-tenths of the manufacturing and four-fifths of the total productive activity are concentrated in the advanced industrial countries, the ideas of symmetry, reciprocity and mutual dependence which are associated with the traditional theory of international trade are of rather questionable relevance to trade relations between centre and periphery.

The point in the international trading system where asymmetries between centre and periphery appeared in sharpest focus was in the terms of trade for primary exports. Empirical studies reported a long-term decline, coupled with high instability, in the terms of trade between primary and manufactured exports. The explanation pointed to price and income inelasticity for the demand of primary commodities. This, combined with competitive market conditions, meant that investment and technical progress, which, in the developed countries, led to higher wages and living standards of those employed, in the developing countries tended to result in lower prices for their exports. The secular tendency for the terms of trade to move against developing countries and especially for those exporting primary products, seriously constrained the capacity of developing countries to import the capital goods needed to accelerate capital formation and to diversify into more dynamic areas of international trade. Given that industrial development offered the best chance of raising productivity growth (through scale economies and innovation), and producing a virtuous growth circle between demand expansion and development of productive capacities, a basic objective of development policy was to find ways of redressing the structural constraints on catch-up growth.[18]

Raul Prebisch developed the policy options for countries locked into a pattern of slow growth

and adverse terms-of-trade movements. Already in the mid-1950s as head of the then Economic Commission for Latin America (ECLA), he had organized a series of country studies examining the disappointing results of the inward-oriented industrialization model adopted in Latin America in the inter-war years. A 1956 report on the Argentinean economy prepared under his guidance outlined an outward-oriented growth strategy which aimed for a better balance between agriculture and industrial development, whilst shifting the orientation of industry from domestic to foreign markets to achieve more dynamic scale economies (Rosenthal, 2003: 181–183).[19]

Linking trade prospects to a structuralist development model also cast the working of the international trading system in a different light. If the consistent application of liberalization measures through universal trade rules and principles, combined with the gradual absorption of imported technologies, could not be relied upon to eliminate the external imbalances accompanying economic development, or to bring about rapid productivity growth and income convergence along the lines achieved by the late industrializing economies in the late nineteenth and early twentieth centuries, then a rules-based system supportive of an industry-led growth strategy for poorer countries would have to accommodate an element of asymmetrical integration into the world economy. As noted in the Report of the Secretary-General of UNCTAD (UNCTAD, 1964: 19),

> The request for reciprocity in negotiations between countries that have no structural disparity in their demands is logical. In the case of trade between the developing and the industrial countries, the situation is different. Since the former tend to import more than they export – owing to the international disparity in demand – concessions granted by the industrial countries tend to rectify this disparity and are soon reflected in an expansion of their exports to developing countries. In other words, the developing economies, given their potential demand for imports, can import more than they would otherwise have been able to do had these concessions not been granted. Thus there is a real or implicit reciprocity, independent of the play of conventional concessions.

Multilateral efforts at designing this new trading geometry culminated in the First UNCTAD

Conference in 1964. The Report to the Conference, entitled *Towards a New Trade Policy for Development*, set out to show that the free play of international economic forces would not by itself lead to the most desirable utilization of the world's productive resources, given the structural obstacles to growth at the domestic and international levels. It also spelt out the implications for trade and related finance if the minimum target of 5 per cent growth for developing countries was to be achieved.[20] In specifying what was to be done, the Report rejected both the import substitution model handed down from the inter-war period and the openness model embodied in the GATT. Instead, it spelt out an alternative strategy which would help poorer countries develop outwardly through strong capital formation and continuing and accelerated expansion of exports – both traditional and non-traditional. Central to that agenda was the idea that if developing countries were to rely on their own efforts, they would need to have sufficient policy space to accelerate capital formation, diversify their economic structures and give development a greater "social depth". There would also need to be a change in the orientation of international cooperation to ensure that this strategy was consistent with the international goal of poverty alleviation (UNCTAD, 1964: 64).

> The Report to UNCTAD I recognized that any new trade geometry in support of development would hinge on fast and stable growth in the developed countries.

This reorientation would require a much more flexibly managed trading system to accommodate countries at different levels of development. In a sense, a case for greater flexibility had already been accepted by advanced industrial economies in the GATT when they sought more orderly adjustments for their own peripheral areas and sunset activities.[21] Such flexibilities were provided by non-application of the Agreement between particular Contracting Parties under Article XXXV and the Grandfather Clause, under which original contracting parties to the GATT agreed to apply major obligations of the agreement only to the extent of their consistence with existing national legislation. This was most notably applied in the case of agriculture. Favourable terms were also extended to textiles and clothing, which were eventually accorded their own separate trade regime. Extending

this idea of preferential treatment to industries in developing countries would, however, have to accommodate the wider productivity gaps – due to structural differences and differing technological densities – which existed with the advanced economies. Allowing more favourable access to their markets would be one way to overcome initial cost disadvantages. Additionally, appropriate fiscal support and other incentives for infant industries would be needed, along with supplementary measures, where possible, to ensure a more effectively managed exchange rate. All such measures would have to be carefully monitored and subject to clear bounds in line with improving technological capacities and productivity improvements.

The UNCTAD agenda also addressed the interdependence of trade and finance, given that, particularly in the early stages of industrialization, imports would almost certainly grow faster than exports, and that financing the resulting trade gap would be key to accelerating growth. This would require additional development assistance or compensatory finance for deteriorating terms of trade and debt relief. The Report to UNCTAD I also recognized that any new trade geometry in support of development would hinge on fast and stable growth in the developed countries, and that the international financial arrangements would require sufficient resources to prevent disruptive stop-go cycles in those countries. Furthermore, it raised concerns about the adequacy of balance-of-payments financing in light of the growing volume of trade, persistent trade surpluses in some economies, and the need to supplement gold reserves with new instruments to allow for additional credit expansion by international financial institutions.

In the absence of sufficient finance for meeting the structural demands of developing countries, external equilibrium could only be maintained through the suspension of commitments made in the multilateral trading system (Johnson, 1967: 114–115). The GATT had accepted this principle for developed countries in support of the post-war full-employment agenda. For example, Article VII provided for exchange controls and trade restrictions when the currency required to finance external imbalances was declared "scarce".[22] This implicit acceptance of the priority of meeting financial obligations over the observance of commitments to free trade was reflected in GATT Articles XII (Restrictions to Safeguard the Balance of Payments) and XV (outlining the terms of GATT and IMF collaboration on exchange rate questions). These exemptions were granted, essentially, to address temporary liquidity problems. Similar exemptions for longer run adjustments, included in the ITO proposals, had not been incorporated into the GATT, and were only seriously considered after the creation of UNCTAD. It was only in 1979 that special and differential treatment was accepted as a general requirement for enabling the beneficial participation of developing countries in the post-war international trading and financial system.

The creation of UNCTAD was part of the post-war reformist wave, which extended the search for multilateral solutions to the economic challenges of an interdependent world to encompass development problems largely ignored at Bretton Woods. Its starting point was the need to address the structural obstacles to catch-up growth, and particularly those enforced through international market forces. Rebalancing the system required a strategic pattern of integration in line with levels of industrial development and favourable terms of market access, as well as appropriate levels of development finance. But just as importantly, as noted by Edward Heath, Head of the British delegation to UNCTAD I, it required that the richer countries begin to see "fuller cooperation and greater interdependence" as common allies in the fight for a more prosperous and fairer world.

D. Interdependence after Bretton Woods

As noted in the previous section, a central feature of the Bretton Woods system was affording sufficient space to policy-makers to meet employment, inflation and growth targets, accepting that, in an increasingly interdependent global economy, policies should be employed with a clear sense of any potential negative externalities they might generate.[23] This was achieved through a system of fixed but adjustable exchange rates, with tight controls on international capital movements along with the global provision of liquidity, enabling countries to pursue expansionary policies that would bring positive externalities for trading partners (Stiglitz, 2003). On this basis, an early Washington policy consensus – articulated by Treasury Secretary Morgenthau and the chief United States negotiator at Bretton Woods, Harry White – allowed for restrictions on destabilizing

capital flows and placed clear limits on the surveillance and conditionality attached to international lending. According to White, as cited in Felix (1996: 64),

> To use international monetary arrangements as a cloak for the enforcement of unpopular policies, whose merits or demerits rest not on international monetary considerations as such but on the whole economic program and philosophy of the country concerned, would poison the atmosphere of international financial stability.

This consensus quickly unravelled with the collapse of the Bretton Woods system in the early 1970s, and the transfer of the management of foreign exchange risk to the private financial sector (Eatwell and Taylor, 2000). The collapse was followed by the removal of capital controls, and by a move to financial deregulation in the developed economies, which was transmitted swiftly to the rest of the world, in no small part thanks to the efforts of the international financial institutions to lock in "the freedom of capital movements already achieved and encourage wider liberalization" (Camdessus, 1995). These efforts implied a shift in focus from guaranteeing systemic financial stability to catalysing private capital flows by building confidence, including through intrusive adjustment programmes in debt-ridden developing countries.

> The removal of controls over international capital was followed by a marked increase in flows to developing countries in the 1970s.

This change of direction assumes that financial deepening, brought about by the liberalization of domestic financial markets and the opening up of the capital account, would lead to a more efficient allocation of resources and faster and more stable growth.[24] The removal of controls over international capital was followed by a marked increase in flows to developing countries, beginning with syndicated bank lending in the mid-1970s, and, since the late 1980s, in equity flows and FDI (*TDR 1999*). This has frequently led to comparisons with the earlier period of rapid globalization under the gold standard, when large private capital flows underpinned strong economic performances, including on the periphery. This parallel implies the presence of a number of features in current arrangements: first, capital flows are predominantly long-term, triggered by productive profit opportunities in an emerging international division of labour, and supported by complementary trade and labour flows; second, stability rests on strong domestic capital accumulation, which is not sacrificed to emerging trade imbalances; and third, short-term capital flows play a subordinate and stabilizing role.

Under the gold standard, such flows and adjustments were managed through a "socially-constructed" monetary arrangement that included a simple set of rules around which core lenders and borrowers could build expectations of a stable future. It also included a willingness to subordinate domestic policy goals in times of crisis; and there was a lead economy with a vested economic interest in maintaining a stable currency and free trade, even as it was channelling domestic savings abroad.[25] Strong States channelled funds into productive public investment, while they used policy space to manage a fast pace of capital accumulation and to encourage exporting that could help service the capital flows needed to cover large trade deficits.

The diversity of economies that make up the contemporary international financial system – at least as measured by income gaps between the main debtors and creditors – is probably greater than under the gold standard (World Bank, 1999). However, the greater part of contemporary financial flows are short term, among the developed countries themselves, and even the greater part of global FDI is accounted for by mergers and acquisitions (M&As) amongst the advanced industrialized countries. On balance, the liberalization of capital movements has had little impact on levels of development finance, and the balance-of-payments constraint of developing countries has not been removed. Moreover, no major region has successfully forged strong linkages between net capital inflows, capital formation and industrialization.

Behind these trends lies an emerging picture of transnational finance (Kregel, 1994), with activities focused on providing hedging on foreign-exchange risk across a diversified international portfolio of foreign assets, and with a greatly expanded capacity to operate in a global market for funding sources, borrowing in any currency and lending in any other currency. While the extent of transnational finance remains the subject of ongoing empirical analyses (Felix, 2001), there has been a trend of de-linking international trade and financial flows. This is most clearly the case with short-term flows, where over 80 per cent of transactions relate to round-trip operations of a week or less, motivated by hedging, arbitrage and speculative considerations. But it is also true of some longer term flows. A significant share of FDI flows has been absorbed by M&As and the increased capacity of transnational corporations (TNCs) to combine financial and locational engineering in international production networks has often produced footloose productive assets and ambiguous effects on balance-of-payments positions (Kregel, 1996b; *TDRs 1999* and *2002*). Moreover, and despite the belief that a more open economic environment with unrestricted capital flows would demonstrate the superiority of markets over government intervention, the period since the collapse of the Bretton Woods system has been marked by an increasing incidence of financial crises (in both developed and developing countries), and their growing virulence in terms of lost output and jobs (*TDRs 2000* and *2001*; Eichengreen and Bordo, 2002).

After the rapid opening up of their economies in the 1980s, many developing countries became increasingly preoccupied with ensuring sufficient flows of external funds, rather than improving domestic resource accumulation and productivity growth. In particular, foreign capital flows were regarded as an instrument for accelerating growth. The monetary conditions created by these flows and the policies to attract them were not considered to hinder domestic investment. It was believed that high nominal and real interest rates, a rather stable nominal exchange rate and fiscal restraint should attract capital inflows and assure foreign investors about the seriousness of policy efforts to leave the legacy of hyperinflation behind. In some countries, domestic monetary policy was completely abandoned, and the exchange rate anchor was supposed to stabilize the price level through competition from cheap imports. In addition, it was expected that the sale of State assets and a reduction of government intervention would improve the overall efficiency of the market system. But, the flip side of this "sound policy approach" was that it directly lowered profits and profit expectations of domestic companies and prevented the profit-investment nexus from evolving. Eventually, the efficiency gains of the pro-market policy could not make good the overall restrictive stance of economic policy and the pressure from foreign competitors.

An imbalanced concentration on sound economic policies to fight inflation, and on "getting

> After the rapid opening up of their economies in the 1980s, many developing countries became increasingly preoccupied with ensuring sufficient flows of external funds.

relative prices right" by increasing the efficiency of resource allocation, came at the expense of the overall dynamics of the economy, because macroeconomic prices – the real interest rate and the real exchange rate – were not appropriate to this end. Thus, the necessary conditions to foster productivity growth and to combine international competitiveness with strong growth of domestic demand and company profits were not in place. The "sound macroeconomic fundamentals" did not translate into sound fundamentals capable of producing an environment for firms that was conducive to increasing investment, introducing new technologies and expanding exports.

Macroeconomic policy was successful in fighting and eliminating hyperinflation, but once price stability had been achieved, it did not take account of the fact that, in the global market, competition puts downward pressure on prices via cost competition and the creation of excess supplies; this shifts the balance of risks from inflation and excess demand towards deflation and lack of demand. Under these conditions, the increasing importance of international production chains did not allow the rapid introduction and full exploitation of technology for upgrading domestic industry, because most basic research and the more technology- and skill-intensive slices of the production chain remained in the more advanced economies.

The "consensus" during the 1990s has been that there was no alternative to these orthodox policies. Many observers presumed that interest rates and monetary policy cannot be relaxed without a loss of exchange rate stability, price stability and positive capital inflows. However, the combination of low-income growth, an overvalued exchange rate and high interest rates inhibited investment incentives and the restructuring of the domestic productive sector. It also made it virtually impossible to meet the conditions required to stabilize or reduce the debt burden relative to national income (as real interest rates remained above real growth rates) in the medium term.

Because considerable emphasis was placed on fighting inflation through the establishment of sound macroeconomic fundamentals, such as fiscal restraint, control of monetary expansion and anchoring of the nominal exchange rate, the negative impact on the sustainability of the external balance was neglected. Although external balances generally improved during periods of declining inflation, this was usually achieved by reducing overall income growth sufficiently to compress imports, rather than by raising exports. This is precisely the opposite of the justification for opening the economy to make trade an engine of growth, more specifically to expand manufactured exports in order to be able to increase imports of capital goods for investment and restructuring. These policies also had an adverse impact on the shift from State-led development to market-led development based on international competition. High interest rates were detrimental not only to the industrial sector, but also to primary commodity producers' attempts to modernize their machinery and equipment. Overvalued exchange rates often gave foreign competitors an absolute advantage that could not be compensated by endeavours at the micro level.

In the presence of free capital flows it has been difficult for many developing countries to avoid overvaluation, whether because of excessive optimism about domestic prospects or because of excessive pessimism about prospects in developed countries. Although the international trading system of rules and regulations has always included clauses that allow countries to opt out of their obligations and commitments to free trade when they are faced with extreme balance-of-

> Establishing a virtuous interaction between international finance, domestic capital formation and export growth has proved surprisingly uncommon since the collapse of Bretton Woods.

payments difficulties and dangerous declines in their foreign-exchange reserves, these clauses were not applied. Moreover, there were no regulations allowing a country to temporarily opt out of free international capital flows when such flows created excessive movements in exchange rates that had an impact on its external competitiveness and its balance of payments. Measures to keep outflows to magnitudes that are commensurate with a country's ability to maintain external balance have not been part of the rules and regulations of the international trading system and of the international financial system in the post-Bretton Woods era.[26]

Overall, establishing a virtuous interaction between international finance, domestic capital formation and export growth has proved surprisingly uncommon since the collapse of Bretton Woods. In developing countries, dependence on external capital flows has led markets to impose a risk premium on domestic interest rates that has reduced the space for domestic economic policy and, in some cases, constrained growth, fixed investment and job creation. As a profit-investment nexus failed to take root, development policies became hostage to maintaining a steady increase in capital inflows and to retaining the confidence of the financial institutions providing them. This is highlighted by Latin America which has exhibited a particularly high foreign-debt-to-export ratio and a greater vulnerability to external shocks (IMF, 2002). Additionally, this combination of forces pushes policy-makers to pursue policies that enhance the short-term ability to pay, but they will pay the price of maintaining the confidence of financial markets in terms of reduced policy space to manage any future shocks (Kregel, 1996b).

E. Interdependence, international collective action and policy space

Pressures for greater openness, particularly in an uncertain economic environment and an era of dynamic structural change, have made it increasingly difficult for countries to pursue their own national policies for development and integration into the global economy. The openness agenda overlooks the fact that the advanced industrial economies engaged in very active economic policies in pursuit of their development, and it ignores their history of building "hard States" to guide that process (see Chang, 2002; and Bayly, 2003).[27] Instead, by concentrating on market forces and "getting prices right" to maximize the gains from a given pattern of factor endowments, the openness agenda has perpetuated a lopsided view of the forces driving economic integration. It stresses the potential gains from participation in international markets while downplaying adjustment costs, and it stresses convergence tendencies while ignoring potential sources of cumulative divergence.

As the previous sections have suggested, this approach has its limitations. Trade is just one among several interrelated factors shaping integration. Its impact is largely contingent on the presence of dynamic forces – specialization, learning and innovation, scale economies and capital formation – that do not respond in a simple or predictable way to the incentives generated from rapid opening up. Strengthening these forces requires a series of complementary institutional reforms and discretionary macroeconomic, industrial and social policy measures. This implies considerable diversity in the pattern of integration, even among countries at similar levels of economic development.

Development strategies that successfully harness trade to a strong growth dynamic will necessarily lead to closer links with the wider international economy, especially with neighbouring economies. This will make the success or failure of those strategies increasingly dependent on trends and policies elsewhere. Moreover, as more countries establish successful growth regimes, an expansion of trade will be accompanied by increased cross-border flows of investment, technology and finance. As a result, a country's "internal performance" (as measured by investment levels, productivity growth, employment creation and technological upgrading) and its "external performance" (as measured by the trade balance, net capital flows and exchange rate stability) become much more closely intertwined and the policy trade-offs considerably more challenging.

It is unlikely that the policy trade-offs will ever be satisfactorily resolved by privileging external goals, even as countries seek to maximize the benefits from closer participation in the international division of labour. Rather, stability will depend, in part, on the ability and willingness of

> Trade is just one among a number of interrelated factors shaping integration.

individual countries to pursue policies that are compatible not only with their own national objectives, but also with the objectives and policies of other countries. It is therefore necessary to find common objectives among countries at varying levels of development around which a stable pattern of integration can be built.

The openness agenda has sought consensus around common policy instruments and universal price incentives. However, experience shows that there is a need for policy instruments specifically designed with the aim of helping countries at lower stages of development to converge on the levels of efficiency and affluence achieved by the more advanced economies, and to improve the welfare of all groups of the population. Making this the principle for policy design at both the domestic and the international level requires recognition of the fact that successful development and integration of the developing countries is in the mutual interest of all countries, as longer-term growth and trading opportunities of the more advanced economies also depend on the expansion of industrial capacity and markets in the poorer economies.

Under the gold standard, unprecedented private capital and labour flows helped establish mutually beneficial linkages between a wealthy industrial core, primary exporters and a small group of late industrializing economies. And even though the economic gap was relatively narrow, the latter were free to establish industrial capacity behind high and enduring levels of tariff protection, while exporters were allowed unrestricted access to the markets of the industrial core. The openness agenda during the inter-war period failed to strike the right balance between market forces, policy space and collective international action. Later, under the Bretton Woods system, both private capital flows and the movement of labour were sharply curtailed, but policy space was extended to allow both developed and developing countries to pursue a broad economic agenda, and an institutional framework was set up for collective international action in support of growth and stability and for managing economic integration.

As discussed earlier, this required a degree of flexibility in the workings of those arrangements in recognition of the differences in initial conditions and the varying pace of economic and industrial progress.

In today's world of increased interdependence dealing with the trade-offs between domestic and external objectives requires a much more pragmatic approach to policy-making than that suggested by the openness agenda. In the absence of easy growth and adjustment formulas for economic catch-up through industrialization, strategies that seek to make convergence a common policy objective have to allow a good deal more room for experimentation and discrimination in favour of countries with lower efficiency and income levels. To this end, policy-makers need to adopt a more pragmatic "rule of thumb" approach to designing useful interventions consistent with the practical world of politics (Krugman, 1987).

> The entire international economic system must be capable of supporting growth and convergence across a wide spectrum of countries making up the international division of labour.

Since developing countries have become more vulnerable to external shocks, and the potential costs of adjusting to those shocks are significant and unevenly distributed, there is a danger that countries will try to use their available policy space to solve economic problems at the expense of other countries through "beggar-thy-neighbour" policies. Accordingly, much like integration at the national level, which requires arrangements to ensure that all regions and social groups benefit from growth, efforts to bring progress, stability and predictability to an increasingly interdependent world also have to involve more collaborative and cooperative arrangements among countries.

As more countries seek to build domestic productive capacity and potential conflicts and rivalries increase, success in moving towards more open multilateral economic arrangements implies more than aiming at agreements dealing with reductions of tariffs, quotas and subsidies, and other impediments to the expansion of trade. And attracting more FDI is not a substitute for rapid domestic capital accumulation. Rather, the entire international economic system should be capable of supporting growth and convergence across a wide spectrum of countries making up the international division of labour, with appropriate flexibilities built in to accommodate the diversity of conditions. Currently, only a handful of States are sufficiently large and dynamic enough to harness international forces to economic objectives, and even fewer are able to dictate the terms of integration and, consequently, to influence the prospects of other countries. Under such conditions, a critical ingredient of stable multilateralism is that the leadership of the strongest participants must be oriented in the right direction (Kindleberger, 1986).

> The search for economic stability is not between autarky and surrendering national sovereignty to the expansive logic of markets.

Not only are the leading economies in a better position to bear the short-term costs of the collective actions needed to guarantee the long-term health of a more interdependent economic system, they also have an asymmetric bearing on growth prospects in the weaker economies through their share in world demand, their level of technological development and control over capital. They therefore have the added responsibility of pursuing policies in a way that does not damage the growth and stability of the weaker economies. Of particular concern are the potentially destabilizing and deflationary feedbacks between trade and finance, which often create impediments to development. Financial crises in the developing countries frequently result, at least in part, from various shocks and policy changes that originate in the major reserve currency countries. But at present, there is no system of multilateral surveillance that can insist on greater coherence in the latter's monetary and exchange rate policies. In the absence of more balanced representation in multilateral institutions, there is a need for arrangements that make it possible to accommodate the kind of discretionary policy action on the part of countries at lower levels of efficiency and income that was an important ingredient of the successful integration of the more advanced economies into the international economy.

Thus, contrary to the thrust of the openness model, the search for economic stability and balance is not between autarky and surrendering national sovereignty to the expansive logic of markets. Nor does the latter provide the institutional standard against which development success should be judged. Rather, in an interdependent world, the balance between economic welfare at the national level and integration at the international level will continue to hinge on an appropriate mix of market forces, policy space and collective actions. ∎

Notes

1   A recent review of the voluminous body of modelling exercises, country studies and regression analyses, all reporting a strong link between increased trade openness and economic welfare (both positive and negative), concludes that the whole case has been "exaggerated" (Freeman, 2003). For a review of the evidence see Kozul-Wright and Rayment, 2004.

2   For more on the profit-investment nexus in the development process, see *TDRs 1996* and *1997*; Amsden, 2001; and Ros, 2002.

3   Economic development is complicated by social and political changes, particularly where this involves the separation of large numbers of people from the land and their growing concentration in urban centres, and by the steady, albeit punctuated, rise of democratic institutions; for a seminal discussion, see Polanyi, 1944; and Moore, 1966.

4   The literature describing this history is vast; see, for example, Rowthorn and Chang, 1993; Reinert, 1999; Gomory and Baumol, 2000; and Bayly, 2003.

5   Over 40 per cent of the French labour force was in farming, and the figure was even higher on the European periphery and in the white-settler colonies. Even in the United States, where total farm mortgages had risen from $3.3 billion in 1910 to $9.4 billion in 1925, the agricultural sector accounted for a quarter of total employment and farm exports for over one quarter of farm incomes. With slower growth, weak international prices and protectionism in some leading markets, the burden of external debt-servicing rose steadily for most primary exporters in the 1920s (Kindleberger, 1987: 84–87).

6   According to Bairoch (1993: 4–5), the weighted average of customs duties on manufactures in continental Europe was 24.6 per cent in 1913 and 24.9 per cent in 1927, and the figures were almost certainly lower in 1928 and 1929. As Bairoch notes, however, there was plenty of variation around these average figures, as was the case before 1914.

7   Germany returned to its pre-war parity in 1924 as part of the Dawes Plan, and the United Kingdom a year later. Much of the debate in the United Kingdom at the time, and since, has been about whether prices had reached a level that justified returning to parity with the dollar. However, the return to pre-war parity was not motivated by trade considerations, but was part of the confidence-building exercise needed to restore London as the centre of international finance. In the changed post-war trading environment, and given the failure to re-establish an export-based investment-profit nexus, the consequence was that a growing share of the United Kingdom's invisible earnings were absorbed by trade deficits, resulting in sharply reduced current account surpluses which failed to cover long-term security issues on London capital markets. Its need to resort to short-term borrowing to close this gap became its Achilles' heel once the gold standard was restored.

8   This also allowed some room for a degree of countercyclical monetary policy (Kenwood and Lougheed, 1994: 113–115).

9   This term is derived from an investment swindle, whereby investments are pocketed and interest or profits are paid to investors out of new money flowing into the scheme.

10   This had been a familiar situation in peripheral economies under the gold standard, where erratic export earnings and doubts about the commitment to stay on gold could bring capital flows to a rapid halt and spark financial crisis. However, when shocks did occur on the periphery they were isolated and relatively easy to contain (Eichengreen and Bordo, 2002).

11   Strictly speaking GATT and ITO discussions were parallel negotiating tracks under the auspices of ECOSOC. The former was in fact the first to kick off, involving 23 countries, guided by the United States Trade Agreements Act of 1934 which allowed

the United States Administration to negotiate reciprocal tariff reductions with other countries. The first session was successfully concluded in Geneva in 1947. It was presumed GATT would apply until the full ITO was concluded. Meanwhile, although international commodity schemes disappeared from the agenda, grants of commodities (produced predominantly in the United States) represented a significant component of the European Recovery Programme (Kenwood and Lougheed, 1994: 242).

12 This was helped by a degree of forced policy realism after sterling convertibility linked to the Anglo-American Financial Agreement ended in suspension in 1949, opening the way to a more general wave of devaluations to accommodate balance-of-payment distortions. The start of the Korean War in 1950 also acted as a timely global stimulus.

13 The majority of the 28 developing countries present were small South American economies; India and South Africa were still formerly under British rule and Egypt and Iraq were closely aligned; Cuba, Liberia and the Philippines were closely aligned to the United States. The protocol to implement the GATT was signed by 53 countries with a greater developing-country weight.

14 It is also worth noting that the World Bank lacked a mandate to deal with debt rescheduling or the management of capital flows, both potentially important concerns for developing countries.

15 Kenwood and Lougheed (1994: 254) estimate that between 1945 and 1960 around $26 billion were granted in aid to developing countries (i.e. less than $2 billion annually).

16 One of the first to voice this concern was Brazilian President Getulio Vargas in 1951, who complained that Brazil had experienced a negative net capital flow continuously from 1939 (with the exception of 1947) (Kregel, 2004). For further information on the structuralist approach, see Palma, 1989; and Rosenthal, 2003.

17 The Report led to a number of institutional changes in the GATT aimed at better addressing the concerns of developing countries, see Kenwood and Lougheed (1994: 276).

18 The empirical debate on the movement in the terms of trade has been running for some time, and the pre-war evidence on which Prebisch (and separately Hans Singer) built his initial argument is still a subject of dispute. For critical assessments of the early evidence, see Johnson, 1967; Bairoch, 1993; and Spraos 1980. More recently, Hadass and Williamson (2001) and Blattman et al. (2003) have taken a more favourable view of the Prebisch-Singer data; see also *TDR 2002*.

19 James (2000: 145–158) provides an interesting comparison of the divergent performance of Argentina and Brazil in the 1930s and Prebisch's own experience therein, which, at the time, cast him as an opponent of import substituting industrialization (ISI). On Prebisch's contribution and its distortion by mainstream trade theorists, see the various papers in ECLAC, 2001.

20 The Report's structural emphasis was complemented by a historical perspective, showing how structural growth forces had interacted differently in different periods: in the nineteenth century, when a resource-scarce and free-trading United Kingdom exported manufactures in exchange for food and raw materials from the periphery; in the inter-war period, dominated by a resource-rich and protectionist United States and by the collapse of trade following the Great Depression, growth followed a more inward orientation; and in the contemporary multilateral era, dominated by a rapidly modernizing Europe, openness and the application of reciprocity and mutual dependence reinforced first-mover advantages while it subjected late-comers to the problem of mounting indebtedness.

21 On the nature of managed trade under the GATT, see *TDR 1984*: 70–75; and Cornford, 2004.

22 The concept of currency scarcity was embodied in the IMF Charter, which allowed for its management under certain circumstances (Article VII. 3a, b and c).

23 Unlike the management of trade relations, where opinion over the choice of policies and institutions was quite sharply divided after the war, the failure of financial markets to prevent currency disorders and contagion in the 1930s was widely accepted as the basis for putting in place multilateral financial arrangements (Nurkse, 1944).

24 Much like the literature on the links between trade liberalization and growth, there has been a shift in emphasis from the direct benefits to growth from financial liberalization – which have proved difficult to detect – to the indirect benefits in terms of raising institutional quality (King and Levine, 1993; Prasad et al., 2003).

25 The extent of British dominance of the international financial system was unprecedented, not only relative to other financial centres but also relative to the United Kingdom's own domestic investment, when at times, in the early 1900s, it was investing a higher proportion of savings abroad than at home.

26 For much of the Bretton Woods era, under fixed exchange rate regimes and capital controls, the accumulated stocks of external sovereign debt remained very low, and the majority of capital flows involved direct investments. This could still give rise to a benign form of speculative financial fragility covered by official development assistance (ODA), although this appears to have been uncommon. Under these conditions, devaluation was equivalent to a partial default on debt service to non-resident holders of domestic assets. However, after the col-

lapse of this system in 1973, default on domestic-currency-denominated external commitments became acceptable in the form of flexible exchange rates, with the risk of default shifting onto the individual borrower.

27 The contrast between "hard" and "soft" States in the development process was first made by Gunnar Myrdal.

Chapter IV

FOSTERING COHERENCE BETWEEN THE INTERNATIONAL TRADING, MONETARY AND FINANCIAL SYSTEMS

Developing countries depend on a favourable international trading environment to reap the full benefits of their integration into the world economy. Equally important for their successful integration is the creation of strong supply capacities. An essential lesson from the experiences of countries that combined successful integration into the world economy with sustained growth is the critical role of active and well sequenced policies to augment the existing stock of physical and human capital, enable the use of more efficient technologies, and shift resources from traditional, low-productivity activities towards activities that offer a high potential for productivity growth.

This chapter examines the problem of insufficient coherence between the international trading, monetary and financial systems, and how it affects the formulation and successful implementation of national development strategies. It is argued that rapid financial liberalization, inasmuch as it makes developing countries vulnerable to sharp and abrupt shifts in the direction of largely autonomous short-term private international capital flows, can have negative effects on their trade performance. As demonstrated by the Asian cri-sis, such vulnerability can arise even in countries with sound macroeconomic and external positions, and can contribute to problems in managing interest rates and exchange rates. Managed currency depreciations, proceeding on a smooth, long-term basis, can strengthen the international cost competitiveness of domestic exporters and generally improve developing countries' trade performance. However, this is not the case for the sharp and abrupt exchange rate depreciations that have occurred in many financially open developing countries over the past three decades; they did not result in proportionally larger improvements in trade performance. This is because they were often accompanied by sharp declines in imports and reduced access to trade finance and working capital, which compromised the ability of domestic exporters to benefit from their increased international cost competitiveness stemming from the depreciation. Finally, the chapter draws some conclusions on how developing-country policymakers can avoid a situation where insufficient coherence in the international monetary and financial system jeopardizes the successful implementation of national development strategies designed to foster domestic supply capacities.

A. Building the international competitiveness of developing-country exporters

Historical evidence shows that countries raise the standard of living of their populations by raising labour productivity. This is associated with a substantial change in the sectoral pattern of production and employment, from agricultural to industrial products, and a shift from labour-intensive activities to a growing range of capital- and technology-intensive activities. As discussed in *TDR 2003* (chapter V), the production structure of an economy is of key importance for the development process, because, at any point in time, both the level of productivity and the potential for technical progress and productivity growth vary significantly across agriculture, industry and services, as well as within these sectors. The pace and scale of economic development varies substantially across countries. Many factors account for this diversity in performance, which, apart from a number of structural elements (such as resource endowments, economic size and geographical location), include variables that are susceptible to policy influences and choices. Of paramount importance among these variables are the pace and innovativeness of capital accumulation, human capital formation and the international competitiveness of domestic exporters.

Transformation of the production structure requires entrepreneurs who are capable and willing to invest in activities that are new to the domestic economy. Indeed, Schumpeter (1911) pointed to the importance of innovative investment for economic development, and Baumol (2002) argues that innovation, and the consequent rise in productivity, account for much of the extraordinary growth record that has occurred in various parts of the world since the Industrial Revolution. He suggests that market pressures arising from oligopolistic competition force firms to integrate innovative investment into their routine decision processes and activities – thus, the innovation process is neither largely autonomous nor largely fortuitous. Market forces achieve much of this through financial incentives, by providing higher pay-offs to those firms that are more efficient and whose products are most closely adapted to the wishes of consumers.

However, the occurrence of innovative investment is not automatic; it could encounter structural and institutional impediments. Moreover, the macroeconomic environment could be inappropriate for encouraging and supporting investors seeking to create or expand productive capacity and, in particular, to increase productivity and international competitiveness. The main incentive for investors to discover a more efficient way of producing an existing good or to produce a new good arises when they can appropriate at least part of the rent generated by the creation of new knowledge. Within this framework, for an innovative entrepreneur to enjoy such benefits, a number of conditions must apply at different levels, as discussed in detail in annex 1 to this chapter.

Entrepreneurs invest in the industrial sector of that country in which they expect to realize the highest return on their investment. Cross-country differences in the expected return on investment, expressed in a common currency, are determined by a number of factors, including relative rates of income growth; relative wages and labour productivity; macroeconomic and institutional factors that influence the average level of nominal labour costs in an economy as a whole; relative costs of intermediate production inputs; relative transaction costs associated with information, communications, transportation and distribution; and the use of different currencies. Moreover, market access and entry conditions and the availability of trade finance also determine whether improved cost competitiveness translates into improved export performance. This shows that a wide range of conditions must combine for firms that are competitive on the domestic market to become successful exporters.

First, the availability of adequate transport and communications infrastructure and information systems has a crucial influence on the ability of developing-country firms to conduct trade and to successfully compete in foreign markets.[1] Innovative investors in economies with comparatively high communication, transport and information costs may need to offset this disadvantage by paying lower wages or reducing costs elsewhere in the production process in order to be able to compete in world markets. Firms in countries that are landlocked or geographically distant from major international shipping routes are particularly disadvantaged in this respect. While this is a well-known problem, the impact on trade flows of other forms of trade facilitation, such as the availability of networked information technology and compliance with product standards, has gained in importance over the past few years.

Second, trade finance provides the liquidity for firms to bring their products to the market. Exporters with limited access to working capital often require credit to buy imported raw materials and intermediate production inputs, as well as financing to manufacture products before receiv-

ing payments. Trade finance may be provided directly through loans from commercial banks, prepayments by buyers, and delayed payments by sellers, or indirectly from either export-credit agencies (in the form of guarantees, insurance and government-backed loans), private insurance companies, or multilateral development banks.

Third, assuming constant nominal exchange rates, preserving the international cost competitiveness of domestic firms requires that the ratio of average nominal labour cost growth to average domestic productivity growth in the domestic economy does not rise faster than in the rest of the world. Macroeconomic and institutional factors play an important role in fulfilling this condition. For example, the pressure for sharp general wage increases in an economy approaching full employment is likely to be higher than in an economy with substantial unemployment. Moreover, indexation of wage rises based on factors other than productivity growth is likely to cause substantial and lasting divergence between wage and productivity developments.[2]

Fourth, stable nominal exchange rates are perhaps the single most important condition for the transmission of domestic productivity improvements to gains in international competitiveness. Exchange rate movements alter the relative competitive position of firms in different countries. On the one hand, this implies that a currency appreciation will wipe out improvements in international competitiveness achieved by innovative firms on the basis of improved labour productivity if the change in the exchange rate exceeds the gain in productivity. If technological progress relies on cumulative and incremental innovations that individually lead to comparatively small productivity gains, it does not take exchange rate changes of a spectacular size for this to occur.[3] On the other hand, this implies that currency depreciation can

> A wide range of conditions must combine for firms that are competitive on the domestic market to become successful exporters.

> Stable nominal exchange rates are perhaps the single most important condition for the transmission of domestic productivity improvements to gains in international competitiveness.

give a further boost to the international competitiveness of an innovative firm and maintain the relative competitive position of non-innovative enterprises in the short run. However, there can be little doubt that long-term economic success and maintaining international competitiveness depend on sustained improvements in productivity. Moreover, resorting to currency depreciation may allow for some breathing space to adjust to changes in the relative competitive position of foreign competitors, but it also entails the risk of igniting a process of competitive devaluations.

B. Impacts of monetary and financial factors on developing countries' export performance

Only productivity growth and technological upgrading can ensure sustained improvement in the external balance of developing countries. This can be achieved by a national development strategy that is successful in augmenting the existing stock of physical and human capital, enabling the use of more efficient technologies, and shifting resources away from traditional, low-productivity activities towards activities that offer a high potential for productivity growth. Under some circumstances, and particularly when a period of real currency appreciation has hampered export performance, real currency depreciations can improve international cost competitiveness and boost exports.

The exchange rate has long been recognized as an important policy instrument to make domestic entrepreneurs internationally competitive and provide profit incentives for them to invest in non-traditional export sectors. For example, according to Agosin and Tussie (1993: 22) "The historical record ... shows that ... [a]ll countries that have succeeded in generating a sustained growth of their exports, leading to high rates of growth of output over the long term, have also been able to maintain exchange rates that are attractive to exporters over long periods of time. The exchange rate in such countries has also tended to be fairly stable, enabling producers of tradeables to make long-term investment plans." In a similar vein, Rodrik (2003) argues that countries grow rich by increasing the range of products that they produce, and not by concentrating on what they already do well. Product diversification requires entrepreneurs who are willing to invest in activities that are new to the local economy, and that process may require positive inducements. Rodrik (2003: 21) concludes that "a credible, sustained real exchange rate depreciation may constitute the most effective industrial policy there is."

For successful trade performance, developing countries need to be able to manage their exchange rates in a way that allows them not only to sustain competitive rates over the longer term, but also to retain enough policy space to be able to make orderly adjustments when faced with exogenous shocks. On some theoretical accounts, a regime of freely floating exchange rates and free capital mobility would enable nominal exchange rate movements to stabilize real exchange rates. This argument is based on the premise that movements of the nominal rates eliminate temporary disequilibrium in the pricing of goods in different currencies, and that arbitraging currency speculators speed up the adjustment, thus helping to maintain a correct set of real prices on which international traders and speculators can base their decisions (see, for example, Friedman, 1953).

Floating exchange rates between the main reserve currencies were introduced into the international system of trade and finance in the early 1970s. However, orderly balance-of-payments adjustments, increased real exchange rate stability, greater macroeconomic policy autonomy and removal of persistent currency misalignments and gyrations have not been achieved. This is partly due to the liberalization of capital flows in the last 30 years and to the sizeable increase in the scale and variety of cross-border financial transactions, whose direction can change rapidly in response to shifts in expectations of international portfolio investors. As a result, the currencies of the major developed countries, as well as those of financially open emerging-market economies, have been subject to strong volatility and gyrations, which often represent endogenous responses to large and sharp changes in the direction of international financial flows. These developments are reminiscent of the failure of financial markets to prevent currency disorders and contagion in the 1930s (an insight that was widely accepted as the basis for the attempt to put in place multilateral financial arrangements after the Second World War).

For developing countries, capital inflows, both private and public, can be a source of development finance. However, volatility in international financial markets, and particularly sharp and abrupt shifts in the direction of largely autonomous short-term private capital flows, have frequently contributed to problems in managing interest rates and exchange rates, and to financial crises including in countries with track records of macroeconomic discipline. Since the early 1990s, a number of developing countries, particularly those that had begun liberalizing their financial markets, have experienced substantial movements in their exchange rates. These movements have frequently been characterized by prolonged periods of exchange rate appreciation followed by abrupt and sharp devaluations, often associated with a sizeable slowdown in economic activity.

These episodes of sharp and abrupt currency depreciations include the well-known currency crises when countries abandoned pegged exchange rates, starting with Mexico in 1994, followed by East Asia (1997–1998), the Russian Federation (1998), Brazil (1999), Turkey (2001) and Argentina (2002). There were also instances of unusually sharp depreciations in countries with more flexible exchange rates, such as Mexico and South Africa in 1998.

> The sharpness of recent real currency depreciations brings an additional dimension to the debate on the effect of exchange rate changes on trade flows.

The scale of nominal exchange rate depreciations in many developing countries – even those with a record of macroeconomic discipline – over the past few years has often caused large real exchange rate depreciations. Given that real currency depreciations can generally be expected to improve a country's trade balance, it could be assumed that sharp depreciations of the real exchange rate will provide an even greater impetus to the international cost competitiveness of domestic exporters and a boost to a country's exports.

The main argument of this section is that the sharpness of recent real currency depreciations brings an additional dimension to the debate on the effect of exchange rate changes on trade flows. This is because, in the short term, large depreciations of the real exchange rate can seriously compromise the ability of domestic exporters to benefit from their increased international cost competitiveness stemming from the depreciation. Adverse effects occur at two levels. At the level of individual enterprises, it can take the form of a sharp decline in the availability, and/or a strong rise in the cost, of trade finance and working capital. At the macroeconomic level, close trading relationships can provide a channel for the transmission of financial crises and raise the risk of competitive devaluations, which can offset the rise in demand for exports created by the depreciation. Moreover, the steep decline in economic activity, often associated with sharp and abrupt real currency depreciations, can have an adverse effect on the supply of exports. Such depreciations tend to violate two of the conditions necessary for domestic productivity growth to translate into sustained international competitiveness: access of firms to reliable, adequate and cost-effective sources for financing their investments and stable nominal exchange rates at a level that does not impair the international cost competitiveness of domestic exporters. This section examines more closely the impact that the absence of these two conditions is likely to have on developing-country trade performance.

1. Impacts of exchange rate changes on enterprise investment and competitiveness

Uncertainty in currency markets adversely affects many types of economic activities, particularly those that require forward planning and involve decisions that are only reversible, if at all, at high cost. Long-term investment by enterprises in export production capacity is a noteworthy example of such activities, particularly when their production process utilizes imports from third countries. Consider a production unit whose output would be sold in, for example, the United States for dollars, and which would utilize machinery and equipment purchased from Germany, partly on credit denominated in euros, with intermediate production inputs from Japan denominated in yen, and domestic labour remunerated in domestic currency. In such cases, the estimated rate of return on the investment project would be sensitive to the relative exchange rates between the currencies in which the output is to be sold, the currencies in which imported machinery, equipment and intermediate inputs are invoiced, and the domestic currency. The greater the range of exchange rate variation, the greater is the risk of the project. The project may be profitable only under a given configuration of exchange rates. As a consequence, the investor will realize an extra profit if the exchange rate configuration evolves favourably, but risk bankruptcy in the opposite case. Firm size and financial strength, diversification of operations across products and markets, managing assets and liabilities in different currencies, as well as the use of other risk management techniques, can limit exchange rate risk. But these measures entail additional costs and do not provide complete protection.

Monetary factors in the form of nominal exchange rate changes can thus have a major impact on enterprise investment and international competitiveness. The form and strength of this impact depends on a variety of factors operating through two channels: (i) marginal cost, where the impact partly depends on the firm's ratio of imported to domestically sourced production inputs, the share of financing denominated in foreign currency, and the impact of exchange rate changes on domestic monetary conditions; and (ii) a possible mark-up of price over marginal cost. These factors can pull in opposite directions, and their relative strength can change with the length of time that elapses after the exchange rate change. Moreover, they affect the instruments that firms can use to foster international cost competitiveness in a sustainable way (i.e. making productivity-enhancing investment) and to fend off temporarily adverse influences on their competitiveness (i.e. accepting a profit squeeze or resorting to wage suppression or labour shedding).

(a) The cost channel

Regarding production costs, depreciations of the domestic currency lower the cost of domestic inputs and increase the cost of imported inputs. However, an enterprise can postpone the depreciation-induced price increase of imported inputs measured in domestic currency until it needs to rebuild its stock of such inputs.[4] Moreover, this effect is reduced if the foreign producers of imported machinery and intermediate goods respond to the depreciation of the domestic currency by lowering their prices denominated in domestic currency.

Empirical evidence supports the argument that large depreciations increase the cost of imported inputs relative to other factors of production. Using input-output tables for Argentina, Chile, Mexico and the Republic of Korea, Burstein, Neves and Rebelo (2004) show that nominal exchange rate changes have a much larger impact on prices of capital goods than consumption goods, and that this impact is strongest for tradable capital goods. Given that developing-country firms import a large share of their machinery and equipment, an increase in the cost of imported capital goods is likely to have an adverse effect on investment dynamics, and hence on the firm's path of technological upgrading.

In addition to their effect on production costs, adverse impacts of sharp currency depreciations can render it difficult, if not impossible, for firms to obtain financing to increase productive capacity or even to obtain enough working capital to purchase the inputs necessary for maintaining production at pre-depreciation levels. Depreciations have an adverse effect on the financial position of firms, in particular when companies borrow abroad and have high unhedged debt exposure in foreign currency. In this case, sharp depreciations have balance-sheet effects, increasing the relative burden of repaying existing foreign-currency debt, and make the substitution of domestic for foreign sources of financing more onerous. Moreover, depreciations increase the cost of new loans as they reduce collateral values.

A growing concern for a number of developing countries is to ensure that, in the aftermath of sharp currency depreciation, reliable trade finance is available at an adequate level, a reasonable set of conditions and cost. According to a recent study (IMF, 2003: 17–18), bank-financed trade credits declined by as much as 30 to 50 per cent in Brazil and Argentina in 2002, by about 50 per cent in the Republic of Korea in 1997–1998, and by over 80 per cent in Indonesia during the Asian crisis; sharp declines in trade finance were also observed in the Russian Federation, the Philippines and Thailand in 1997–1998, and in Turkey in 2000–2001. The provision of short-term credit for trade financing has traditionally been considered a routine operation, because it is secured by contracts for the sale of goods that earn foreign exchange. Since this represents an implicit hedge for both the borrower and the lender, the default rate on this category of financing has been low. Thus the scale of the decline in trade finance seems to be disproportionate to the

> Sharp currency depreciations can render it difficult for firms to obtain financing ...

> ... to increase productive capacity and take advantage of lower dollar export prices ...

level of risk. Most importantly, a sharp decline in trade finance seriously compromises the ability of firms involved in foreign trade to maintain their investment, production and trade activities. As a result, this loss of financing may offset the stimulus for export expansion stemming from the currency depreciation.

During the years prior to the Asian crisis of 1997–1998, trade finance to developing countries rose sharply, with commitments from commercial banks increasing the fastest (World Bank, 2004: 128). This change in the composition of trade finance partly reflected the overall surge in commercial bank lending to developing countries until 1997, and the shift in such lending away from long-term finance, now predominantly provided by bond holders, towards short-term finance. As discussed in some detail in previous *TDR*s, supply-side factors, such as the emerging widespread availability of derivative instruments and the recession-related adoption of low interest rates by the major developed countries, were an important driving force behind this surge in short-term bank lending in the early 1990s. Financial liberalization, along with relatively high domestic nominal interest rates and comparatively stable nominal exchange rates, made a number of developing countries attractive locations for capital flows that were driven by short-term arbitrage motivations.

At the same time, documentation requirements for trade financing loans by commercial banks sharply declined. Given that an increasing share of world trade has been associated with international production networks and their often relatively long-term trading relationships, the share of commercial-bank trade-financing transactions relying on traditional documentary procedures (such as letters of credit) fell from about 90 per cent of all transactions in the late 1980s to about 30 per cent in the late 1990s (World Bank, 2004: 129–130). The less cumbersome, and often less costly, trade financing relationship, mostly with foreign commercial banks, became increasingly attractive for export-oriented domestic firms also when these firms' export earnings represented an implicit hedge against foreign-exchange risk associated with borrowings in foreign currency. Thus, as happened in the build-up to the Asian crisis (*TDR 1998*: chapter III), assuming relatively stable exchange rates and sustained high export growth, generally, neither exporting firms nor their creditors consider it necessary to explicitly hedge credit risk due to currency fluctuations.

Views differ among market participants as to which factors were predominantly responsible for the shortages of short-term finance during recent currency crises, as discussed by Auboin and Meier-Ewert (2003: 6–8). However, there is widespread agreement that supply-side factors were primarily responsible for the sharp decline in trade finance. For example, international banks – the primary sources of trade credit to emerging markets – engaged in herd behaviour, characterized by a general withdrawal from all lending to developing countries. Their rush to exit was based on an assessment of economy-wide prospects, rather than of the financial conditions of their individual corporate clients. As a result, the majority of international banks, confounding country risk with credit risk, limited their overall exposure to the crisis-ridden markets, rather than maintaining a selective presence on the basis of the true risk profile of their clients.

It is likely that the reduced documentation requirements for trade finance, discussed above, have made it more difficult for commercial banks to distinguish between trade finance and other types of short-term finance. These changes largely explain the uncertainty among international lenders about the continued creditworthiness of domestic firms and about whether crisis-affected countries would continue granting reimbursement priority to trade credit over other types of short-term financing. Indeed, as noted by the World Bank (2004: 14): "One reason that trade credit was not always afforded differential treatment in the 1990s was that the easing of capital controls (under

which trade finance transactions often enjoyed preferential access to scarce foreign exchange) and the movement away from detailed documentation requirements underlying trade finance transactions have blurred the lines between trade credit and other forms of short-term financing."

Domestic lenders may not be in a position to offset the sharp decline in the provision of trade finance from international banks because of adverse changes in domestic monetary conditions. A common feature of most of the recent large depreciations, and especially currency crises, is that they were accompanied by a contraction in domestic lending and/or a sharp increase in domestic interest rates. In some cases, the contraction in lending was a market response to the capital outflows that generated the currency depreciation. In others, the increase in interest rates was a policy response designed to reverse capital outflows, halt the depreciation of the currency's value and reduce expenditure imbalances between imports and exports.[5] Furthermore, some of the measures introduced to strengthen the financial system, such as the imposition of stringent capital requirements on banks, have tended to seriously reduce the availability of domestic credit. Evidence from the Asian crisis, for example, suggests that currency depreciation inflicted much less damage on firms than the rise in interest rates and cut-backs in domestic credit lines, because many firms with large foreign indebtedness were export-oriented (Choi and Kang, 2000). If credit lines had been maintained, greater competitiveness and growing export revenues would have provided a cushion against the rise in liabilities, measured in domestic currency, caused by the currency depreciations.

The above discussion documents the adverse effects on enterprise investment and international competitiveness that monetary factors originating in other countries can have. Perhaps most importantly, it shows that sharp currency depreciations have effects that can seriously compromise the ability of domestic exporters to take advantage of their increased international cost competitiveness stemming from the depreciation.

> ... or even to obtain enough working capital to purchase the inputs necessary for maintaining production at pre-depreciation levels.

(b) The profit channel

Regarding profits and sales prices, the impact of large changes in nominal exchange rates on enterprise investment depends on the firm's price-setting strategy and the persistence of the exchange rate change. Firms that set sales prices in foreign markets by adding a mark-up on domestic unit labour costs can temporarily insulate their competitive position from adverse movements in nominal exchange rates, if they limit the exchange rate pass-through into sales prices denominated in foreign currency. In other words, a strategy of "pricing to market" (i.e. discriminating between destination countries by setting different prices on different markets) allows exporters to maintain their price competitiveness even in the aftermath of an exchange rate appreciation. Exchange rate pass-through is complete when the exporter allows prices denominated in foreign currency to adjust entirely in line with exchange rate variations, while there is no pass-through if prices measured in foreign currency remain stable and the exchange rate change is absorbed entirely by a fall in profits.

However, individual firms can use pricing to market only for a limited period of time, because such a strategy has adverse effects on company profits. By using incomplete exchange rate pass-through in order to defend price competitiveness in the short run, firms expose themselves to a high degree of variability in – or even a complete loss of – their profit margins, which is likely to depress investment, and thus adversely affects competitiveness in the long run. This means that if a currency appreciation persists, firms may eventually have to give up pricing to market and transmit the appreciation into higher foreign-currency-denominated sales prices; this would, however, entail the risk of losing their market shares.

Pricing-to-market strategies reduce the visible impact of exchange rate changes on trade flows. The question therefore arises as to how common is their actual use. Cross-country differences in strategic pricing behaviour are likely to reflect differences in the industry composition of exports, because high-technology-intensive differentiated products, which are typically produced in developed countries, provide more scope for price discrimination. Thus, systematic empirical evidence on the use of pricing to market is limited to exporters of large developed countries, indicating that "in many cases half or more of the effect of an exchange rate change is offset by destination-specific adjustments of mark-ups over costs" (Goldberg and Knetter, 1997: 1270). Regarding empirical evidence for developing countries, changes in the difference between the real exchange rate, expressed in relative unit labour costs, and the real exchange rate, expressed in relative consumer price, provide an approximate indirect measure of the impact of exchange rate changes on profits of developing-country exports. As shown in *TDR 2003* (fig. 5.3), the large currency depreciations in Mexico in 1994–1995 and in the Republic of Korea in 1997 restored profit margins earned by exporters of manufactures, which had been eroded in the years prior to the exchange rate crises.

In addition to strategic pricing behaviour, shifts in the marginal cost curves, due to changes in imported input costs stemming from the exchange rate change, may give rise to incomplete exchange rate pass-through. Campa and Goldberg (1999) show that for major developed countries, the importance of the exchange rate for marginal profitability and for investment responsiveness to exchange rates varies over time: positively in relation to sectoral reliance on export share, and negatively with respect to the share of imported inputs in production. Moreover, in low price-over-cost mark-up sectors, mark-ups are relatively unresponsive to exchange rate changes, whereas investment is strongly affected. By contrast, high mark-up industries absorb much of the exchange

> "Pricing to market" allows exporters to maintain price competitiveness even after an exchange rate appreciation ...

> ... but trying to do so over a longer period of time risks compromising profit-related incentives for investment.

rate fluctuations in mark-ups and relatively little through real investment. Although systematic evidence for developing-country imports is not available, it is possible that foreign suppliers selling in large developing countries with sizeable import-competing sectors may engage in strategic pricing to market for selected important differentiated manufactured products. To the extent that this is the case, the price effect of exchange rate changes for domestic producers in import-competing industries and in export industries that have a large import content of differentiated products will be diminished.

Enterprises that cannot outweigh the adverse effect of exchange rate changes on competitiveness through productivity-enhancing investment or a squeeze in profit margins may need to resort to wage compression or labour shedding in order to stay in business. Assessments of the wage and employment response to real exchange rate movements often analyse net changes in wages per worker or employment across manufacturing industries. For example, *TDR 2003* (table 5.7) showed that wages were reduced in many African and Latin American countries in order to increase international competitiveness.

In brief, the impact of exchange rate changes on enterprise profits and investment varies across firms. Firms can limit the adverse effects of currency appreciations on their international cost competitiveness temporarily, if they are able to follow a pricing-to-market strategy and absorb at least part of the exchange rate change by a squeeze in profit margins. But trying to do so over a longer period of time risks compromising profit-related incentives for investment. On the other hand, firms may not be able to benefit from sharp real currency depreciations if the goods that they export have a large import content, so that the net effect of the currency depreciation on the firms' international cost competitiveness is very small. More importantly, recent experience shows that adverse impacts of sharp real currency depreciations can compromise the ability of firms to expand production capacity or even maintain production at pre-depreciation levels. Indeed, the easing of capital controls, combined with the movement away from detailed documentation requirements for trade financing transactions, have seriously compromised the availability of trade finance from

international sources in the aftermath of sharp currency depreciations. In addition, the tightening of domestic monetary conditions associated with the depreciation has made it difficult for domestic lenders to maintain their provision of short-term lending.

2. Sharp exchange rate changes and developing countries' export performance

At the macroeconomic level, maintaining a stable exchange rate at an appropriate level is crucial for successful exporting and structural change towards high-productivity sectors. Discussions on the impact of exchange rate changes on trade flows have frequently emphasized the effect of exchange rate volatility on trade, or the contribution of currency depreciations to the removal of temporary imbalances in a country's current account. Typically, the focus has been on the impact of exchange rate changes that are relatively small compared to the large gyrations in developing countries' real exchange rates that have frequently occurred since the early 1990s. This section briefly addresses the two issues discussed in the traditional debate, with its emphasis on relative small exchange rate movements. However, its main focus is on large changes in real exchange rates, often associated with sharp and abrupt changes in the direction of short-term private international capital flows. Such changes can cause substantial shifts in relative production costs and output prices across countries, and hence in relative competitive positions.

In its review of the impact of exchange rate volatility on trade, a recent study by the IMF (2004: 7) concludes: "On balance, it is not clear whether the major changes in the world economy over the past two decades have operated to reduce or increase the extent to which international trade is adversely affected by fluctuations in exchange rates." The study argues that, on the one hand, the liberalization of capital flows in the last 30 years, and the ensuing strong growth in the scale and variety of cross-border financial transactions have clearly increased the magnitude of exchange rate movements in some countries; the recent currency crises in emerging market economies being especially notable for their large exchange rate volatility. On the other hand, the proliferation of financial hedging instruments has made it possible for firms to reduce their vulnerability to the risks arising from volatile currency movements. Moreover, the fact that a growing proportion of international transactions is undertaken by TNCs, and exchange rate fluctuations may have mutually offsetting effects on their profitability, may have further reduced the impact of exchange rate volatility on world trade. However, it is likely that trade involving developed countries is relatively less sensitive to the adverse effects of exchange rate volatility, because most TNCs are based in developed countries, and hedging instruments are more readily available for the currencies of these countries. The results of their empirical analysis of trade and exchange rate volatility at the bilateral level led the authors of the IMF study to conclude that there is a generally small negative effect of exchange rate volatility on trade, but that this evidence is not robust across different model specifications.[6]

In its treatment of the impact of exchange rate changes on international trade flows, standard international trade theory emphasizes the mechanism that removes temporary imbalances in a country's current account. It shows that a real depreciation of the domestic currency reduces import demand and increases export demand for goods and services, thus restoring the current account balance if the sum of the relative price elasticities of export and import demand exceeds unity. Empirical estimates for price elasticities for international trade in manufactured goods by developed countries generally show that a real appreciation is likely to worsen the trade account. Conversely, a real depreciation is likely to improve it, except over short periods where the elasticities are typically too small to satisfy the elasticity condition, thereby causing the trade account to deteriorate immediately following a real depreciation.[7]

There has long been a debate in the literature on the ability of changes in the real exchange rate to improve the merchandise trade balance of developing countries in the medium and long run.[8]

Elasticity pessimists have argued that in developing countries, (i) the elasticity of import demand is low because most imports are production inputs, and the elasticity of substitution in production between imports and domestic value added is essentially zero; (ii) the elasticity of export supply is low because exports are concentrated in a few primary products with a very low domestic supply response; and (iii) the elasticity of export demand is low because world demand is inelastic, with respect to both income and prices, for the products exported by developing countries. Indeed, many developing-country exporters of primary commodities appear to be trapped in a vicious circle, where real exchange rate changes can play a fairly small role in increasing exports and reducing imports at the same time. The existing production structure in these countries can generate little diversification and export growth in the absence of new investment in industry, which requires substantial imports and foreign exchange. Export growth is thus constrained by the inability to increase imports due to inadequate export earnings. This dilemma is accentuated when the loss of the purchasing power of exports is not compensated, and imports have to be reduced.[9] In countries that face this dilemma, the persistent excessive reliance on exports of primary commodities to finance imports of goods and services has contributed to the accumulation of unsustainable debt burdens. However, while this is likely to limit, sometimes substantially, the positive response of the trade balance to real currency depreciations, empirical evidence shows that, in general, a real depreciation of the domestic currency improves the merchandise trade balance of developing countries (Ghei and Prichett, 1999).

The large size of recent real exchange rate changes brings an additional dimension to the traditional elasticity debate for at least two reasons. First, the external trade position of countries that are not directly subject to a sharp exchange rate change themselves can, nevertheless, be adversely affected. Second, the impact of sharp and abrupt exchange rate changes on the economy of the depreciating currency is more complex than the ad-

> Sharp currency depreciations are often associated with economic recession and a sharp decline in the availability of trade finance.

justments resulting from small exchange rate fluctuations, because sharp currency depreciations are often associated with economic recession and, as discussed in some detail in the preceding section, with a sharp decline in the availability of trade finance.

Looking first at the effects of crisis on countries other than the crisis-hit country, the literature shows that financial crises can be transmitted through trade linkages from a directly affected country to other countries that export similar goods, even if those countries have relatively good fundamentals. The way in which changes in relative prices and/or quantities of goods traded by a crisis-hit country can have spillover effects in other economies operates through a number of distinct channels that can counteract each other (see, for example, van Wincoop and Yi, 2000).

For example, sharp exchange rate changes have a significant impact on relative output prices. These, in turn, affect the relative competitiveness of countries' exports, even if a country does not directly compete with exports from the crisis-affected country in any specific market. This is because the depreciation reduces the relative price of a country's exports, and therefore shifts demand away from countries that produce similar goods. If exports from the crisis-affected country constitute a large enough share of global markets in a given industry, prices in that industry will fall worldwide (for a numerical example, see Pesenti and Tille, 2000: 9). One example of this is the electronics sector in the aftermath of the Asian crisis. Barth and Dinmore (1999) show, for instance, that part of the reason for the price slump in electronic components was the glut in supply created by the troubled Asian economies in their attempt to pursue export-led recoveries from the recession.

A diametrically opposite effect occurs when a country not affected by crisis imports produc-

> Both external demand and the competitiveness of domestic exporters have a significant impact on developing countries' export performance ...

> ... but the relative importance of these two factors differs, depending on the composition of exports and different periods of time.

tion inputs from a crisis-affected country. The decline in prices of these imported inputs, resulting from the crisis, leads to a change in relative inputs prices, so that the effect is equivalent to that of a positive productivity shock.

Finally, a crisis-affected country may experience a sharp contraction in economic growth and a reduction in aggregate demand, followed by a reduction in import demand. If imports by the crisis-affected country constitute a large enough share of global markets in a given industry, prices in that industry will fall worldwide. For example, the Asian crisis was followed by a widespread and pronounced fall in commodity prices, which was reflected in a decline in the price index for non-oil commodities by about 30 per cent (*TDR 2000*: 33). This price slump created balance-of-payments and fiscal difficulties for a number of commodity-exporting developed and developing countries.

There is an ongoing debate as to whether these trade linkages have been large and/or significant determinants of how different countries were affected by recent financial crises. The debate is unresolved partly because of the difficulty in disentangling trade and financial linkages. In spite of variations in currency crisis events, approaches and estimation techniques, most empirical studies have, nevertheless, found support for the importance of trade in the international transmission of crises.[10]

One recent study on the Asian crisis (Duttagupta and Spilimbergo, 2004) emphasizes competitive depreciations as an important form of contagion through trade linkages. This means that countries whose exporters compete directly with those in the crisis-affected country face pressure to depreciate their currencies as well, in order to allow their firms to reduce export prices and avoid a loss in international competitiveness. On the other hand, this also means that exporters in the crisis-affected country do not experience a rise in demand for their products, as would have been the case had the competitive depreciations not enabled their competitors to cut prices.

Turning to the impact on trade performance of the country with the strongly depreciating currency, the large size of recent real exchange rate changes complicates empirical analysis. This concerns, for example, statistical measurement, given that comprehensive data on the price and volume components of export values are not available. One study shows that changes in export prices, rather than changes in export volumes, were mainly to blame for the poor performance of dollar-denominated export revenues in Hong Kong (China), Indonesia, Malaysia, the Republic of Korea, Singapore, Taiwan Province of China and Thailand in the aftermath of the East Asian crisis in 1997–1998. The export prices of these six economies fell by 4.8 per cent in 1997 and by a further 9.1 per cent in 1998. Thus, while aggregate export revenue for these six economies was nominally up by 6.1 per cent in 1997 and fell by 3.6 per cent in 1998, export volumes rose by 8.8 and 0.7 per cent respectively in these two years (Barth and Dinmore, 1999).

> Major exchange rate depreciations neither give a sizeable additional boost to export performance nor result in proportionally larger improvements in the trade balance.

The UNCTAD secretariat conducted some econometric estimations with the basic objective of assessing the impact of changes in international cost competitiveness on developing countries' merchandise trade performance for the period 1970–2002. Annex 2 to this chapter explains the set-up of these estimations, where international cost competitiveness is measured by the exporting country's real effective exchange rate, and merchandise trade performance is captured by four variables: (i) the merchandise trade balance; (ii) total merchandise exports as a percentage of nominal income; (iii) total merchandise imports as a percentage of nominal income; and (iv) the country's market share in total world manufactured exports. Due to its strategic importance for policy-making and the development of external indebtedness, the current account balance was included in the estimations as a fifth dependent variable. Given that cross-country variations in the rate of real income growth are also likely to influence countries' trade flows, the estimations also consider the impact of changes in world income and in the exporting country's income. Following the discussion above, the anticipated impact of real exchange rate changes on the trade performance variables is that a depreciation increases exports and export market shares, while it reduces imports; these effects combined imply that a depreciation is expected to improve the merchandise trade balance, as well as the current account balance. At the same time, accelerated domestic (world) income growth is expected to boost imports (exports).

It is not immediately clear whether the econometric estimation can be expected to reveal the anticipated inverse relationship between changes in competitiveness, as measured by the real effective exchange rate, and changes in a country's share in world exports of manufactures. Firstly, the market share of a country whose currency depreciates declines due to a statistical effect. For example, if a country's currency depreciates by 10 per cent vis-à-vis the dollar, its market share, measured in dollar terms, also drops by 10 per cent. However, a statistical method that would allow taking account of this effect is not available. Secondly, cross-country differences in the rise of export market shares following a currency depreciation are influenced by differences in the growth rate of aggregate demand in the exporting country's trading partners. Thirdly, the entry of countries into the world trading system automatically reduces the market shares of the other countries, as occurred when China and the countries of the former Council For Mutual Economic Assistance (CMEA) began to participate more actively in world trade.

Fourthly, Kaldor found that between 1956 and 1976 the United States and the United Kingdom suffered a decline in their share of manufactured exports to major developed-market economies, while they became more competitive – as measured by changes in relative unit labour costs – and Germany, Italy and Japan saw a rise in their market shares, while they became less competitive on this measure. Based on these findings (frequently referred to as the 'Kaldor paradox'), Kaldor (1978: 104) argued that "the changes in exchange rates and in 'competitiveness' as conventionally measured were not the cause, but the consequence of differing *trends* in the market shares of different industrial countries, and the 'trends' themselves must then be due to factors not susceptible to measurement."

However, this argumentation does not take account of the level from which changes have occurred. At the beginning of the 1970s, the currencies of both Germany and Japan were undervalued by more than 10 per cent (Williamson, 1983), so that currency appreciation had substantial leeway to reduce these countries' advantage in exchange-rate-based competitiveness before eliminating or even reversing it. Thus part of the explanation of this "paradox" is likely to be found in the fact that the observed currency movements implied a correction of previously accumulated misalignments, rather than movements away from an equilibrium value. Moreover, Kreinin (1977) estimated for the early 1970s that the exchange rate pass-through to United States import prices was only 50 per cent, and to German and Japanese import prices about 60–70 per cent. This means that exporting firms transmitted exchange rate changes only partially to sales prices measured in foreign currency, and absorbed the other part through changes in their profit margins.[11]

The relationship between the real exchange rate and market shares in world manufactured exports in developing countries diverges widely, as shown in figure 4.1 for six major developing-country exporters of manufactures. In East Asia, relatively stable real effective exchange rates accompanied the dramatic rise of the share in world manufactured exports of the Republic of Korea and Taiwan Province of China between the early 1970s and the late 1980s. But most East Asian economies, in order to maintain their cost competitiveness, have successfully stabilized their real exchange rates – although sometimes at an undervalued level – through a consensus based on nominal wage increases, in line with productivity growth, capital controls and interventions in the currency market. Following the Asian crisis in 1997–1998, the experience of the Republic of

Korea and Taiwan Province of China has been characterized by a combination of a trend towards real currency depreciation and an increase in market share. For Brazil, India and Turkey, periods of rapidly increasing market shares in world manufactured exports have broadly coincided with periods of real currency depreciations. Mexico is the only country in the figure where, during the second half of the 1990s, a rise in market shares was accompanied by real currency appreciation. However, as discussed in previous *TDR*s, given that Mexico's exports of manufactures increased rapidly following the entry into force of the North American Free Trade Agreement (NAFTA) in 1994, and since they have a significant import content and comparatively little domestic value added, it is no surprise that real currency appreciation had no significant adverse impact on the evolution of market shares. Taken together, the figure provides broad statistical evidence to support the argument that, over the long term, increases in market shares in world manufactured exports are associated with periods of real currency depreciations.

This contrasts with the results of the econometric estimation in table 4.1, which shows that, in general, over the period 1971–2002 as a whole, exchange rate changes had no statistically significant impact on changes in the share of world manufactured exports for the selected 28 developing economies and Central and Eastern European countries (CEECs). Looking at the results for different country groups, this finding also holds for the group of Asian and Latin American economies included in the sample. Similar to the above discussion of the Kaldor paradox, a possible explanation for this finding is that the analysis focuses on changes in the real effective exchange rate, but does not take account of the level from which these changes occurred. As already mentioned, the growth of exports from East Asian economies was associated with a strategy of maintaining real exchange rate stability, sometimes at an undervalued level. This implies that these countries' market shares were able to increase even with a slight real currency appreciation. In contrast, in much of Latin America, periods of sometimes prolonged exchange rate overvaluation, followed by real currency depreciations, may not have led to increasing market shares for their exports.[12]

Figure 4.1

EXCHANGE RATES AND SHARE IN WORLD EXPORTS OF MANUFACTURES, SELECTED DEVELOPING ECONOMIES, 1970–2002

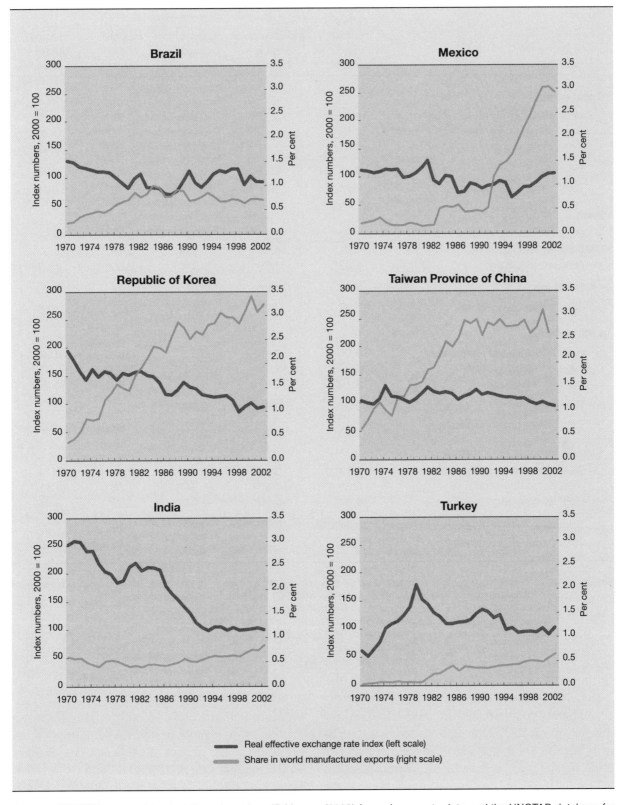

Real effective exchange rate index (left scale)
Share in world manufactured exports (right scale)

Source: UNCTAD secretariat calculations, based on JP Morgan (2003) for exchange rate data; and the UNCTAD database for trade data.

Table 4.1

IMPACT OF CHANGES IN EXCHANGE RATES AND INCOME ON
EXTERNAL PERFORMANCE: ESTIMATION RESULTS, 1971–2002[a]

	Share in world manufactured exports	Merchandise trade balance	Current account balance	Income share of exports	Income share of imports
Total sample					
Real effective exchange rate	0.01	-0.35*	-0.23*	-0.59*	-0.17**
Real domestic income	0.94*	-1.02*	-0.90*	-0.32**	0.76*
Real world income	1.81*	2.67*	1.25*	2.56*	-0.42
R-square	0.25	0.21	0.26	0.27	0.09
Total panel observations	679	677	585	679	684
Asia					
Real effective exchange rate	-0.02	-0.28*	-0.18*	-0.47*	-0.14
Real domestic income	1.51*	-0.57*	-0.66*	0.05	0.61*
Real world income	1.82*	2.55*	0.74**	2.50*	-0.03
R-square	0.47	0.24	0.38	0.28	0.08
Total panel observations	330	328	247	330	328
Latin America					
Real effective exchange rate	-0.05	-0.46*	-0.33*	-0.82*	-0.28**
Real domestic income	-0.20	-2.73*	-1.83*	-1.20*	1.41*
Real world income	3.19*	5.28*	3.81*	2.89*	-2.29*
R-square	0.06	0.37	0.39	0.37	0.13
Total panel observations	192	192	167	192	192
Central and Eastern Europe					
Real effective exchange rate	0.30**	-0.18	-0.24	-0.42*	-0.14
Real domestic income	0.39	-1.33	-1.04***	-0.76	-0.11
Real world income	-4.84*	-0.96	-1.03	2.89**	3.44*
R-square	0.51	0.27	0.27	0.36	0.30
Total panel observations	46	46	46	46	46

Source: UNCTAD secretariat calculations, based on JP Morgan (2003) for exchange rate data; IMF, *International Financial Statistics* database for current account data; and the UNCTAD database for trade and income data.

  a For Central and Eastern Europe, estimations refer to the period 1995–2002.
    * Denotes significant at the 1 per cent level.
   ** Denotes significant at the 5 per cent level.
  *** Denotes significant at the 10 per cent level.

The estimation results in table 4.1 also show that, as anticipated, depreciations led to a statistically significant improvement in the merchandise trade balance, as well as in the current account balance. However, contrary to expectations, the results show that depreciations led to a rise – in most cases statistically significant – in the income shares of both imports and exports. But this result for the entire sample period masks a noteworthy evolution of the impact of exchange rate changes on the income shares of imports and exports (table 4.2). Looking only at the 1970s, the results show that depreciations led to the anticipated decline in the income share of imports and to a rise in the income share of exports, although the coefficient on imports is statistically not significant. The coefficient on the income share of exports rises in size and maintains both its sign and statistical significance for the 1980s and for the period 1990–2002. By contrast, the coefficient on the income share of imports changes its sign, and for the period 1990–2002 the results show that depreciations led to a statistically significant rise in the income share of imports. It is likely that this evolution in the impact of exchange rate changes on imports mirrors the increased import content of developing-country exports, which has occurred with the rising importance of developing-country participation in international production networks since the mid-1980s. High import intensity of exports makes imports and exports move in the same direction, independently of the direction of exchange rate changes.

Concerning the impact of changes in income on trade performance, the results in table 4.1, for the entire sample and for the group of Latin American countries, show that, as expected, rising growth in domestic demand led to growing income shares of imports and declining income shares of exports. For the group of Asian economies, higher domestic (world) demand had no statistically significant impact on the income share of exports (imports). The increasing importance of changes in regional income for the trade performance of these countries might explain this finding. The results also show that an increase in world income leads to a sharply rising income share of exports in both regions and to a strong improvement in the merchandise trade balance.

Possible lagged reactions of trade performance can reverse the impact that occurs immediately after exchange rate changes (i.e. J-curve effects may arise). Imposing time lags on the exchange rate variable to detect such lagged reactions reveals that statistically significant effects on exports occur in the same period as the exchange rate change as well as in the subsequent period, while the effects on imports are statistically significant up to three years after the exchange rate change. The combined effect of these cumulative changes implies that a 10-per-cent depreciation leads to an improvement in the trade balance by more than 0.6 percentage points in the year following the depreciation, and that this improvement remains

Table 4.2

IMPACT OF CHANGES IN EXCHANGE RATES AND INCOME ON INCOME SHARES OF IMPORTS AND EXPORTS: ESTIMATION RESULTS FOR SELECTED PERIODS

	Income share of exports	Income share of imports
1971–1980		
Real effective exchange rate	-0.28*	0.10
Real domestic income	0.09`	1.07*
Real world income	1.98*	-2.62*
R-square	0.17	0.13
Total panel observations	192	192
1980–1990		
Real effective exchange rate	-0.56*	-0.05
Real domestic income	-0.06	0.94*
Real world income	1.70*	1.31*
R-square	0.23	0.23
Total panel observations	208	213
1990–2002		
Real effective exchange rate	-0.97*	-0.46*
Real domestic income	-0.43*	0.98*
Real world income	3.72*	1.31*
R-square	0.72	0.28
Total panel observations	272	272

Source: See table 4.1.
  Note: All results refer to country samples excluding CEECs.
      * Denotes significant at the 1 per cent level.
     ** Denotes significant at the 5 per cent level.
    *** Denotes significant at the 10 per cent level.

at about 0.3 percentage points in the medium term, as shown in figure 4.2. The figure also shows that a 10-per-cent depreciation leads to a cumulative increase in the market share in world manufactured exports by about 0.4 percentage points during the five-year period following the depreciation.

A country's export composition is likely to influence the relative strength of the impact on trade performance of changes in the real exchange rate on the one hand, and of external demand on the other. External demand will tend to be rela-

Figure 4.2

CURRENCY DEPRECIATIONS AND TRADE PERFORMANCE: TIME PATH OF ADJUSTMENT

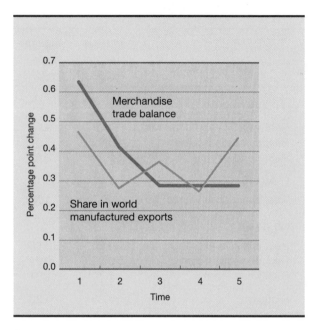

Source: See table 4.1.
  Note: The graph shows the cumulative effect of a 10-percent currency depreciation occurring in time t = 0 on trade performance over the subsequent five years.

tern of the results obtained for the entire sample discussed above. However, the results presented in table 4.3 reveal that, with respect to the relative impact of changes in the real effective exchange rate and in world income on changes in the merchandise trade balance, the former is indeed more important for major exporters of manufactures, while the latter is more important for the other countries. A further noteworthy difference in the trade performance of these two groups of countries relates to the lag structure of the impact of changes in the real effective exchange rate on the countries' share of world export markets. Changes in the real effective exchange rate have a statistically significant impact on changes in the share of major exporters of manufactures in both total world exports and world exports of manufactures over several years, with a 10-per-cent depreciation leading to a cumulative increase in world market shares by about 0.2 percentage points over the subsequent five years (fig. 4.3). By contrast, none of the coefficients on the lagged exchange

tively more important for countries that rely for most of their export earnings on comparatively homogeneous primary products. Changes in supply and demand conditions on world markets determine price changes on the world market for homogeneous products. As a result, rather than boost its export performance, a country's currency depreciations would diminish its export earnings, measured in domestic currency, and hence worsen its barter terms of trade. By contrast, relative changes in domestic production costs of countries' manufacturing exports influence price changes on world markets for manufactures. Hence, price competitiveness (as measured by the real exchange rate) will be a relatively more important determinant of the trade performance of major exporters of manufactures.

Dividing the country sample into countries that are major exporters of manufactures and other countries[13] leads to no change in the general pat-

Table 4.3

IMPACT OF CHANGES IN EXCHANGE RATES AND INCOME ON THE MERCHANDISE TRADE BALANCE: ESTIMATION RESULTS FOR SELECTED COUNTRY GROUPS, 1971–2002

	Merchandise trade balance
Major exporters of manufactures	
Real effective exchange rate	-0.43*
Real domestic income	-0.69*
Real world income	2.63*
Other countries	
Real effective exchange rate	-0.24***
Real domestic income	-1.89*
Real world income	3.92*
R-square	0.24
Total panel observations	631

Source: See table 4.1.
  Note: See table 4.2.

rate variable is statistically significant for the share of other countries in total world exports.

Concentrating on the income share of exports, the results in table 4.2 discussed above show that real currency depreciation boosted exports, but that export growth was particularly sensitive to an increase in world income. In this sense, while both factors had a significant impact, external demand appears to have been a relative more important factor influencing merchandise trade performance than the competitiveness of domestic producers. On the other hand, comparing the size of the coefficients for the real effective exchange rate and world income growth for the 1970s and for the period 1990–2002, reveals that the relative strength of the effects of improved domestic supply capacity increased and that of greater external demand decreased. This is true for all the developing countries combined, as well as for the group of Latin American and Asian countries and economies taken separately. By contrast, splitting the country sample into the group of major exporters of manufactures and other countries reveals that this pattern applies to the former group, while for the export performance of developing countries that rely on primary commodities, the impact of external demand became increasingly pronounced (table 4.4). This shows that both external demand and the competitiveness of domestic exporters have a significant impact on developing countries' export performance, but their relative importance differs, depending on the composition of exports and different periods of time.

Separating changes in the real exchange rate based on changes in fundamental factors (such as relative productivity and wage developments) from those based on other factors would ideally rely on an assessment of changes in the equilibrium exchange rate and deviations from the equilibrium rate. However, there is no agreement as to whether, or how, an equilibrium exchange rate can be determined theoretically, and the data required to test existing concepts empirically are often not available for developing countries or incomplete. A second way of gaining a general insight into when exchange rate changes are unrelated to changes in fundamentals that do not depend on the credibility of any particular estimates of an equilibrium exchange can be based on the assumption that changes in those funda-

Figure 4.3

CURRENCY DEPRECIATIONS AND EXPORT MARKET SHARES: TIME PATH OF ADJUSTMENT FOR MAJOR EXPORTERS OF MANUFACTURES

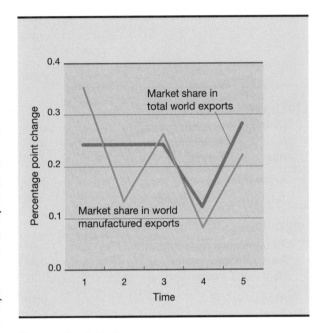

Source: See table 4.1.
Note: See figure 4.2.

mentals are usually not very large. Hence, it can be assumed that changes in the real exchange rate that exceed a certain threshold level are unlikely to reflect changes in fundamentals; rather they are likely to reflect substantial changes in the nominal exchange rate, partly due to changes in the demand for currencies as capital assets.

Consequently, in order to separate major from minor changes in the real effective exchange rate, the following analysis defines "major changes" as any change in a three-month period during 1970–2002, when a country's real effective exchange rate depreciated or appreciated by 15 per cent or more.[14] The resulting list of major changes in real effective exchange rates (table 4.5) includes the well-known recent currency crises, such as the series of devaluations in East Asia in 1997–1998; the devaluations in Mexico, the Russian Federation, South Africa and Brazil in the late 1990s; and the Argentinean devaluation in early 2002 following the collapse of its currency board. It also includes a number of strong appreciations, some

Table 4.4

IMPACT OF CHANGES IN EXCHANGE RATES AND INCOME ON INCOME SHARE OF EXPORTS: ESTIMATION RESULTS FOR SELECTED COUNTRY GROUPS AND PERIODS

	Country groups by geographical region		Country groups by export structure	
	Asia	Latin America	Major exporters of manufactures	Other countries
1971–1980				
Real effective exchange rate	-0.11	-0.25**	-0.19	-0.32*
Real domestic income	0.37	-0.50	0.29	-0.39
Real world income	2.03**	2.58*	1.93*	2.02**
R-square	0.20	0.17	0.19	0.16
Total panel observations	100	60	110	82
1980–1990				
Real effective exchange rate	-0.31*	-0.95*	-0.48*	-0.75*
Real domestic income	0.48**	-1.53*	0.30	-0.89**
Real world income	1.97*	4.12*	1.38**	2.45***
R-square	0.28	0.49	0.24	0.31
Total panel observations	110	66	121	87
1990–2002				
Real effective exchange rate	-0.91*	-1.18*	-0.83*	-1.06*
Real domestic income	-0.27*	-0.94*	-0.55*	-0.29*
Real world income	3.28*	4.82*	3.49*	4.35*
R-square	0.77	0.69	0.64	0.73
Total panel observations	140	78	153	119

Source: See table 4.1.
Note: See table 4.2.

of which reflect a sharp rebound of the exchange rate following a currency crisis (as in Indonesia in 1998). It is interesting to note that there were more than twice as many major depreciations than there were appreciations. Moreover, the fact that almost one third of the major depreciations during the 33-year period occurred after the Mexican crisis at the beginning of 1995 reflects the increasing frequency of exchange rate crises or their contagion effects. While each of these episodes had its own special characteristics, two common features are: (i) that the crises were preceded by periods of sharply increasing capital inflows attracted by an interest rate differential (i.e. a relatively high level of domestic interest rates, of-

ten in the context of tight monetary policy designed to attain or maintain price stability), and associated with a slow but continuous appreciation of the real exchange rates, and (ii) that they were triggered by a sharp swing in expectations of international investors – often associated with rising international rates and a deterioration of domestic macroeconomic conditions resulting from the effects of the capital inflows, rather than with shifts in domestic policies – which led to large-scale selling of the country's currency (*TDR 2003*, chapter VI).

The varying impact on trade performance between major and other real currency deprecia-

Table 4.5

MAJOR CURRENCY DEPRECIATION AND APPRECIATION EVENTS, SELECTED ECONOMIES, 1970–2002

	Major depreciations					*Major appreciations*		
Argentina	1975 (2)	1977 (1)	1981 (2)	1989 (2)	2002 (1)	1976 (1)	1988 (3)	1990 (2)
Brazil	1971 (4)	1983 (1)	1999 (1)	2002 (3)		1990 (1)		
Chile	1973 (3)					1972 (2)		
China	1986 (3)	1988 (2)						
India	1991 (3)							
Indonesia	1978 (4)	1983 (2)	1986 (4)	1997 (4)		1971 (1)	1998 (4)	2001 (3)
Mexico	1976 (4)	1982 (3)	1995 (1)					
Morocco	1974 (2)							
Pakistan	1972 (2)							
Republic of Korea	1998 (1)							
Russian Federation	1998 (3)					1995 (2)		
Saudi Arabia						1974 (4)	1976 (3)	
South Africa	1984 (3)	1998 (3)	2001 (4)			1986 (1)		
Taiwan Prov. of China						1974 (1)		
Thailand	1997 (3)					1974 (1)		
Turkey	1994 (1)					2002 (1)		
Venezuela	1984 (1)	1987 (1)	1989 (2)	1996 (2)	2002 (3)			

Source: UNCTAD secretariat calculations, based on exchange rate data from JP Morgan (2003).
Note: Major depreciation or appreciation events here are defined as a change in the real effective exchange rate of 15 per cent or greater in any three-month period between 1970 and 2002; the three quarters following such an event are excluded, so that there can be at most one event within any four-quarter period. The numbers in brackets indicate the quarter in which the event occurred.

tions is illustrated in figure 4.4, which shows the experience of four countries recently affected by a currency crisis: Brazil (1999), Indonesia (1997), Mexico (1995) and the Republic of Korea (1998). While the underlying mechanisms are undoubtedly complex, partly due to the varying divergence of the exchange rates from their equilibrium values prior to the currency crisis, some general observations can be made. Looking only at the relationship between changes in the real exchange rate and in the merchandise trade balance (represented by the ratio of merchandise exports to imports), Mexico and the Republic of Korea experienced a sharp real depreciation and a strong improvement in the trade balance during the period 1990–2002. The improvement in the trade balance of Brazil and Indonesia associated with

the sharp currency depreciation, is also large, but smaller than in Mexico and the Republic of Korea. This may be due to the fact that the share of manufactures in total merchandise exports of the latter two countries was considerably larger than that in Brazil and Indonesia. Overall, this could lead to the conclusion that, regarding their impact on trade performance, sharp real depreciations are simply extreme examples of real depreciations of a more ordinary size.

However, looking at the evidence more closely reveals two specific features of sharp real currency depreciations. One is that they were accompanied by a sharp decline in real domestic income in all four countries shown in the figure, except Brazil. Moreover, the income share of imports increased

Figure 4.4

TRENDS IN THE REAL EFFECTIVE EXCHANGE RATE, INCOME AND TRADE PERFORMANCE, SELECTED DEVELOPING COUNTRIES, 1990–2002

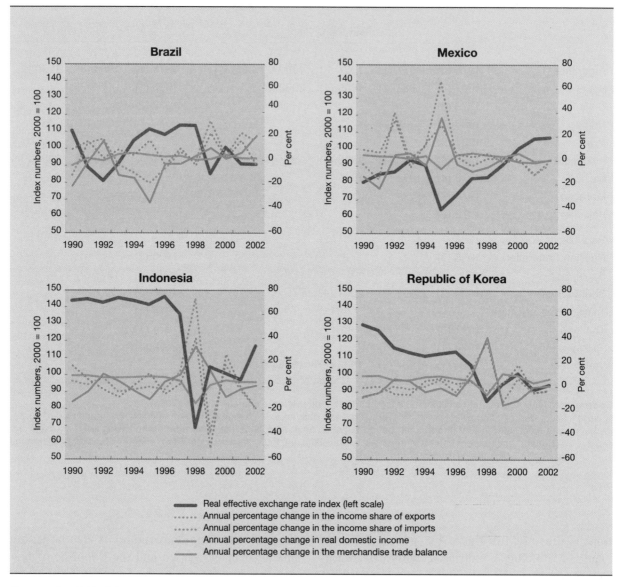

Source: See table 4.1.

much less than the income share of exports. Thus, contrary to more ordinary real currency depreciations, sharp real currency depreciations are often accompanied by a decline in domestic economic activity and imports. Combined with the sharp decline in the availability of trade finance, which often follows sharp currency depreciations, as discussed above, this is likely to hamper the supply response of the country with the depreciating currency.

The results of the estimations relating to the impact on trade performance of these major exchange rate changes as compared to others, are shown in table 4.6. They show that major currency depreciations boosted countries' export performance only slightly more than more normal depreciations. Most importantly, contrary to depreciations of relatively small size, major depreciations did not lead to a statistically significant improvement in the trade balance. By contrast,

Table 4.6

IMPACT OF CHANGES IN EXCHANGE RATES AND INCOME ON EXTERNAL PERFORMANCE: ESTIMATION RESULTS FOR DIFFERENT SIZES OF EXCHANGE RATE CHANGE, 1971–2002

	Merchandise trade balance	Current account balance	Income share of exports	Income share of imports	Share in world manufactured exports
Major appreciations and depreciations					
Real effective exchange rate	-0.30	-0.08	-0.56*	-0.26	-0.18
Real domestic income	-2.27*	-1.79*	-1.77*	0.65	0.51
Real world income	3.91*	2.47**	5.75*	1.15	0.38
Other appreciations and depreciations					
Real effective exchange rate	-0.31*	-0.23*	-0.49*	-0.11	0.07***
Real domestic income	-0.88*	-0.83*	-0.05	0.86*	1.00*
Real world income	2.57*	1.09*	2.34*	-0.58**	1.80*
R-square	0.22	0.24	0.31	0.10	0.27
Total panel observations	677	585	679	684	679
Major appreciations					
Real effective exchange rate	-0.13	0.13	-0.44	-0.29	-0.27
Real domestic income	-1.54	-1.26	-0.72	0.86	1.01
Real world income	2.57	2.41	5.51**	2.69	1.22
Major depreciations					
Real effective exchange rate	-0.45	-0.41*	-0.86*	-0.46	-0.19
Real domestic income	-2.85*	-2.13*	-2.24*	0.78	0.41
Real world income	3.70**	0.57	4.23**	-0.37	0.16
Other appreciations and depreciations					
Real effective exchange rate	-0.31*	-0.22*	-0.49*	-0.10	0.07
Real domestic income	-0.89*	-0.84*	-0.06	0.86*	1.01*
Real world income	2.62*	1.16*	2.41*	-0.56***	1.79*
R-square	0.23	0.26	0.31	0.10	0.27
Total panel observations	677	585	679	684	679

Source: See table 4.1
   Note: * Denotes significant at the 1 per cent level.
         ** Denotes significant at the 5 per cent level.
        *** Denotes significant at the 10 per cent level.

changes in domestic income and world income had a sizeable and strongly significant impact on the ability of exporters to take advantage of increased international price competitiveness. Indeed, the results show that following major currency movements, a rise in the income share of exports was strongly and adversely affected by changes in domestic demand, while changes in domestic demand had no statistically significant impact on the income share of imports.[15] Thus currency depreciations and changes in domestic income and world income had a markedly different short-term

Table 4.7

IMPACT OF CHANGES IN EXCHANGE RATES AND INCOME ON THE MERCHANDISE TRADE BALANCE: TIME PATH OF ADJUSTMENT, 1971–2002

	Merchandise trade balance
Major appreciations and depreciations	
Real effective exchange rate	-0.10
One year lagged	-0.51
Two years lagged	0.32
Three years lagged	0.23
Four years lagged	0.20
Five years lagged	-0.89**
Real domestic income	-2.65*
Real world income	5.20*
Other appreciations and depreciations	
Real effective exchange rate	-0.26*
One year lagged	-0.26*
Two years lagged	0.22*
Three years lagged	0.13**
Four years lagged	0.11**
Five years lagged	-0.01
Real domestic income	-0.79*
Real world income	1.19*
R-square	0.31
Total panel observations	547

Source: See table 4.1

Note: * Denotes significant at the 1 per cent level.
  ** Denotes significant at the 5 per cent level.
  *** Denotes significant at the 10 per cent level.

impact on countries' trade performance when they were associated with major exchange rate changes rather than with comparatively smaller ones.

This finding is supported by the results in table 4.7, which show that comparatively small exchange rate changes improved the trade balance in the short run, while there was no similar statistically significant effect of major exchange rate changes. The results in table 4.6 also show that, contrary to their impact on the trade balance, major currency depreciations led to a statistically significant improvement of the current account balance. This is likely to be related to the decline in the commissions and fees such as for letters of credit or lines of credit that accompanied the sharp decline in the access of firms to trade finance and working capital provided by foreign banks in the aftermath of financial crises. It may also reflect changes in the provision of services with a relatively high elasticity with respect to changes in exchange rates and income.

The finding that, compared to depreciations of a more normal size, major exchange rate depreciations neither give a sizeable additional boost to export performance nor result in proportionally larger improvements in the trade balance is likely to reflect also the impact of at least one other factor discussed earlier. The observed worsening of firms' access to trade finance from both international and domestic sources in the aftermath of major currency depreciations makes it difficult for those firms to expand or even merely maintain activity levels. This seriously inhibits their supply response to benefit from lower dollar-denominated export prices.

C. Policy adjustment with open capital accounts

For policy makers in developing countries, the fact that exchange rate changes can influence the overall competitiveness of a country and have the potential to directly improve the overall trade performance of the majority of their firms and the balance of payments is a promising prospect. On the other hand, the use of the exchange rate as a powerful tool of economic policy is often strictly limited by the influence that the global capital market and the policy of other countries exert on that rate. The exchange rate of any country is, by definition, a multilateral phenomenon, and any rate change has multilateral repercussions.

In the last three decades, developing and emerging-market economies in all the major regions have had to struggle with financial crises or their contagion effects once they have tried to manage the exchange rate unilaterally or even opted for free floating. Nevertheless, in the Bretton Woods era, as well as in the period of floating or managed floating thereafter, some patterns of successful adjustment to the vagaries of the international capital market emerged, which have been increasingly adopted by developing countries' economic and financial policies. Since the Second World War, some experiences of successful catching up – such as by Western Europe, Japan and the NIEs – suggest that, among other factors, long-lasting currency undervaluation can be extremely helpful to fully reap the benefits of open markets. Today, as multilateral arrangements do not exist on a global scale, a strategy to avoid overvaluation by any means has become the preferred tool of many governments and central banks.

This is in stark contrast to the experience of the 1990s in Latin America. During that decade many Latin American countries maintained hard or soft currency pegs with some overvaluation during the 1990s, and used the exchange rate as a nominal anchor to achieve rapid disinflation. This led to an impressive improvement in their monetary stability (Fischer, 2001: 9; Mussa et al., 2000) but also to currency appreciations that impaired the competitiveness of exporters in these countries. Today, with inflation rates being relatively low and stable due to favourable domestic conditions, adopting a strategy designed to avoid currency overvaluation has become feasible for a much larger number of developing countries. Indeed, many developing countries (such as China, Brazil and South Africa) have recently sought to avoid a revaluation of their currencies through direct central bank intervention, with the result that they have accumulated substantial amounts of foreign-exchange reserves.

It is clear that for these countries, avoiding currency overvaluation is not only a means to preserve or improve macroeconomic competitiveness, but also an insurance against the risk of future financial crises. The accumulation of current account deficits, and frequent financial crises, with overshooting currency depreciations, proved very costly in the past. Surges in inflation, huge losses of real income, and rising debt burdens have been a common feature of all recent financial crises.

However, a strategy of avoiding currency overvaluation cannot easily be implemented if the capital account is open. If inflation rates in developing countries exceed those in the developed world, or if there are expectations of an imminent currency appreciation, monetary policy will often face a dilemma in trying to keep the exchange rate stable and yet at a level that preserves the international cost competitiveness of the country's exporters.

1. The dilemma posed by capital account openness

Even a slightly diverging inflation trend between two open economies is sufficient for highly volatile short-term international capital flows to force the central bank of the country with high inflation to give up its undervaluation strategy or to face the severe fiscal costs that can be associated with this strategy.[16] Differences in inflation rates are usually reflected in differences in nominal interest rates, with the high-inflation country having higher interest rates than the low-inflation country, even if both countries have similar growth trends and a similar monetary policy stance (e.g. if they try to apply a Taylor rule[17]). The reason for this is that nominal interest rates have to be higher in the high-inflation country if the central bank is to bring the domestic real interest rate in line with the given real growth rate and degree of capacity utilization.

However, short-term capital flows are not driven exclusively by interest rate differentials. Speculators may attack the currencies of countries that follow an undervaluation policy, because they expect a revaluation to occur sooner or later. This means that, contrary to textbook scenarios, in the real world, international investors do not form short-term exchange rate expectations on the basis of the purchasing power parity (PPP) rule.

Since the PPP rule is relevant only over the long term, policy-makers in financially open developing countries need to be aware that international investors in short-term deposits base their

decisions on the expected nominal return rather than the expected real return on investments. This is because portfolio investors do not intend to buy goods in the country in which they invest, but simply invest money for a day, a week or three months. If, during that period of time, the inflation divergence between the high-inflation and the low-inflation country does not trigger the generally expected depreciation of the high-inflation country's currency, portfolio investment will be more attracted to the high-inflation than to the low-inflation country. As discussed in *TDR*s *1998* and *2001*, most of the financial crises in the post-Bretton Woods era have been characterized by unsustainable nominal interest rate differentials. The differential in nominal interest rates attracts portfolio investment in the currency of the high-inflation country. This, in turn, improves the short-term attractiveness of the high-inflation country's currency, because an appreciation would increase the expected return from such an investment. On the other hand, if governments try, from the outset, to limit the extent of an appreciation of the domestic currency by buying foreign currencies, this will usually add to the confidence of international investors as the high-inflation country's international reserves increase.

Thus, independently of whether high nominal interest rates or the expectation of a revaluation attract short-term capital inflows, the currency of the high-inflation country will tend to appreciate in the short-term.[18] This undermines the fundamental external equilibrium between the high-inflation and the low-inflation country and risks increasing the volatility of the nominal and real exchange rates. The presence of an interest-rate differential, which determines the movement of the real exchange rate in the short term, does not preclude the exchange rate from eventually returning to PPP. In the medium term, the clearly visible deterioration of the international competitive position of the high-inflation country will reverse expectations of international investors: they will lose "confidence" in the high-inflation country's currency, thus making a correction of the overvaluation unavoidable.

> International investors in short-term deposits base their decisions on the expected nominal return rather than the expected real return on investments.

Even in the absence of short-term capital flows, internal and external equilibrium cannot be achieved at the same time by adjusting interest rates, if inflation rates in the two countries diverge, for example, because of different institutional arrangements on the labour market. This is because the central bank cannot fight inflation without attracting capital inflows in the short term, and provoking volatility of capital flows and exchange rates in the medium term. Neither can it lower interest rates without running the risk of failing to reach the inflation target.[19]

Independently of whether a high-inflation country with a fully liberalized capital account chooses to fight inflation by maintaining high interest rates, or to keep the real interest rate at a level at least as high as in the low-inflation country, its currency will attract international investors in short-term assets. The high-inflation country can achieve domestic price stabilization only if it maintains nominal interest rates at a level higher than those of the low-inflation country. But if, in the short run, the inflation differential between the two countries is not matched by a corresponding expectation of depreciation of the high-inflation country's currency, the occurrence of a fundamental disequilibrium will be unavoidable. However, choosing the alternative approach and trying to fix the nominal exchange rate is, in this framework, also very costly. Intervention by the central bank of a developing country implies buying foreign currency against bonds denominated in domestic currency that bear relatively high interest rates, and investing the foreign currency purchased at a lower interest rate in the developed country. Thus a strategy of intervening in currency markets and accumulating foreign currency reserves amounts to a permanent subsidization of foreign investors with domestic taxpayers' money.

Free capital flows between countries with differing rates of inflation usually break the link between interest rate differentials and the risk of currency depreciation, because exchange rates do not follow PPP in the short term. Introducing PPP as a "theoretical norm" (Schumpeter, 1939) or a political target is the only way out. With exchange rate expectations being "rational" in terms of PPP, exchange rate expectations should always equal the interest rate differential and the price level differential. But this solution does not apply in

reality. Expectations are not formed rationally along the lines of PPP, as unhedged borrowing offers a short-term profit in most exchange rate regimes only if major imbalances have not occurred.

2. Patterns of adjustment

The UNCTAD secretariat conducted some calculations in order to examine the evolution of returns on short-term international portfolio investment in a number of developing countries over the period 1995–2003. As a first step, assuming exchange rates to remain stable, the real interest rate that is relevant for the decision of an investor from the United States to make, for example, a three-month investment in a developing country, is the three-month nominal interest rate in the developing country minus the inflation rate in the United States. International investors base their decisions on the inflation rate in their home country, and not on the rate in the country in which they invest, because they intend to reimport the invested money at the end of the investment period rather than to buy goods in the country in which they invest.[20]

The results of these calculations are shown in figure 4.5 for six countries. The exchange rate regimes that govern the relationship between the dollar and the currencies of these six countries strongly differ. China has maintained a stable currency peg against the dollar for a long time. The figure indicates that from the financial side, this peg is sustainable, as China does not offer real interest rates for international investors that could directly endanger the peg. The incentive to invest in China on a short-term basis, as reflected by the line showing the real interest rate for United States investors, has consistently been either only marginally positive or even negative. By contrast, Mexico and Brazil maintained a very high real interest rate for international investors throughout the second half of the 1990s. Even Argentina maintained positive real interest rate differentials during this period – reflected by the difference between the two solid lines in the figure – despite its hard currency peg with the dollar. Indeed, the real interest rate that underlies decisions of United

Figure 4.5

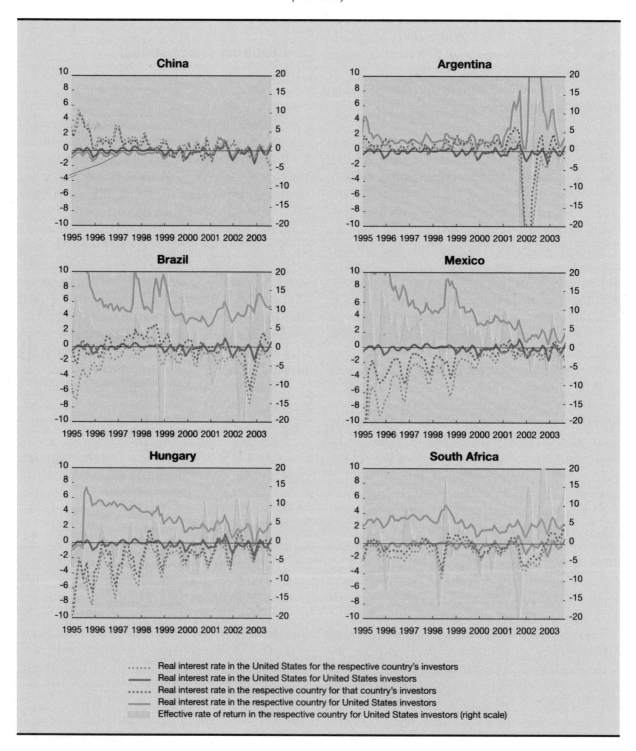

INCENTIVES FOR SHORT-TERM INTERNATIONAL PORTFOLIO INVESTMENT IN SELECTED COUNTRIES, 1995–2003

(Per cent)

.... Real interest rate in the United States for the respective country's investors
——— Real interest rate in the United States for United States investors
.... Real interest rate in the respective country for that country's investors
——— Real interest rate in the respective country for United States investors
░░░ Effective rate of return in the respective country for United States investors (right scale)

Source: UNCTAD secretariat calculations, based on data from IMF, *International Financial Statistics*; and Thomson Financial Datastream.

Note: The scenario that underlies the figure is based on a 3-month investment horizon. Real interest rates lower than minus 10 per cent or higher than plus 10 per cent, and effective returns lower than minus 20 per cent or higher than plus 20 per cent are not shown for expositional clarity.

States investors to invest in the Latin American countries has, in many instances, been much higher than in the United States over a long period. Thus transactions of a huge size must have taken place, assuming that the money and currency markets operated efficiently. The crises in Mexico (in the mid-1990s), Brazil (1999), and Argentina (2001–2002) demonstrate that, as a rule, financial crises and the collapse of the exchange rate are preceded by phases of enormous effective returns and extremely high interest rates for foreign investors. Only in 2002 did Mexico manage to bring inflation and its short-term interest rate down, and to avoid attracting foreign investors with offers of high financial yields. Brazil, on the other hand, still offers investors very attractive conditions.

In addition to the interest rates calculated at a fixed exchange rate, a second step in the calculations takes account of the actual change in the bilateral exchange rate in order to calculate the effective rate of return for United States investors in the developing country. This rate (shown by the shaded area in figure 4.5) reflects the ex-post observed change in the exchange rate, but provides no information on the rate that the investors expected. Indeed, the calculations are based on *ex post* known interest and exchange rates, which may differ from the rates the investors expected. As such, the results of the calculations do not allow any assessment of the actual size of capital flows that may have been induced by the configuration of these rates at any point in time. At some points there may have been huge flows, while at others there may have been no flows at all. While these limitations need to be kept in mind when interpreting the results, the calculations reveal the dilemma of developing countries that liberalize their capital account without being able to keep their inflation rate at the level of the developed economies.

Hungary and South Africa are examples of countries with rather flexible exchange rate regimes and high de facto exchange rate volatility. Since 2002, both countries have tried to reduce domestic inflation by maintaining relatively high interest rates. This has resulted in a decline in competitiveness due to real currency appreciation. Figure 4.5 shows that the real interest rate incentive for foreign investors is significant and induces

short-term capital inflows, causing an adverse impact on the real exchange rate. During 2003, for example, a three-month investment in South Africa could yield as much as 10 to 20 per cent, which may add up to an annual rate far beyond 50 per cent.

Argentina and Brazil followed similar approaches in the second half of the 1990s but with varying rigour. Argentina fixed its exchange rate very strictly to the dollar, offering a positive and, over many years, fairly stable real rate of return to foreign investors; this rate increased sharply in the run-up to the crisis of its currency board system and led to the collapse of that system. Brazil adopted a crawling peg, visible in the stable difference between the real interest rate for United States investors and the effective rate of return. This system per se was less restrictive than the Argentinean one on the external side, but had to be complemented by higher domestic interest rates to avoid a return of inflation. Under conditions of free capital flows, the Brazilian soft peg offered very high real rates of return until the beginning of the crisis in 1999. However, even after the crisis, the Brazilian central bank did not fundamentally change its policy of maintaining a high level of interest rates relative to that in the United States. The resulting recent rise in capital inflows has put sharp pressure on the Brazilian real to appreciate.

Looking at the experience of a larger group of economies, figure 4.6 reveals sharp differences in patterns of adjustment. In this figure, the real interest rate for a United States investor is correlated with the effective rate of return for that investor. The economies are grouped according to the attractiveness of their currencies for international portfolio investors. If the nominal exchange rate is perfectly stable, there is no scattering of the points and the correlation is very high, as is the case for China. The position of the curve (right of the zero point or on the zero point) indicates whether, in terms of the interest rate differential, the country has been attractive (Argentina, Brazil) or not (China) for international investors. In group 1 (column 1 of the figure), the countries aim at a rather low nominal interest rate, with or without fixing the exchange rates. In Malaysia, Singapore and Chile, the exchange rate is not as stable as in China, but these three countries' cen-

Figure 4.6

ALTERNATIVE EXCHANGE RATE REGIMES AND INCENTIVES FOR SHORT-TERM PORTFOLIO INVESTMENT IN SELECTED ECONOMIES, 1995–2003

(Per cent)

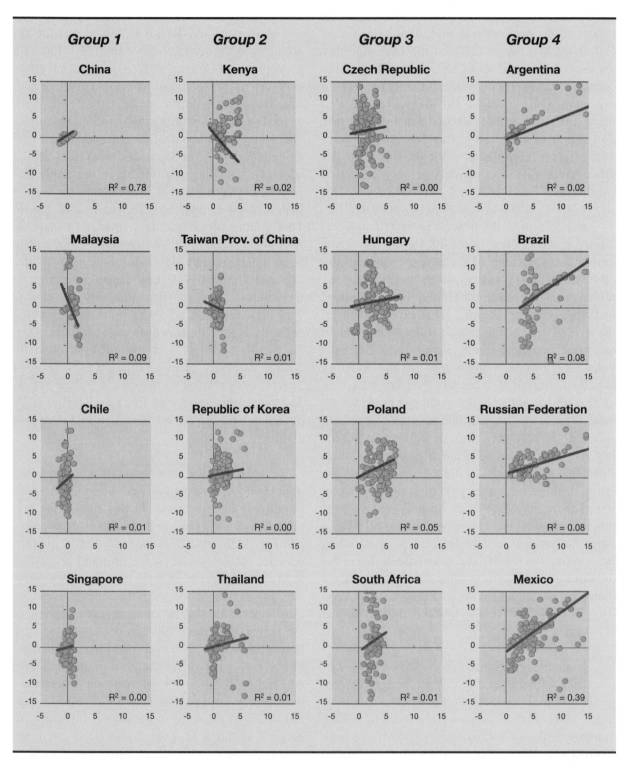

Source: See fig. 4.5.
Note: For the calculation of the real interest rate and the effective rate of return, see text. Vertical scale: effective rate of return in the respective economy for United States investors; horizontal scale: real interest rate in the respective economy for United States investors.

tral banks avoid giving incentives to foreign investors to speculate on an overvaluation.

In group 2, the interest rate incentives are fairly small and the effective returns (including exchange rate changes) scatter quite remarkably along the vertical axis. This means that these economies – as demonstrated by the Republic of Korea, Taiwan Province of China and Thailand – avoid one-sided flows by maintaining high exchange rate volatility and low interest rates.

Countries in group 3, consisting mainly of transition economies, have adopted a floating exchange rate regime but with some interest rate incentives for international investors, as the inflation rate in these countries was relatively high during the 1990s.

The fourth group of countries follows a different approach. By keeping the exchange rate fairly stable and offering incentives for financial investors, their central banks try to use the exchange rate to stabilize inflation. This implies prolonged periods of rather risk-free arbitrage for international investors. These hard or soft pegs are sustainable only if the high interest rate does not depress the rate of domestic investment, or if an appreciation of the real exchange rate can be avoided. In most cases, however, these conditions do not apply. Sooner or later, the currency peg, soft or hard, has to be discontinued and replaced by a new system.

The examples of intermediate systems of managed floating (as in Poland, Hungary, the Czech Republic, South Africa, or in Brazil and Argentina after their currency crises) show that the variability of the exchange rate may increase the risk for the international investor at certain points, but it may increase the reward as well. If, for example, the country with the floating currency has been going through a crisis phase with real depreciation, the exchange rate expectation tends to turn around for a time, as the international investors expect revaluation and not a new devaluation. This has been the recent experience of Brazil and South Africa. To avoid a quick and strong real currency revaluation, which would destroy the gains in competitiveness the country has just achieved, the monetary authorities intervene by buying foreign currency and piling up interna-

tional reserves. This is costly for the country involved, as its interest rates are higher than the rates it can earn by recycling the money to the country of origin or to another safe haven. In these circumstances, it is difficult, if not impossible, to strike a balance between the domestic needs to fight inflation and the negative repercussions of incentives for foreign investors in portfolio capital on domestic growth and employment.

3. Multilateral solutions are the answer

The message of the preceding analysis is a simple one. If the nominal short-term interest rate in a financially open emerging-market economy exceeds that in a developed country by more than the growth differential, the nominal exchange rate of the former should depreciate at a (annual) rate that equals the difference in (annual) interest rates. If this is not the case, the situation is not sustainable, as either the high interest rate or the overvalued exchange rate hampers sustainable economic development in the emerging market economy.

Hence the political choice to combine floating of the currency with restrictive domestic monetary policy to bring down inflation will destabilize the external account. Speculation on uncovered interest rate parities will yield high returns to arbitraging international portfolio investors, as nominal and real interest rates in the developing economies are higher than in the leading industrialized economies. The currencies of the high-inflation countries will tend to appreciate, thereby, temporarily, even increasing the incentive for foreign investors to buy domestic assets and the incentive of domestic borrowers to borrow abroad.

Overall, the dilemma for developing-country policy-makers of a situation in which international investors earn high rates of return in their countries, despite falling real income, domestic profits and employment, cannot be resolved under conditions of free capital flows. Developing-country policy-makers are usually unable to reduce interest rates to stop the speculative capital inflow, because doing so would endanger the credibility of their monetary policy domestically. The political will to achieve economic stability is reflected in the decision to keep nominal interest rates high. How long an external economic imbalance following an exchange rate peg or an appreciation can be sustained is an open question. With growing visible external imbalances the developing country's exchange rate policy will begin to lose credibility in markets. Once investors are convinced that the anchoring country will not be able to manage slowing down the growth of its external debt smoothly, confidence will deteriorate. This will lead to renewed crisis, a reduction of reserves and eventually a depreciation of the country's exchange rate.

In any case, exchange rate changes are necessary to compensate for the opening scissor blades of the price and cost developments between a high-inflation and a low-inflation country. As long as developing countries are not able to perfectly converge in nominal terms with the developed countries, devaluations are unavoidable in order to preserve the competitiveness of the high-inflation countries. However, exchange rate changes, and in particular, real exchange rate changes, that determine the competitiveness of the whole economy, cannot be left to the market. Given the arbitrage opportunities between high- and low-inflation countries, a rule of competitive neutrality of the exchange rate, like the PPP rule, has to be enforced by governments and/or central banks. Ideally, such a rule should be the result of multilateral agreements, as exchange rate changes always have multilateral repercussions. But if the international community is not able to agree on rules to avoid competitive devaluations and huge destabilizing shocks, countries will continue to manage the floating of their currencies unilaterally.

Managed floating, however, faces an adding-up problem on the global scale. Not all countries can simultaneously manage the movements of their exchange rate and achieve their targeted rates. The exchange rate, by definition, is a multilateral phenomenon, and attempts by many countries to keep their currencies at an undervalued rate may end up in a race to the bottom – or in competitive devaluations – that would be as harmful for the world economy as in the 1930s. Moreover, given the size of international short-term capital flows and the inherent volatility of these flows, only those developing countries that are big and competitive enough to withstand strong and sustained attempts of the international financial markets to move the exchange rate in a certain direction will be able to manage the floating successfully. A small and open developing economy will hardly be able to continue fighting a strong tendency to appreciate over many years or even decades.

Multilateral or even global arrangements are clearly the best solutions to this problem. The idea of a cooperative global monetary system would be to assure, on a multilateral basis, the same rules of the game for all parties involved, more or less in the same way as multilateral trade rules apply to every party equally. That is why the main idea behind the founding of the International Monetary Fund in the 1940s was to avoid competitive devaluations. In a well-designed global monetary system, the need and the advantages of the currency depreciation of one country have to be balanced against the disadvantages to the others. As changes in the exchange rate, deviating from purchasing power parity, affect international trade in exactly the same way as changes in tariffs and export duties do, such changes should be governed by multilateral regulations. Such a multilateral regime would, among other things, require countries to specify their reasons for real devaluations and the dimension of necessary changes. If such rules were strictly applied, the real exchange rate of all the parties involved would remain more

> To combine floating of the currency with restrictive domestic monetary policy to bring down inflation will destabilize the external account.

> If the international community is not able to agree on rules to avoid competitive devaluations, countries will continue to manage the floating of their currencies unilaterally ...

or less constant, as strong arguments for creating competitive advantages at the national level would rarely be acceptable.

In a world without a multilateral solution to the currency problem, the only way out for high-inflation or high-growth countries that are not members of a regional monetary union is to resort to controls of short-term capital flows or to follow a strategy of undervaluation and unilateral fixing.

> ... managed floating, however, faces an adding-up problem.

If developing countries are able to avoid destabilizing inflows and outflows, either by taxing those flows or by limiting their impact through direct intervention in the market, the hardest choices and misallocations due to erratic exchange rate changes can be avoided; but the resort to controls or permanent intervention should not replace the search for an appropriate exchange rate system at the regional or global level. ■

Notes

1   Local wholesale and distribution costs also affect trade costs. But since they apply to both imports and domestic goods, they do not affect relative prices to buyers and international competitiveness.

2   This is the case, for example, if wage increases are indexed to inflation, and if external supply shocks such as price increases of imports (e.g. oil) have a strong impact on inflation.

3   For example, according to Gordon (2003: 208), the average annual rate of growth of labour productivity in the United States during the period of the information and communications technology boom (1995–2000) was about 2.5 per cent.

4   See Forbes (2002a) for a theoretical model and econometric evidence for this argument.

5   However, as discussed in *TDR 1998* (chapter III), the sharp rise in domestic interest rates may prove largely unsuccessful in stopping the downward spiral in exchange rates, as demonstrated by the 1997–1998 East Asian crisis.

6   The conclusion that the finding of an adverse impact of exchange rate volatility on trade flows is not robust relies on the result of one out of seven regressions. This result has by far the lowest level of statistical significance among the regressions that rely on the chosen model specification. Moreover,

the authors note that the set-up chosen for this regression may not be able to reveal the entire negative effect of exchange rate volatility on trade (IMF, 2004: 49–50).

7   This initial deterioration of the trade account following a real depreciation is known as the J-curve effect, and the mentioned elasticity condition is known as the Marshall-Lerner condition.

8   Ghei and Pritchett (1999) review the literature and discuss factors that determine whether real depreciations improve the trade balance in developing countries, as well as the empirical challenges in measuring these effects.

9   For a full discussion of this dilemma faced by many African countries, see *TDR 1998*.

10 Especially those by Glick and Rose (1999), Forbes (2002b), and Duttagupta and Spilimbergo (2004). Other studies find that trade linkages have some role, but are overshadowed by financial linkages and/or macroeconomic variables (*TDR 1998* (chapter II); van Rijckegham and Weder, 2001; and Caramazza, Ricci and Salgado, 2004). Baig and Goldfajn (1998) are among the few authors who do not find support for the importance of trade in the international transmission of crises, but their evidence is contradicted by Duttagupta and Spilimbergo (2004).

11   Indeed, similar "paradoxes" regarding persistent external imbalances, in spite of substantial movements in relative exchange rates among major currencies, have become a frequent feature of the world economy. For example, the strong appreciation of the yen against the dollar in 1985 and 1994–1995 was not followed by a collapse in Japanese output of traded goods relative to the United States and other countries. Similarly, the recent strong depreciation of the dollar and the strong appreciation of the euro have had only a modest impact on trade flows. While the reasons for these developments are undoubtedly complex, incomplete exchange rate pass-through appears also to have played an important role in all these instances, as documented for Japan by Athukorala and Menon (1994) and Goldberg and Knetter (1997), and for the euro area by Faruqee (2004).

12   For the group of CEECs, the results indicate a statistically significant positive relationship between real currency appreciations and increases in export-market shares – a finding in line with the Kaldor paradox. However, as data for earlier years were not available, the results for the CEECs refer to a relatively short period (i.e. 1995–2002). More importantly, during the early 1990s these countries carried out major exchange rate depreciations to facilitate the massive industrial restructuring associated with their transition from a centrally planned system to a market economy system. In addition, their gain in market shares in world manufactured exports during the 1990s was in large part due to a reorientation of their trade flows towards developed and developing countries, and away from their traditional trading partners in the former CMEA. Intra-CMEA trade flows were not market-driven, and valuations on the basis of so-called transfer roubles were arbitrary. Conversion to dollar values were, moreover, complicated by inconsistent national rouble/dollar cross rates. These specific circumstances largely explain why the CEECs included in the sample experienced, on average, a combination of real currency appreciation and rising shares in world manufactured exports during the period 1995–2002.

13   This division is based on the country classification used in the UNCTAD *Handbook of Statistics*. Wollmershäuser (2004) uses different categories and classifies countries for each individual year, based on whether manufactures, fuels, or non-fuel primary products account for the highest share in the country's total merchandise exports in a specific year. However, he obtains similar results.

14   This resembles the approach of Forbes (2002c: 218), who determined yearly dummy variables for depreciation events on the basis of monthly data, and defined a depreciation event as a 10-per-cent or greater increase in a country's exchange rate versus the dollar in any four-week period during the sample period.

15   This is likely to reflect a decline in both imports and domestic income.

16   Diverging inflation trends in open economies are much more important for the viability of an exchange rate strategy than the usually discussed "asymmetric shock", first introduced by Mundell in his paper on optimum currency areas (Mundell, 1961). With diverging inflation trends grounded in different labour market regimes, the arguments used to defend hard pegs or dollarization (e.g. Calvo, 1999) no longer apply, as long-lasting remedies to preserve competitiveness are sought and not just one-off measures.

17   The monetary policy rule presented by Taylor (1993) postulates that the central bank should base the setting of the short-term interest rate on the current situation with regard to inflation and the business cycle.

18   A striking example of this is Hungary's recent switch from a crawling peg to a flexible exchange rate following a strategy of inflation targeting. Immediately after the move, although the country had an inflation rate of around 10 per cent (compared with 2 per cent in its main trading partner Germany), its currency appreciated sharply, as Hungary offered much higher nominal interest rates than Germany.

19   Laursen and Metzler (1950: 277–278) summarize the experience of the 1930s in a similar way: "Exchange rates at that time underwent frequent and substantial fluctuations ... the fluctuations that occurred nevertheless created serious doubts concerning the effectiveness of a flexible-exchange system in equalizing a country's international payments and receipts". They conclude that "a regime of flexible exchange rates would not be successful unless capital movements were subject to some kind of control".

20   The same reasoning applies for a developing-country enterprise seeking a low-interest, short-term credit. In other words, the enterprise will have an incentive to obtain the credit in the United States if the nominal interest rate in the United States is lower than in its home country.

THE CONCEPT OF COMPETITIVENESS

Linkages between investment, productivity growth, successful integration into the international trading and financial systems, and economic development have been seen in recent years through the lens of international competitiveness. A wide range of criteria and measures of the competitiveness of countries have been elaborated, some of which have been extensively publicized. Indeed, "competitiveness" has become not only a management buzzword, but also a term widely used in economics and economic policy-making.

The concept of competitiveness can contribute to an understanding of the distribution of wealth, both nationally and internationally, if it is recognized that: (i) it can be applied at both the enterprise and the country level, (ii) when applied at the enterprise level, it relates to profits or market shares, (iii) when applied at the country level, it relates to both national income and international trade performance, particularly in relation to specific industrial sectors that are important in terms of, for example, employment or productivity and growth potential, (iv) it is based on a Schumpeterian logic that sees the nature of capitalist development as a sequence of innovative investments associated with dynamic imperfect competition and productivity gains, and that sees a major role for public policy in facilitating productivity-increasing investment,[1] and (v) not all countries can simultaneously improve the competitiveness of their firms or sectors relative to other countries, but all countries can simultaneously raise productivity and wages to improve their overall economic welfare without altering their relative competitive positions.

If new technology in the form of added capital per worker (or embodied technological change) is at the heart of the development process through which nations become rich, and if embodied technological change is driven by investment based on either innovation of domestic entrepreneurs or putting imported capital equipment to efficient use, then approaching the concept of competitiveness in the context of economic development needs to take account of the interdependence of investment, trade, finance and technology.

Looking at competitiveness from the perspective of interdependence, two key questions relate to how different price, wage, exchange rate and trade arrangements (i) influence the determinants of innovative investment, and (ii) determine whether productivity gains of individual firms translate into benefits for the overall economy, as reflected in rising living standards, while maintaining external balance.

Emphasizing interdependence also implies that competitiveness in international markets is determined by both real and monetary factors. Competitiveness may increase as a result of the relatively strong productivity performance of companies or the national economy as a whole. But greater competitiveness can result also from a depreciation of a country's real effective exchange rate following either a depreciation of its nominal effective exchange rate or a smaller rise in the ratio between wages and productivity (i.e. unit labour costs) than in other countries.

There have been strong objections to the use of the concept of competitiveness at the level of countries rather than at the level of individual firms. Some of these objections raise valid concerns. Indeed, caution is needed in presenting the concept as one of the economic challenges facing developing countries. The first major objection is that countries, unlike companies, do not compete with each other (Krugman, 1994). This means that, strictly speaking, if the international mobility of labour was very high, and the monetary and trading conditions in the world economy mirrored exactly those that apply within national economies, the concept would be useful only to define the position of individual enterprises vis-à-vis each other. By contrast, it would not be useful for comparisons between national economies, or even between industries comprising many firms with different characteristics.

However, most of the factors underlying the competitiveness of individual enterprises are determined at the level of the national economy, implying that the national economy is indeed a meaningful entity for the concept of competitiveness.[2] More precisely, one characteristic of the world economy today is that labour mobility is much lower across, than within, countries. Where labour mobility is relatively low even within countries, rules and regulations that govern labour costs are designed to apply at the level of the national economy.[3] Moreover, most national economies are individual currency areas, so that fluctuations and misalignments of nominal exchange rates directly influence the competitiveness of firms operating in different countries, even if factors determining competitiveness at the firm level are similar. Further, government interventions that affect the determinants of trade flows and exchange rates usually have a similar effect across all sectors and enterprises of the national economy. However, from an individual firm's perspective, it may matter little whether its international competitiveness improves through productivity growth, lower labour costs or a devaluation of the currency. But from a broader, socioeconomic point of view, these have different implications for national economic development, as well as for systemic stability and welfare in the global economy.

The second major objection raised against the concept of competitiveness is that international trade is not a zero-sum game, and it is therefore meaningless to say that a national economy is becoming more or less competitive. In traditional trade theory, relative changes in the importance of different sectors reflect changes in relative resource endowments; in a general equilibrium framework, this simply implies a shift from one setting of optimal resource allocation to another. As such, sector-specific changes imply shifts in the countries' relative positions of comparative advantage, but the underlying general equilibrium framework does not allow for any definition of national competitiveness. However, as argued by Krugman (1996: 18), these mechanisms come into play only in perfect markets, while in imperfect markets, "involving imperfect competition, external economies, or both", there are valid concerns about national competitiveness. Of the many departures from perfect markets in actual economic relations – including scale economies, externalities and linkages, product differentiation, cumulative learning and first-mover advantages, and technological leads and lags – technology factors are of key importance in the concept of competitiveness, because it is mainly technological innovations that drive productivity gains, which provide the microeconomic basis for improved competitiveness.

All this implies that developing countries have valid concerns about their external economic performance. First, countries in the early stages of industrialization require foreign-exchange earnings from exports to finance machinery and equipment imports that enable innovative investors to obtain productivity gains. Second, countries further advanced in industrialization, and strongly integrated into international trading and financial markets, may find it difficult to maintain a sufficient degree of flexibility in their monetary, wage and trade policies. Flexibility is needed to accommodate price adjustments that arise from productivity-enhancing investment and to prevent profits earned through innovative investments from being spent on luxury imports rather than being reinvested. Third, and most importantly, changes in the relative importance of different economic sectors are a key factor for rapid and sustained productivity growth and higher living standards. This implies that the concept of competitiveness is of immediate policy relevance. It can be used to analyse under which conditions productivity gains at the microeconomic level translate into structural change at the level of the national economy and enable upgrading of the technology content of a country's export basket. It is also useful for identifying policy measures that reduce the vulnerability of national economies to disturbances emanating from the international economy and which may have adverse effects on national economic development.[4]

Given the complexity of the issue of competitiveness, it is not surprising that there is a multitude of competitiveness indicators. Some analysts use competitiveness indices that combine several dozens of individual measures spanning across a wide range of economic and non-economic factors.[5] However, the indicator that is most widely used in applied economic analysis is the real exchange rate, based on either relative consumer price or relative unit labour cost indices expressed in a common currency.

1. Conditions for competitiveness at the microeconomic level

Linkages between capital accumulation, technological progress and structural change constitute the basis for rapid and sustained productivity growth, rising living standards and successful integration into the international economy. Investment holds a central place in this interplay, because it can simultaneously generate income, expand productive capacity, and carry strong complementarities with other elements in the growth process, such as technological progress, skills acquisition and institutional deepening.

However, a given rate of investment can generate different growth rates, depending on its nature and composition as well as the efficiency with which production capacity is utilized. Particularly important for productivity growth and structural change is investment in new techniques and/or new products. This is because new procedures generally reduce production costs of established products, while new products are often more attractive to consumers than any of the previously available alternatives. Assuming constant wages, successful innovative investment will be reflected in growing market shares, if the investor chooses to pass on innovation rents in the form of lower prices; or it will lead to (temporary) monopoly profits, if the investor chooses to leave sales prices unchanged and enjoy innovation rents from the rising revenue-cost ratio until competitors succeed in imitating the innovator. Which of these strategies the investor chooses will depend on the intensity of competition. This means that in the microeconomic sphere, changes in competitiveness relate to changes in relative labour productivity across different firms, and that technological progress and the ensuing growth in labour productivity (i.e. the drivers of sustainably rising competitiveness) are associated with oligopolistic, rather than perfect, competition.

Innovative investment in developed countries extends the technological frontier. By contrast, in developing countries it generally relates to the adoption, imitation and adaptation of technology invented elsewhere. While this does not affect the key importance of productivity-enhancing investment for competitiveness at the firm level, or significantly alter the determinants of investment decisions, there are three issues that specifically concern productivity-enhancing investment in developing countries. First, in building their industrial capacity and competitive strength, newly industrializing countries must typically import a large volume of capital goods and intermediate inputs. However, an inability to obtain additional export earnings (i.e. if the country's products are not competitive on international markets or face prohibitive market access or entry barriers), and thus to finance these imports, may be a serious constraint on the industrialization process. The extent of this balance-of-payments constraint and dependence of developing countries on foreign technologies embodied in imported capital goods are perhaps greatest during the initial stages of industrialization. However, the need for large-scale imports of machinery and equipment persists throughout much of the industrialization process, especially when catching up is based on imitating technological leaders.

Second, in addition to directly facilitating a rise in the level of technology used by domestic firms, developing-country imports of goods that embody foreign technology positively affect domestic imitation and innovation. For example, a notable feature of the process of technological improvement in the East Asian economies in the early stages of their industrialization was their emphasis on research and development (R&D) spending, not only for backward engineering but also to match or surpass the product quality of foreign manufacturers by adapting and improving imported technology. The former enabled firms, for example, to fully assess the merits of a new foreign technology and thus to determine whether to secure a licence or not, and to unbundle foreign technology, thereby enhancing their bargaining power in negotiating with suppliers. As the industrialization process unfolded and firms came to master imitation, an increasing share of R&D spending was channelled into own innovation (*TDR 1994*, Part Two, chapter one). Taking a wider geographical perspective, and looking at a large number of countries from all developing regions, a recent empirical study (Connolly, 2003) also reveals the positive impact of technology imports from developed countries on domestic imitation and innovation in developing countries.

Third, the realization of technological improvements in developing countries is closely related both to the skill level of their labour force – which determines the amount and degree of sophistication of technology that can be adopted and efficiently used – and to managerial capabilities, which must meet the requirements to function effectively in new sectors and new markets. As such, technological upgrading in developing countries is usually associated with a painstaking and cumulative process of technological learning. Human capital formation, including through learning, is instrumental in preventing a decline in the marginal product of capital, despite the rapid growth in the capital-labour ratio generated by rapid accumulation of physical capital. It also helps prevent a decline in the marginal product of labour, despite the rise in wages that results in a higher standard of living.

The competitiveness of affiliates of foreign TNCs is likely to be significantly higher than that of domestic firms. Labour productivity in TNC affiliates tends to be higher than in their domestic counterparts, because they can combine the comparatively lower general level of labour costs in the host country[6] with the advanced production technology and management techniques used in their home countries, and with supplies of raw materials and intermediate production inputs from the cheapest sources.[7] Indeed, in the context of the concept of competitiveness, the decision of a foreign company to invest abroad is generally based on the objective to reduce unit labour costs in production. Setting aside other host country characteristics (such as income or corporate tax treatment or provision of infrastructure), this implies that for FDI to occur, the investor must expect the ratio between labour productivity and wages in the affiliate to exceed that in the parent company. In other words, if expected unit labour costs in the host country are lower than in the TNC's home country, the TNC will consider moving part of its production activities abroad.

2. Competitiveness of firms at the level of the national economy

At the level of the national economy, the decisive factor for realizing technological upgrading and productivity-driven structural change is the ability of investors to sell the products resulting from their product or process innovations without a significant change in cost conditions (i.e. to enjoy a (temporary) monopoly profit). In other words, if an economy is characterized by high domestic labour mobility and by a similar level of wages for workers with similar qualifications across the economy, its dynamic development will be driven by profit differentials, rather than wage differentials. Indeed, as noted by Keynes (1930: 141), "the departure of profits from zero is the mainspring of change in the ... modern world. ... It is by altering the rate of profits in particular directions that entrepreneurs can be induced to produce this rather than that, and it is by altering the rate of profits in general that they can be induced to modify the average of their offers of remuneration to the factors of production."

Hence, the closer actual conditions on the labour markets get to the law of one price, the stronger will be the effects of profit differentials on the evolution of economic systems.[8] The observed asymmetry between uneven productivity growth and the more even growth in wage rates across enterprises or industrial sectors is frequently emphasized as providing an important source of both structural change in the domestic economy and changes in the comparative cost advantages of different countries in specific industrial sectors. Uneven productivity growth across firms, combined with more even growth in wage rates, implies that workers in industries with relatively high productivity growth are not fully compensated.

Under this scenario, innovative investors may decide to leave sales prices unchanged and obtain a sizeable extra profit equal to the difference between their productivity gain and the economy-wide average growth in productivity. Alternatively, they may prefer to reduce sales prices by the amount to which their cost per unit of output falls, and thus, assuming normal price elasticities of demand, increase their market share. This will lead to a rise in their absolute level of profits in line with the rise in sold output. This potential for extra profits is the major incentive for starting the process of "creative construction" or "destruction" along Schumpeterian lines, and hence for making innovative investments. By contrast, if wages in each firm rise more in line with firm-specific productivity gains, innovative investors will obtain a much lower extra profit, which will be much less of an incentive for innovative investment.

Enterprises whose productivity gains fall short of the national average will experience shrinking profits if labour costs rise at equal rates across firms. These enterprises will therefore attempt to raise the sales prices for their goods so as not to risk a complete erosion of profits.[9] This implies that sectorally uneven productivity gains, combined with even labour cost increases across the entire economy, generate price pressures in non-innovative sectors. However, the net impact of this supply-side effect on price pressure depends on effects originating from the demand side. Rising labour productivity induces increases in income, and hence consumption. If demand for innovated and non-innovated goods were to grow at the same rate, demand effects would not skew price pressure towards one or the other group of goods, thus the supply-side effect would dominate. By contrast, if demand for the innovated good were to grow faster than for the other goods, the supply-side effect would be offset, partly or completely. And if demand were biased towards goods for which productivity gains were low (such as services), the demand effect would reinforce the supply effect. This will be the case particularly when productivity gains are high in the traded sector, while domestic consumption demand is biased towards non-traded goods.

A second important condition for innovative investment to govern the evolution of the economic system is that firms should have access to reliable, adequate and cost-effective sources for financing their investments. This condition is best met when profits themselves are the main source of investment financing. Indeed, if an investment-profit nexus can be ignited, profits from innovative investments simultaneously increase the incentive for firms to invest and their capacity to finance new investments.[10] When enterprises are heavily dependent on borrowing to meet their needs for fixed investment and working capital, as is the case of new enterprises, the stance of domestic monetary policy is of crucial importance, because high levels of nominal and real interest rates tend to increase production costs. In addition to its adverse impact on the cost of capital, a restrictive monetary policy may bias investment decisions in favour of financial assets, or fixed investment in production activities with known cost and demand schedules over innovative production activities for which investors face uncertainty as to the volume of sales and the true costs of production.

To understand how the mechanisms discussed in this annex work in practice, it is useful to consider a two-country world comprising a developing country, with a low average level of both labour costs and labour productivity, and a developed country, with a high average level of labour costs and labour productivity. Expressed in a common currency, these levels are assumed as 5 and 10 in the developing country and 50 and 100 in the developed country (case 1 in table 4.A1). Further, assuming that in both countries the average

level of labour costs reflects the average level of labour productivity, firms in both countries face the same average level of unit labour costs (i.e. 0.5 currency units). If labour is the only internationally immobile production factor, these assumptions imply that firms from both countries are, on average, internationally competitive. Moreover, if firms set sales prices on the basis of a mark-up of 100 per cent over labour costs, the absolute level of profits in the developed country will be 10 times higher than in the developing country.[11]

Case 2 in the table introduces the effects of innovative investment by assuming that productivity increases by 20 per cent in innovative firms of both countries. If the weight of these firms in their domestic economies is too small for these productivity gains to have a marked impact on the economy-wide average level of productivity, nominal labour costs will remain unchanged, and unit labour costs in the innovative firms will decline by 20 per cent. Profits per unit of output will also remain unchanged if the innovative firms reduce their sales prices in line with the decline of their unit labour costs. This implies that the innovative firms from both countries will experience an increase in both their export-market shares and their absolute level of profits. By contrast, non-innovative firms will suffer a decline in export-market shares and in profit levels due to the increase in their sales prices relative to those of the innovative firms.

Case 3 in the table shows that affiliates of TNCs can gain considerable advantages in international competitiveness by combining developed-country technology with developing-country labour costs. The level of the affiliate's unit labour costs will be substantially lower than that of either its parent company in the developed country or of domestic firms in the developing country. While it is unlikely that the relatively less educated workers in the developing country can match the productivity level of workers in the developed country, it is probable that the TNC will experience a strong reduction of its unit labour costs by moving its labour-intensive production activities to a low-wage country.

Changes in the nominal exchange rate that are caused by "autonomous" capital flows (i.e. that are unrelated to the flow of goods) can offset the

Table 4.A1

INNOVATIVE INVESTMENT, EXCHANGE RATE CHANGES, AND
INTERNATIONAL COMPETITIVENESS: A NUMERICAL EXAMPLE

	Case 1		Case 2				Case 3
	No innovative investment		Innovative firm average[a]		Non-innovative firm average		TNC affiliate investing in developing-country export-oriented production
	Developing country	Developed country	Developing country	Developed country	Developing country	Developed country	
Productivity	10	100	12	120	10	100	120 > productivity > 10
Nominal labour costs	5	50	5	50	5	50	5
Unit labour costs	0.5	0.5	0.4	0.4	0.5	0.5	0.5 > ULC > 0.04
Profits per unit of output	5	50	5	50	5	50	115 > profits > 5
Price	1	1	1-x	1-y	1+x	1+y	1-z
1. Unchanged nominal exchange rate							
Export market share	unchanged	unchanged	up	up	down	down	up
2. Nominal exchange rate[b] appreciation by more than 20 per cent							
Export market share	down	up	down[c]	up[c]	down[c]	up[c]	up
3. Nominal exchange rate[b] depreciation by more than 20 per cent							
Export market share	up	down	up[c]	down[c]	up[c]	down[c]	up

Source: UNCTAD secretariat calculations.

   Note: x and y are the shares of the innovative investors' products in the total consumption of their respective economies. z is the share of the multinational firm's reimported product in the total consumption of the economy of the parent company.

    a The scenario in the table is based on the assumption that innovative investors fully transmit gains in profits per unit of output into price reductions.

    b Developing-country currency/developed-country currency.

    c The net effect depends on the relation between the gain in productivity and the exchange rate misalignment. The assumption for the effects noted in the table is that the misalignment is far greater than the gain in productivity.

effects discussed above. In case 1, export-market shares will move from firms of the country whose currency appreciates towards firms of the country whose currency depreciates, even though none of the firms has undertaken productivity-enhancing investments and unit labour costs, measured in domestic currency units, have not changed in any of the firms. More importantly, the innovative firms in case 2 will lose, rather than gain, export-market shares if the appreciation of the exchange rate exceeds productivity gains. For example, assuming the currency of the developing country to appreciate by more than the productivity gains achieved by innovative firms, these firms will lose export-market shares to both the innovative and non-innovative firms of developed countries. This example shows that adverse external monetary shocks can wipe out the gains resulting from an improvement in the international competitiveness of developing-country exporters based on innovative investments and a decline in unit labour costs. ∎

Notes

1 Fagerberg, Knell and Srholec (2004) present a similar argument.

2 The major exception is labour productivity, which can be measured at the level of enterprises and industrial sectors, as well as at the aggregate level of the national economy. Other exceptions include firm-specific capabilities to access international markets.

3 In some countries, such as Germany, such rules and regulations apply at the level of industrial sectors, but developments in leading sectors have a strong impact on other sectors.

4 The concept of competitiveness as defined here is relevant for countries where economic success depends on investment that leads to sustained improvements in productivity. This excludes many of the poorest countries, where capital accumulation can help raise per capita income and living standards simply by allowing a fuller use of underutilized labour and natural resources without altering the efficiency with which resources are utilized.

5 Probably the two best-known competitiveness indices, contained in *The Global Competitiveness Report* of the World Economic Forum and in *The World Competitiveness Report* of the International Institute for Management Development, are frequently invoked in policy discussions and economic policy-making. But the way these indices combine the very wide range of individual indicators is not transparent and, more importantly, the complex theoretical issues that underlie the concept of competitiveness are insufficiently discussed. However, Lall (2001) has significantly contributed to a clarification of how these indices are actually constructed.

6 If labour mobility within the host country is high, the wage level will be determined by the economy-wide average level of labour productivity, rather than by marginal labour productivity.

7 The development effect of FDI for the host economy depends on a range of factors, including the amount of technological spillovers from affiliates to domestic enterprises, the creation of forward and back-ward linkages, and the effects on domestic investment. The large body of literature on this, including successive UNCTAD *World Investment Reports*, provides ambiguous findings, and shows that much depends on host-country characteristics and the way foreign affiliates operate.

8 Looking at developed countries, Scarpetta and Tressel (2004) point out that in addition to wage bargaining regimes, two main aspects of labour-market policy and institutional settings are closely related to the incentives for firms to undertake investment with a view to expanding and innovating production facilities: (i) the stringency of employment protection legislation, which influences the costs of hiring and firing, and (ii) the possible interactions between this legislation and industry-specific technology characteristics. However, a discussion of the importance of these factors for developing countries is beyond the scope of this Report.

9 Note that this example assumes that the innovative and the non-innovative firms operate in different sectors, so that they are not in direct competition. If they operated in the same sector, an attempt to raise sales prices would make the non-innovative firm even more likely to be driven out of the market.

10 As argued by Akyüz and Gore (1996), the presence of such an investment-profit nexus played an important role in East Asian industrialization. The investment-profit nexus played an important role also in the growth performance of Western Europe during the three decades after the Second World War.

11 However, the developed country will tend to employ a higher stock of capital in production than the developing country. Thus the rate of return over capital (i.e. the absolute profit relative to the value of the capital stock) may be very similar in the two countries. In other words, the example relies on the assumption that the internationally immobile factor – labour – absorbs the entire wealth difference between the developed and the developing country, while the internationally mobile factor – capital – obeys the law of one price.

THE SET-UP OF ECONOMETRIC ESTIMATES OF THE IMPACT OF EXCHANGE RATE CHANGES ON TRADE PERFORMANCE

This annex details the set-up of the econometric estimations of the impact of exchange rates on the trade performance of developing countries and CEECs. The results are discussed in section B.2.[1] The basic objective of these panel data estimations is to assess how changes in the competitiveness of producers in an exporting country affect the country's merchandise trade performance. The estimations refer to annual data for the period 1970–2002, based on a sample that includes 22 developing economies and six CEECs; for the latter countries data availability restricts the time period to 1994–2002. This sample of 28 countries includes the 30 leading developing-country exporters, except Nigeria (which exports virtually only crude petroleum, so that its export performance is determined mainly by supply and demand in the global oil market), and the 10 leading CEEC exporters in 2001 for which data on real effective exchange rates were available.[2]

Competitiveness is measured by the exporting country's real effective exchange rate (*REER*) based, in most cases, on relative consumer prices.[3] One of the advantages of using real-exchange-rate indices based on relative consumer prices is the ready availability of data. On the other hand, consumer price indices include not only domestically produced traded goods, but also non-traded domestic as well as imported goods. An alternative measure of REERs is based on relative unit labour costs of different countries, defined as the ratio of employee compensation (including non-wage labour costs) per employee and the volume of output (value added at constant prices) per employee expressed in a common currency. Thus relative unit labour costs depend on relative labour costs per worker, relative labour productivity and the exchange rate. As such, a 10-per-cent slower rise in nominal labour costs, a 10-per-cent depreciation in the exchange rate or a 10-per-cent faster increase in labour productivity all have an identical impact on measured relative unit labour costs. Moreover, the real exchange rate based on relative unit labour costs allows for the decomposing of changes in international competitiveness into the relative impact of changes that emanate from the domestic economy (i.e. productivity gains and nominal wage changes) and those that have their origin in international relations (nominal exchange rate changes).[4]

The above implies that, conceptually, real-exchange-rate indices based on relative unit labour costs are the preferred measure of competitiveness, in particular for economies with a well-established industrial base and strong backward linkages. However, they tend to overestimate the impact of exchange rate changes on the competitiveness of domestic exporters to the extent that exports rely on imported intermediate inputs. A relatively high import content of exports offsets, to a considerable degree, the competitive edge provided by nominal currency depreciations.

Moreover, comprehensive data required to calculate relative unit labour costs are not available. This explains why empirical assessments of changes in real exchange rates usually rely on changes in relative consumer prices.[5]

The exchange rate data used for the estimations are taken from JP Morgan (2003), which cover both a wider range of countries and, for most countries, except for China, the Czech Republic, Hungary, Poland and Slovakia, a longer time period than the IMF's *International Financial Statistics*.[6] Trade performance is measured by four variables: (i) the merchandise trade balance (*MB*) expressed as the ratio of exports to imports; (ii) total merchandise exports as a percentage of nominal income (*EX*); (iii) total merchandise imports as a percentage of nominal income (*IM*); and (iv) a country's market share in total world manufactured exports (*SHARE*). The current account balance, expressed as the ratio of exports to imports, is included as a fifth dependent variable. Given that cross-country variation in the rate of real income growth is likely also to influence countries' trade flows, the estimated equation also includes real world income expressed in dollars

(*WORLD*), and the exporting country's real income expressed in domestic currency (*GDP*). All trade and income data are taken from the UNCTAD *Handbook of Statistics*; current account data are from the IMF's *International Financial Statistics*. The equation is estimated as changes in underlying values in order to eliminate statistical problems, such as non-stationarity, and to allow interpreting the estimated coefficients as elasticities. It can be expressed as follows:

$$d(\ln TRADE_{it}) = \alpha + \beta d(\ln REER_{it}) + \delta d(\ln GDP_{it}) + \gamma d(\ln WORLD_t) + \varepsilon_{it}$$

where *TRADE* represents the four trade performance variables, i and t denote exporting countries and time periods, and ε is an error term. All variables are expressed as logarithms. All estimations were done with both the generalized least square method (GLS) in its simple form (i.e. a common intercept for all countries) with cross-section weights, and GLS with fixed effects (i.e. allowing intercepts to vary across countries). Since tests revealed the presence of fixed effects, only the results of fixed-effect estimations are reported.[7] ∎

Notes

1   This framework is partly based on Wollmershäuser (2004) who also presents a more comprehensive discussion of this relationship.

2   The 22 developing economies are Argentina, Brazil, Chile, China, Colombia, Egypt, Hong Kong (China), India, Indonesia, Malaysia, Mexico, Morocco, Pakistan, the Philippines, the Republic of Korea, Saudi Arabia, Singapore, South Africa, Taiwan Province of China, Thailand, Turkey and Venezuela; and the six CEECs are the Czech Republic, Hungary, Poland, the Russian Federation, Slovakia and Slovenia. For some countries, the first year for which exchange rate data are available is after 1970, namely China (1980), the Czech Republic (1990), Egypt (1994), Hungary (1980), Poland (1980), the Russian Federation (1994), Slovakia (1990), Slovenia (1994) and Turkey (1994).

3   See JP Morgan (2003: 20) for a list of which price index was used for which country.

4   Some analysts, such as Boltho (1996), have argued that using the real exchange rate as an indicator for competitiveness reflects short-term macroeconomic management concerns. However, when countries are subject to frequent external shocks, such as significant volatility in the nominal exchange rate or in commodity prices – that have an adverse effect on the country's terms of trade – or lasting exchange rate misalignments, concerns about the level of the real exchange rate also reflect long-term development objectives.

5   However, Turner and Golub (1997) show that, for most countries for which comprehensive data are available, there is a substantial positive correlation between the two measures of real exchange rates, even though large differences between the two measures occur over the medium term, in particular for developed countries.

6   For the 16 countries included in the sample for which data are available from both sources, the correlation coefficient between IMF and JP Morgan data exceeds 0.95 for 11 and averages 0.75 for the remaining 5 countries.

7   Tests showed that correction for autocorrelation is not necessary. Heteroskedasticity was corrected by using White's covariance estimator.

CONCLUSIONS AND POLICY CHALLENGES

Rapid integration into the world economy, followed by many developing countries as a key element of their economic reform agenda since the mid-1980s, has not had the expected developmental effects. Their increased exposure to international market forces and competition has not enabled these countries to establish the kind of virtuous interaction between international finance, domestic capital formation and export activities that underpinned the successful catching up of Western Europe after the Second World War and of the NIEs during the 1980s and early 1990s. In this context, a fundamental question is how to reinforce coherence between national development strategies and global processes and disciplines, as well as policy coherence among and within the various aspects/sectors of the global economy that impact on development prospects of developing countries. Of particular importance is the interface between the international trading system and the international monetary and financial system.

A key objective of the initial set-up of the post-war multilateral trading system, which adopted the tariff as the only legitimate trade policy measure, was that the allocation of resources on the basis of comparative advantage should not be distorted by selective government intervention. The principle of unconditional, non-discriminatory treatment was an essential component of the tariff-based system. It ensured that all signatories to the GATT would be subject to the obligations resulting from multilaterally negotiated tariff concessions, thus imparting a greater degree of security to the concessions. Special and preferential treatment and other trade preferences in favour of developing countries constituted a variation of, but not a departure from, the basic principle underlying this approach.

The adoption of the tariff as the only legitimate trade policy measure was predicated on the belief that, in conditions of strictly limited private international capital flows, setting-up a new international monetary system on an intergovernmental basis with convertible currencies at fixed, but adjustable, exchange rates would provide a stable monetary environment conducive to trade and investment. Accordingly, it was expected that participants in international trade negotiations would be able to predict the full extent to which the competitive position of domestic industries would be affected by tariff cuts without having to be unduly concerned with other exogenous factors.

This assumption does not hold in the presence of sizeable exchange rate volatility, which in developing countries has taken the form of sharp and abrupt real currency depreciations typically preceded by large shifts in expectations of international portfolio investors, in turn resulting in a sharp and abrupt change in the direction of short-term international capital flows. While the trade performance of developing countries generally improves after "normal" depreciations, major real currency depreciations do not result in proportionally larger improvements, as such depreciations tend to undermine the ability of exporters to take advantage of the rise in international cost competitiveness resulting from them.

In effect, volatility in international financial markets and particularly in short-term private capital flows can reduce international competitiveness and the profit incentive for investors to undertake productivity-enhancing investment in developing countries.[1] Hence, there is inconsistency in the policy advice that encourages developing countries to adopt rapid financial liberalization and yet to increasingly rely on productivity-enhancing investment to strengthen their competitiveness for improved trade performance.

More generally, existing modalities in the multilateral trading system do not address the problems of trade performance that originate in the monetary and financial system. Moreover, there are no mechanisms under the existing system of global economic governance for dispute settlement or redress regarding these impulses. One possible approach to this situation could be a review of the balance-of-payments provisions of the GATT. Articles XII and XV of the GATT 1994 allow a Member to suspend its obligations under the Agreement and to impose import restrictions in order to forestall a serious decline in, or otherwise protect the level of, its foreign-exchange reserves, or to ensure a level of reserves adequate for implementation of its programme of economic development. The provisions of Article XV are directed particularly at payments difficulties arising mainly from a country's efforts to expand its internal market or from instability in its terms of trade. These provisions are designed to prevent situations whereby countries are forced to sacrifice economic growth and development as a result of temporary difficulties originating in the current account of the balance of payments. The issue could be explored whether they could be used also to address problems associated with instability in financial flows (i.e. the capital account of the balance of payments).

Otherwise, developing-country policy-makers who have adopted financial liberalization at an early stage of their integration process may have to consider adopting measures designed to limit the impact of short-term private international capital flows on exchange rate movements that adversely affect their country's balance of payments and the international competitiveness of its exporters. This implies that real exchange rate changes, which determine changes in the competitiveness of the economy as a whole, will not be left to the market alone. Many of the particularly vulnerable developing countries will continue to manage the exchange rate of their currencies unilaterally. As this is a promising strategy only if the currency is undervalued and the country records current account surpluses, there is a latent risk of competitive devaluations and destabilizing shocks both among developing countries and in relation to the developed world.

The changes required in the international trading, monetary and financial systems to enable a more equitable distribution of the benefits from international trade and to maximize the developmental effects of globalization for developing countries call for an integrated treatment of trade problems and the increasingly interlinked issues of development and overall payments balances. One major implication of this approach is that decisions on the international monetary and financial system should not be circumscribed by the perspectives of narrow monetary and financial considerations, and should assume the fact that they have strong and lasting impact on the real sectors in both developed and developing countries.

As discussed in chapter III, the architects of the post-war international economic system already attempted to establish mutually supportive systems governing international trade, monetary and financial relations to ensure high and stable levels of activity and employment, financial and exchange rate stability, and the participation of all countries in the benefits from the growth of international trade. This institutional project has never been completed.

While not being a substitute for arrangements that manage international trade, monetary and financial flows interdependently and on the multilateral level, ensuring sufficient policy space has become the chosen strategy of more and more developing countries. East Asian countries pioneered this approach. They did not apply the "open capital market strategy" at an early stage of their catching-up process, and they tried to avoid dependence on foreign capital flows. This has allowed them to control the real exchange rate, a key determinant of exporters' international cost competitiveness, and the real interest rate, a key determinant of domestic investment, simultaneously.

In the Asian case, the management of the labour market and to a large extent the capital market remained in the hands of national Governments. By adjusting nominal wages to productivity and by influencing the movements of the exchange rate, governments expanded national policy space inasmuch as they reduced their dependence on foreign capital. If governments can prevent a dramatic deterioration in the international competitiveness of a large number of domestic companies, the gains resulting from a favourable investment climate in terms of lower interest rates and higher profits may far outweigh the losses resulting from lower inflows of foreign capital and higher imports.

By the same token, simultaneous opening up of domestic markets to both foreign goods and international capital flows, especially when it is done on a unilateral basis, may cause domestic production capacity to shrink and thus do little to create effective market competition. In such cases, policies to promote the creation of new competitive firms may require active monitoring by the government of the effects of opening up and the possibility of slowing down the process in situations where domestic firms are in danger of being wiped out. Further, the process of opening up has to be supported by policies to strengthen the domestic supply capacity at the national level and to ensure access to the most important export markets at the international level. But even supply capacity and market access may not be sufficient for reaping the benefits of an improved division of labour if there are not enough firms that have a competitive edge resulting from niche production, low production costs or a low exchange rate valuation. ∎

Note

1 Moreover, according to Gourinchas and Jeanne (2004: 23), "it has been argued that far from inducing discipline, the disruption induced by capital flows could have deleterious effects on domestic institutions, policies, and growth."

REFERENCES – PART TWO

Agosin M and Tussie D (1993). An Overview. In: Agosin M and Tussie D, eds., *Trade and Growth – New Dilemmas in Trade Policy*. New York, St. Martin's Press.

Akyüz Y (2004). The rational for multilateral lending: A critical assessment. Mimeo, 2 July. Paper prepared for the UNDP Project "Public Finance in a Globalizing World".

Akyüz Y and Gore C (1996). The profit-investment nexus in East Asian industrialization. *World Development*, 24(3).

Amsden A (2001). T*he Rise of the Rest: Challenges to the West From Late-Industrializing Economies*. Oxford, Oxford University Press.

Athukorala P and Menon J (1994). Pricing to market behaviour and exchange rate pass-through in Japanese exports. *Economic Journal*, 104: 271–281.

Auboin M and Meier-Ewert M (2003). Improving the availability of trade finance during financial crises. *Discussion Paper*, 2. Geneva, World Trade Organization.

Baig T and Goldfajn I (1998). Financial market contagion in the Asian crisis. *Working Paper,* 98/155. Washington, DC, International Monetary Fund.

Bairoch P (1993). *Economics and World History: Myths and Paradoxes*. Chicago, University of Chicago Press.

Barth M and Dinmore T (1999). Trade prices and volumes in East Asia through the crisis. *International Finance Discussion Papers*, 643. Washington, DC, United States Board of Governors of the Federal Reserve System.

Baumol W (1986). Productivity growth, convergence and welfare: What the long-run data show. *American Economic Review*, 76(5): 1072–1085.

Baumol WJ (2002). *The Free-Market Innovation Machine*. Princeton and Oxford, Princeton University Press.

Bayen JW (1954). *Money in a Maelstrom*. London, Macmillan Press.

Bayly C (2003). *The Birth of the Modern World 1780–1914*. Oxford, Blackwell Publishing.

Blattman C, Hwang J and Williamson J (2003). The terms of trade and economic growth in the periphery, 1870–1983. *NBER Working Paper*, 9940. Cambridge, MA, National Bureau of Economic Research.

Boltho A (1996). The assessment: International competitiveness. *Oxford Review of Economic Policy*, 12 (3):1–16.

Burstein A, Neves JC and Rebelo S (2004). Investment prices and exchange rates: Some basic facts. *NBER Working Paper,* 10238. Cambridge, MA, National Bureau of Economic Research.

Calvo GA (1999). On dollarization. University of Maryland, VA. Available at: http://www/bsos.umd.edu/econ/ciecpn5.pdf.

Camdessus M (1995). The IMF in a globalized world economy – The tasks ahead. Address given at the Third Annual Sylvia Ostry Lecture, Ottawa, 7 June 1995. Washington, DC, International Monetary Fund.

Campa JM and Goldberg LS (1999). Investment passthrough, and exchange rates: A cross-country comparison. *International Economic Review,* 40(1): 287–314.

Caramazza F, Ricci L and Salgado R (2004). International financial contagion in currency crises. *Journal of International Money and Finance,* 23: 51–70.

Chang HJ (2002). *Kicking Away the Ladder – Development Strategy in Historical Perspective*. London, Anthem Press.

Choi N and Kang D (2000). A study on the crisis, recovery and industrial upgrading in the Republic of Korea, Chapter 11. In: Dwor-Frécaut D, Colaço F and Hallward-Driemeier M, eds., *Asian Corporate Recovery. Findings from Firm-Level Surveys in Five Countries*. Washington DC, World Bank.

Connolly M (2003). The dual nature of trade: measuring its impact on imitation and growth. *Journal of Development Economics, 72*: 31–55.

Cornford A (2004). Variable geometry for the WTO: Concept and precedents. *UNCTAD Discussion Paper, 171*. Geneva, United Nations Conference on Trade and Development.

Crucini M and Kahn J (1996). Tariffs and aggregate economic activity: Lessons from the Great Depression. *Journal of Monetary Economics, 38*.

Dunning J (1981). *International Production and the Multinational Enterprise.* London, Allen and Unwin.

Duttagupta R and Spilimbergo A (2004). What happened to Asian exports during the crisis? *IMF Staff Papers, 51*(1): 72–95.

Eatwell J and Taylor L (2000). *Global Finance at Risk: The Case for International Regulation.* New York, The New Press.

ECE (1990). *Economic Survey of Europe.* New York and Geneva, United Nations Economic Commission for Europe.

ECLA (1965). *External Financing in Latin America.* New York and Santiago, United Nations Economic Commission for Latin America.

ECLAC (2001). *CEPAL Review, 75*, December. New York and Santiago, United Nations Economic Commission for Latin America and the Caribbean.

ECLAC (2002). *Globalization and Development* (LC/G.2157(SES.29/3) 15 April 2002). New York and Santiago, United Nations Economic Commission for Latin America and the Caribbean.

Eichengreen B (1996). *Globalizing Capital: A History of the International Monetary System.* Princeton, NJ, Princeton University Press.

Eichengreen B (2004). Global imbalances and the lessons of Bretton Woods. *NBER Working Paper, 10497.* Cambridge, MA, National Bureau of Economic Research.

Eichengreen B and Bordo M (2002). Crises now and then: What lessons from the last era of financial globalization? *NBER Working Paper, 8716.* Cambridge, MA, National Bureau of Economic Research.

Fagerberg J, Knell M and Srholec (2004). The competitiveness of nations: Economic growth in the ECE region. Mimeo. Blindern, NO, University of Oslo.

Faruqee H (2004). Exchange-rate pass-through in the Euro area: The role of asymmetric pricing behaviour. *Working Paper* 04/14. Washington, DC, International Monetary Fund, January.

Felix D (1996). Financial globalization versus free trade: The case for the Tobin Tax. In: UNCTAD Review (UNCTAD/SGO/10). United Nations publication, sales no. E.97.II.D.2, New York and Geneva.

Felix D (2001). Why international capital mobility should be curbed, and how it could be done. Mimeo, February. St. Louis, MO, Washington University in St. Louis.

Fischer S (2001). Exchange rate regimes: Is the bipolar view correct? Speech delivered at the meeting of the American Economic Association, New Orleans, 6 January. Available at: http://www.imf.org/external/np/speeches/2001/010601a.htm.

Forbes KJ (2002a). Cheap labor meets costly capital: The impact of devaluations on commodity firms. *Journal of Development Economics, 69*: 335–365.

Forbes KJ (2002b). Are trade linkages important determinants of country vulnerability to crisis? In: Edwards S and Frankel JA, eds., *Preventing currency crises in emerging markets.* Chicago, University of Chicago Press.

Forbes KJ (2002c). How do large depreciations affect firm performance? *IMF Staff Papers, 49*: 214–238.

Freeman R (2003). Trade wars: The exaggerated impact of trade in economic debate. *NBER Working Paper, 10000.* Cambridge, MA, National Bureau of Economic Research.

Friedman M (1953). The case for flexible exchange rates. In: Friedman M, *Essays in Positive Economics.* Chicago, University of Chicago Press.

Ghei N and Pritchett L (1999). The three pessimisms: real exchange rates and trade flows in developing countries. In: Hinkle L and Montiel P, eds., *Exchange Rate Misalignment: Concept and Measurement for Developing Countries.* New York, Oxford University Press.

Glick R and Rose AK (1999). Contagion and trade. Why are currency crises regional? *Journal of International Money and Finance, 18*: 603–617.

Goldberg PK and Knetter MM (1997). Goods prices and exchange rates: What have we learned? *Journal of Economic Literature, 35*: 1243–1272.

Gomory R and Baumol W (2000). *Global Trade and Conflicting National Interests.* Cambridge, MA, MIT Press.

Gordon RJ (2003). Exploding productivity growth: Context, causes, and implications. *Brookings Papers on Economic Activity, 2:* 2003: 207–298.

Gourinchas P and Jeanne O (2004). The elusive gains from international financial integration. *Working Paper, 04/74.* Washington, DC, International Monetary Fund. May.

Hadass Y and Williamson J (2001). Terms of trade shocks and economic performance, 1870–1914: Prebisch and Singer revisited. *NBER Working Paper, 8188.* Cambridge, MA, National Bureau of Economic Research.

Hymer S (1976). *The International Operations of National Firms: A Study of Foreign Direct Investment.* Cambridge, MA, MIT Press.

ILO (2004). *A Fair Globalization: Creating Opportunities for All.* Geneva, International Labour Organization.

IMF (2002), Three essays on how financial markets affect real activity. *World Economic Outlook.* Washington, DC, International Monetary Fund, April.

IMF (2003). *Trade Finance in Financial Crisis: Assessment of Key Issues*. Washington, DC, International Monetary Fund.

IMF (2004). *Exchange Rate Volatility and Trade Flows – Some New Evidence*. Washington, DC, International Monetary Fund.

James H (2000). *The End of Globalization: Lesson from the Great Depression*. Cambridge, MA, Harvard University Press.

Johnson H (1967). *Economic Policies Towards Less Developed Countries*. Washington, DC, The Brookings Institution.

JP Morgan (2003). JP Morgan effective exchange rates: revised and modernized. *Economic Research Note*, 30: 17–20. Available at: http://www2.jpmorgan.com/MarketDataInd/Forex/currIndex.html.

Kaldor N (1978). *Further Essays on Applied Economics*. London, Duckworth.

Kenwood A and Lougheed A (1994). *The Growth of the International Economy, 1820–1990*, 3rd ed. London, Routledge.

Keynes JM (1930). A Treatise on Money – The Pure Theory of Money. In: *The Collected Writings of John Maynard Keynes*, V. London and Basingstoke, Macmillan Press, 1973.

Kindleberger C (1975). *Manias, Panics and Crashes: A History of Financial Crises*. New York, Basic Books.

Kindleberger C (1986). International public goods without international government. *American Economic Review*, 76, March.

Kindleberger C (1987). *The World in Depression, 1929–1939*. Harmondsworth, Pelican Books.

King R and Levine R (1993). Finance, entrepreneurship and growth: Theory and evidence. *Journal of Monetary Economics*, 32.

Kozul-Wright R and Rayment P (2004). Globalization reloaded: An UNCTAD perspective. *UNCTAD Discussion Paper*, 167. Geneva, United Nations Conference on Trade and Development.

Kregel J (1994). Capital flows: Globalization of production and financing development. *UNCTAD Review*. United Nations publication, sales no. E.94.II.D.19, New York and Geneva.

Kregel J (1996a). Germany and the creation of Universal Banks. Chapter 5 of *Origini e sviluppi dei mercati finanziari*. Arezzo, Banca Popolare dell'Etruria e del Lazio – studi e ricerche.

Kregel J (1996b). Some risks and implications of financial globalization for national policy autonomy. *UNCTAD Review*. United Nations publication, sales no. E.97.II.D.2, New York and Geneva.

Kregel J (2004). External financing for development and international financial instability. Research paper for the International Group of Twenty-Four on International Monetary Affairs, XVIII G-24 Technical Group Meeting, 8–9 March. Geneva, United Nations Conference on Trade and Development and Intergovernmental Group of Twenty-Four.

Kreinin ME (1977). The effect of exchange rate changes on the prices and volume of foreign trade. *IMF Staff Papers*, 24: 297–329.

Krugman P (1987). Is free trade passé? *Journal of Economic Perspectives*, 1(2).

Krugman P (1994). *Peddling Prosperity*. New York, W.W. Norton & Company.

Krugman P (1996). Making sense of the competitiveness debate. *Oxford Review of Economic Policy*. 2(3): 17–25.

Lall S (2001). Competitiveness indices and developing countries: An economic evaluation of the Global Competitiveness Report. *World Development*, 29(9): 1501–1525.

Laursen S and Metzler LA (1950). Flexible exchange rates and the theory of employment. In: Metzler LA, ed., *Collected Papers*. Cambridge MA, Harvard University Press, 1978.

Maddison A (1982). *Phases of Capitalist Development*. Oxford and New York, Oxford University Press.

Moore B (1966). *Social Origins of Dictatorship and Democracy: Lord and Peasant in the Making of the Modern World*. Boston, MA, Beacon Press.

Mundell RA (1961). A theory of optimum currency areas. *American Economic Review*, 51: 657–665, September.

Mussa M (1997). IMF Surveillance. *American Economic Review Papers and Proceedings*, May.

Mussa M, Masson P, Swoboda A, Jadresic E, Mauro P and Berg Y (2000). Exchange rate regimes in an increasingly integrated world economy. *Occasional Paper*, 193. Washington, DC, International Monetary Fund.

Nurkse R (1944). *International Currency Experience: Lessons of the Inter-War Period*. Geneva, League of Nations (United Nations Office at Geneva).

Nurkse R (1959). *Patterns of Trade and Development*. Wicksell Lectures, Stockholm.

O'Rourke K (2002). Europe and the causes of globalization, 1790–2000. In: Kierskowski H, ed., *From Europe and Globalization*. Basingstoke, Palgrave.

Palma G (1989). Structuralism. In: Eatwell J et al., *Economic Development*. London, Macmillan Press.

Panic M (1995). The Bretton Woods System: Concept and Practice. In: Michie J and Grieve Smith J, eds., *Managing the Global Economy*. Oxford, Oxford University Press.

Pauly L (1997). *Who Elected the Bankers?* Ithaca, NY, Cornell University Press.

Pesenti P and Tille C (2000). The economics of currency crises and contagion: An introduction. *Federal Reserve Bank of New York Economic Policy Review*, 6(3): 3–16.

Polanyi K (1944). *The Great Transformation*. Boston, MA, Beacon Press.

Prasad E, Rogoff K, Shang-Jin Wei and Aykhan Kose M (2003). *Effects of Financial Globalization on Devel-*

oping Countries: Some Empirical Evidence. Washington DC, International Monetary Fund, March.

Rayment P (1983). Intra-industry specialization and the foreign trade of industrial countries. In: Frowen F, ed., *Controlling Industrial Economies*. London, Macmillan Press.

Reinert E (1999). Increasing poverty in a globalised world: Marshall Plans and Morgenthau Plans as mechanisms of polarization of world incomes. Mimeo. Norway, The Other Canon Foundation.

Rodrik D (2002). Feasible Globalizations. *NBER Working Paper,* 9129. Cambridge, MA, National Bureau of Economic Research.

Rodrik D (2003). Growth strategies. Mimeo. Forthcoming in the Handbook of Economic Growth. Available at: http://ksghome.harvard.edu/~.drodrik. academic.ksg/papers.html.

Ros J (2002). *Development Theory and the Economics of Growth.* Ann Arbor, MI, University of Michigan Press.

Rosenthal G (2003). ECLAC: A commitment to a Latin American Way. In: Berthelot Y, ed., *Unity and Diversity in Development Idea.* Bloomington, IN, Indiana University Press.

Rowthorn R and Chang HJ, eds. (1993). *The State and Economic Change.* Cambridge, Cambridge University Press.

Scarpetta S and Tressel T (2004). Boosting productivity via innovation and adoption of new technologies: Any role for labor market institutions? *Working Paper* 3273. Washington, DC, World Bank, April.

Schumpeter JA (1911). *The Theory of Economic Development*. Cambridge, MA, Harvard University Press (English translation 1936).

Schumpeter JA (1939). *Business cycles. A theoretical, historical, and statistical analysis of the capitalist process*. New York and London, McGraw Hill.

Spraos J (1980). The statistical debate on the net barter terms of trade between primary commodities and manufactures. *Economic Journal*, 90.

Stiglitz J (2003). Globalization and the logic of international collective action: Re-examining the Bretton Woods Institutions. In: Nayyar D, ed., *Governing Globalization: Issues and Institutions.* Oxford, Oxford University Press, Chapter 9.

Taylor JB (1993). Discretion versus policy rules in practice. *Carnegie-Rochester Conference Series on Public Policy*, 39: 195–214.

Turner AG and Golub SS (1997). Towards a system of multilateral unit labor cost-based competitiveness indicators for advanced, developing, and transition countries. *Working Paper* 97/151. Washington, DC, International Monetary Fund, November.

Twomey M (2000). *A Century of Foreign Direct Investment in the Third World*. London, Routledge.

UNCTAD (1964). Towards a New Trade Policy for Development: Report by the Secretary-General of the United Nations Conference on Trade and Development. United Nations, New York and Geneva.

UNCTAD (2001). *Economic Development in Africa: Performance, Prospects and Policy Issues* (UNCTAD/GDS/AFRICA/1). United Nations publication, New York and Geneva.

UNCTAD (2002). *The Least Developed Countries Report, 2002*. United Nations publication, sales no. E.02.II.D.13, New York and Geneva.

UNCTAD (various issues). *Trade and Development Report.* United Nations publication, New York and Geneva.

UNDP (1999). *Human Development Report, 1999*. United Nations publication, New York.

UN-HABITAT (2003). *The Challenge of the Slums: Global Report on Human Settlements 2003*. New York and Nairobi, United Nations Human Settlement Programme.

van Rijckeghem C and Weder B (2001). Sources of contagion: is it finance or trade? *Journal of International Economics,* 54: 293–308.

van Wincoop E and Yi KM (2000). Asia crisis postmortem: Where did the money go and did the United States benefit? *Federal Reserve Bank of New York Economic Policy Review,* 6(3): 51–70.

Williamson J (1983). *The Exchange Rate System*. Washington, DC, Institute for International Economics.

Winters A (2001). Coherence with no "here": WTO cooperation with the World Bank and the IMF. Mimeo. Murphy Institute Conference on the Political Economy of Policy Reform. New Orleans, LA, Tulane University, 9–10 November.

Winters A (2004). Trade liberalization and economic performance: An overview. *Economic Journal*, 114.

Wolf M (2004). *Why Globalization Works.* New Haven, CT, Yale University Press.

Wollmershäuser T (2004). Exchange rate changes and trade flows: Evidence from emerging market economies. Mimeo. Background paper prepared for the UNCTAD *Trade and Development Report, 2004.* Geneva, United Nations Conference on Trade and Development.

World Bank (1999). *Global Development Finance.* Washington, DC.

World Bank (2002). *Globalization, Growth and Poverty: Building an Inclusive Global Economy.* New York, World Bank/Oxford University Press.

World Bank (2004). *Global Development Finance.* Washington, DC.

WTO (1998). *Annual Report, Special Topic: Globalization and Trade.* Geneva, World Trade Organization.

Young A (1928). Increasing returns and economic progress. *The Economic Journal*, 38: 527–542.

UNITED NATIONS CONFERENCE ON TRADE AND DEVELOPMENT

Palais des Nations
CH-1211 GENEVA 10
Switzerland
(www.unctad.org)

Selected UNCTAD Publications

Trade and Development Report, 2003   United Nations publication, sales no. E.03.II.D.7
ISBN 92-1-112579-0

Part One   Global Trends and Prospects

I   The World Economy: Performance and Prospects

II   Financial Flows to Developing Countries and Transition Economies

III   Trade Flows and Balances
Annex: Commodity prices

Part Two   Capital Accumulation, Economic Growth and Structural Change

IV   Economic Growth and Capital Accumulation

V   Industrialization, Trade and Structural Change

VI   Policy Reforms and Economic Performance: The Latin American Experience

Trade and Development Report, 2002   United Nations publication, sales no. E.02.II.D.2
ISBN 92-1-112549-9

Part One   Global Trends and Prospects

I   The World Economy: Performance and Prospects

II   The Multilateral Trading System After Doha

Part Two   Developing Countries in World Trade

III   Export Dynamism and Industrialization in Developing Countries
Annex 1:   Growth and classification of world merchandise exports
Annex 2:   United States trade prices and dynamic products
Annex 3:   International production networks and industrialization in developing countries

IV   Competition and the Fallacy of Composition

V   China's Accession to WTO: Managing Integration and Industrialization

Trade and Development Report, 2001   United Nations publication, sales no. E.01.II.D.10
                                                                              ISBN 92-1-112520-0

Trade and Development Report, 2000   United Nations publication, sales no. E.00.II.D.19
                                                                              ISBN 92-1-112489-1

******

These publications may be obtained from bookstores and distributors throughout the world. Consult your bookstore
or write to United Nations Publications/Sales Section, Palais des Nations, CH-1211 Geneva 10, Switzerland
(Fax: +41-22-917.0027; E-mail: unpubli@un.org; Internet: www.un.org/publications); or from United Nations
Publications, Two UN Plaza, Room DC2-853, Dept. PERS, New York, NY 10017, USA (Tel. +1-212-963.8302 or
+1-800-253.9646; Fax +1-212-963.3489; E-mail: publications@un.org).

G-24 Discussion Paper Series

Research papers for the Intergovernmental
Group of Twenty-Four on International Monetary Affairs

No. 30	June 2004	Andrew CORNFORD	Enron and Internationally Agreed Principles for Corporate Governance and the Financial Sector
No. 29	April 2004	Devesh KAPUR	Remittances: The New Development Mantra?
No. 28	April 2004	Sanjaya LALL	Reinventing Industrial Strategy: The Role of Government Policy in Building Industrial Competitiveness
No. 27	March 2004	Gerald EPSTEIN, Ilene GRABEL and JOMO, K.S.	Capital Management Techniques in Developing Countries: An Assessment of Experiences from the 1990s and Lessons for the Future
No. 26	March 2004	Claudio M. LOSER	External Debt Sustainability: Guidelines for Low- and Middle-income Countries
No. 25	January 2004	Irfan ul HAQUE	Commodities under Neoliberalism: The Case of Cocoa
No. 24	December 2003	Aziz Ali MOHAMMED	Burden Sharing at the IMF
No. 23	November 2003	Mari PANGESTU	The Indonesian Bank Crisis and Restructuring: Lessons and Implications for other Developing Countries
No. 22	August 2003	Ariel BUIRA	An Analysis of IMF Conditionality
No. 21	April 2003	Jim LEVINSOHN	The World Bank's Poverty Reduction Strategy Paper Approach: Good Marketing or Good Policy?
No. 20	February 2003	Devesh KAPUR	Do As I Say Not As I Do: A Critique of G-7 Proposals on Reforming the Multilateral Development Banks
No. 19	December 2002	Ravi KANBUR	International Financial Institutions and International Public Goods: Operational Implications for the World Bank
No. 18	September 2002	Ajit SINGH	Competition and Competition Policy in Emerging Markets: International and Developmental Dimensions
No. 17	April 2002	F. LÓPEZ-DE-SILANES	The Politics of Legal Reform
No. 16	January 2002	Gerardo ESQUIVEL and Felipe LARRAÍN B.	The Impact of G-3 Exchange Rate Volatility on Developing Countries
No. 15	December 2001	Peter EVANS and Martha FINNEMORE	Organizational Reform and the Expansion of the South's Voice at the Fund
No. 14	September 2001	Charles WYPLOSZ	How Risky is Financial Liberalization in the Developing Countries?
No. 13	July 2001	José Antonio OCAMPO	Recasting the International Financial Agenda
No. 12	July 2001	Yung Chul PARK and Yunjong WANG	Reform of the International Financial System and Institutions in Light of the Asian Financial Crisis

G-24 Discussion Paper Series

Research papers for the Intergovernmental
Group of Twenty-Four on International Monetary Affairs

* * * * * *

G-24 Discussion Paper Series are available on the website at: www.unctad.org. Copies of *G-24 Discussion Paper Series* may be obtained from the Publications Assistant, Macroeconomic and Development Policies Branch, Division on Globalization and Development Strategies, United Nations Conference on Trade and Development (UNCTAD), Palais des Nations, CH-1211 Geneva 10, Switzerland (Fax: +41-22-907.0274; E-mail: mdpb-ed.assistant@unctad.org).

UNCTAD Discussion Papers

No. 171	May 2004	Andrew CORNFORD	Variable geometry for the WTO: concepts and precedents
No. 170	May 2004	Robert ROWTHORN and Ken COUTTS	De-industrialization and the balance of payments in advanced economies
No. 169	April 2004	Shigehisa KASAHARA	The flying geese paradigm: a critical study of its application to East Asian regional development
No. 168	Feb. 2004	Alberto GABRIELE	Policy alternatives in reforming power utilities in developing countries: a critical survey
No. 167	Jan. 2004	R. KOZUL-WRIGHT and P. RAYMENT	Globalization reloaded: an UNCTAD perspective
No. 166	Feb. 2003	Jörg MAYER	The fallacy of composition: a review of the literature
No. 165	Nov. 2002	Yuefen LI	China's accession to WTO: exaggerated fears?
No. 164	Nov. 2002	Lucas ASSUNCAO and ZhongXiang ZHANG	Domestic climate change policies and the WTO
No. 163	Nov. 2002	A.S. BHALLA and S. QIU	China's WTO accession. Its impact on Chinese employment
No. 162	July 2002	P. NOLAN and J. ZHANG	The challenge of globalization for large Chinese firms
No. 161	June 2002	Zheng ZHIHAI and Zhao YUMIN	China's terms of trade in manufactures, 1993–2000
No. 160	June 2002	S.M. Shafaeddin	The impact of China's accession to WTO on exports of developing countries
No. 159	May 2002	J. MAYER, A. BUTKEVICIUS and A. KADRI	Dynamic products in world exports
No. 158	April 2002	Yilmaz AKYÜZ and Korkut BORATAV	The making of the Turkish financial crisis
No. 157	Nov. 2001	Heiner FLASSBECK	The exchange rate: Economic policy tool or market price?
No. 156	Aug. 2001	Andrew CORNFORD	The Basel Committee's proposals for revised capital standards: Mark 2 and the state of play
No. 155	Aug. 2001	Alberto GABRIELE	Science and technology policies, industrial reform and technical progress in China: Can socialist property rights be compatible with technological catching up?
No. 154	June 2001	Jörg MAYER	Technology diffusion, human capital and economic growth in developing countries

******

Copies of **UNCTAD Discussion Papers** may be obtained from the Publications Assistant, Macroeconomic and Development Policies Branch, Division on Globalization and Development Strategies, UNCTAD, Palais des Nations, CH-1211 Geneva 10, Switzerland (Fax: (+41-22) 907.0274; E-mail: mdpb-ed.assistant@unctad.org). The full texts of UNCTAD Discussion Papers from No. 140 onwards, as well as abstracts of earlier ones, are available on the UNCTAD website at: www.unctad.org.

QUESTIONNAIRE

Trade and Development Report, 2004

In order to improve the quality and relevance of the Trade and Development Report, the UNCTAD secretariat would greatly appreciate your views on this publication. Please complete the following questionnaire and return it to:

Readership Survey
Division on Globalization and Development Strategies
UNCTAD
Palais des Nations, Room E.10011
CH-1211 Geneva 10, Switzerland
Fax: (+41) (0)22 907 0274
E-mail: tdr@unctad.org

> The questionnaire can also
> be completed on-line at:
> www.unctad.org/tdr/questionnaire

Thank you very much for your kind cooperation.

1. What is your assessment of this publication?

	Excellent	*Good*	*Adequate*	*Poor*
Overall	☐	☐	☐	☐
Relevance of issues	☐	☐	☐	☐
Analytical quality	☐	☐	☐	☐
Policy conclusions	☐	☐	☐	☐
Presentation	☐	☐	☐	☐

2. What do you consider the strong points of this publication?

    _____
    _____
    _____

3. What do you consider the weak points of this publication?

    _____
    _____
    _____

4. For what main purposes do you use this publication?

    Analysis and research ☐   Education and training ☐
    Policy formulation and management ☐   Other (s*pecify*) _____

5. Which of the following best describes your area of work?

    Government ☐   Public enterprise ☐
    Non-governmental organization ☐   Academic or research ☐
    International organization ☐   Media ☐
    Private enterprise institution ☐   Other (*specify*) _____

6. Name and address of respondent (*optional*):

    _____
    _____
    _____

7. Do you have any further comments?

    _____
    _____
    _____